RUSSIAN-ENGLISH DICTIONARY OF
CONTEMPORARY SLANG

RUSSIAN-ENGLISH DICTIONARY OF CONTEMPORARY SLANG

A Guide to the Living Language of Today

by 'UFO'
(Valery Nikolski)

SECOND EDITION revised and enlarged
by **James Davie**

Bramcote Press
Nottingham

Dictionary of Contemporary Russian Slang first published by
Panorama Publishing House, Moscow, 1993
Copyright © V. Nikolski 1993

This edition published 1997 by
**BRAMCOTE PRESS, 27 Seven Oaks Crescent,
Nottingham NG9 3FW**
All new material copyright © James Davie 1997

*Cover design by David Gibbons,
DAG Publications Ltd.*

Printed in Great Britain by
**Antony Rowe Ltd, Bumper's Farm, Chippenham,
Wiltshire SN14 6QA**

British Library Cataloguing in Publication Data.
A catalogue record for this book is available from the
British Library

ISBN 1 900405 03 2

Contents

About the Author and the Editor   vi

Introduction to the Second Edition   vii

How to use the Dictionary   xi

DICTIONARY   **1**

Sources and References by UFO   135

Additional Bibliography by James Davie   138

ABOUT THE AUTHOR

In the first edition of the Dictionary 'UFO' describes himself as follows:

Valery Nikolski was born on 2 October 1953 and is a native of Altai, Russia. He has a unique life experience that helps to compile the Dictionary.

From 1971 to 1981, he studied Applied Mathematics in Saint Petersburg University. After two years of active duty as a military interpreter in Soviet Army, he was imprisoned by KGB in 1979 for a year in a labour camp near Nizhny Novgorod. From 1980 to 1983, he was placed several times in a mental hospital for political reasons. He received public reputation as a leading member of the Soviet hippies' movement appeared on Leningrad TV in 1987. In hippy circles known as UFO.

Since 1988 he is Publisher of the 12 'Zine dedicated to the problems of young men in the country. The publication receives support of International Foundation Cultural Initiative, Moscow.

Valery Nikolski is inhabiting with his wife and three kids in Pskov, Russia.

ABOUT THE EDITOR

James Davie graduated in Russian and French (BA Hons) at the University of Strathclyde in 1993. From November 1993 to 1996 he worked as Research Assistant to the University of Portsmouth's successful *Ab initio* Russian Project, during which time he also commenced PhD research on Russian youth slang.

He is currently completing his doctoral project at the University, where he now also lectures in Russian language and society. His other research interests include the Russian criminal and professional argots of the nineteenth and twentieth centuries, Soviet and post-Soviet youth culture, Russian lexicology, and Russian language teaching methodology and related matters. He is a contributor of nonstandard Russian to the latest phase of the *Oxford Russian-English Dictionary* Project.

He lives in Southsea with his wife, Ruth.

Introduction to the Second Edition

Perhaps one of the greatest pleasures anyone interested in lexicology or language in general can have is to edit and revise a dictionary. Whilst this task undoubtedly brings with it many hours of deliberation and agonizing over such aspects as the translation of the seemingly untranslatable, for instance, it does allow the editor a golden opportunity to go beyond what appears on any given page and somehow to take an inquisitive look into the mind of the original compiler: to ask how he came across the vocabulary in the first place; to wonder why he chose the items he did for inclusion (as well as to wonder about those he omitted); to enquire about what prompted him to compile the dictionary; and to ponder both what the compiler of the original dictionary thought of his task, and how he went about completing it.

In editing and revising UFO's *Dictionary of Contemporary Russian Slang*, I have been mindful of exactly these points. Indeed, as with any other reader, I have come to my own set of conclusions, both about what the UFO dictionary represents, and about the person who actually compiled it. My own first impression concerns the uniqueness of the original UFO volume (Moscow: 'Panorama', 1993). Whilst this work contains some vocabulary to be found in other glossaries of contemporary nonstandard and demotic Russian, it none the less has a distinctly autobiographical flavour (one which most others lack), in that it contains much information based on the original compiler's experiences in the Soviet army, Soviet youth subculture and the Soviet prison system. Of course, UFO is not the only lexicographer to have compiled a dictionary based on personal experience. None the less, in his dictionary, one finds that the focus is not on any one argotic lexicon (e.g. criminal argot), but that all manner of worlds are referred to in a single volume, which itself comes to represent a mirror of sorts reflecting both the dominant and counter-cultural ways of Soviet and post-Soviet life. Indeed, I would add that it is perhaps as a result of this mixture of the countercultural and the mainstream— reflected in the synthesis of argotic and demotic language encountered by UFO in his many 'life experiences'—that we can come to appreciate a curious flavour which is particular to this volume alone.

My second impression concerns both the role and the *tone* of the dictionary. That it has as its main focus various types of nonstandard Russian—particularly criminal argot, youth slang, army jargon and general popular Russian—is also interesting. This allows the reader some insight into the various nonstandard lexicons of contemporary Russian, and thus serves to heighten awareness (especially that of non-native speakers) of the various potential stylistic and sociolinguistic aspects of modern-day usage.

In addition, although the original edition does have a personal aspect to it, it is also part of a wave of new analyses of a language form which was deliberately ignored or under-researched for so long under the Soviet régime. Fortunately, times appear to have changed and attitudes towards the use and study of nonstandard language are more open. New dictionaries are coming to the fore where, as in UFO's work, there is no disapproval of or moralising about sub- or counter-culture, as one might find in those treatments of nonstandard Russian of the Soviet era. It is to be hoped that, in just giving us the info, and letting us *get on with it*, UFO (and other commentators) have set a healthy precedent.

My third and final impression relates to the academic aspect of UFO's work. As my comments above indicate, analysis of non-standard language is presently gaining some popularity—despite intermittent calls for linguistic purism—and several dictionaries of *slang* are now available to the reader. In common with other ventures, the UFO dictionary also signifies a real attempt to unshackle nonstandard Russian and to take it to audiences both Russian and non-Russian. Through such ventures, we can all therefore arrive at a greater understanding of that form of living language which exists beyond the parameters of standard Russian and, if we want to, take a few steps of our own in this newly reclaimed land. So UFO's dictionary not only plays some part in communicating information about the development of what many feel is a rapidly changing Russian language and society, but also presents us with a new possibility, in that it helps us to understand one of those fields of *rusistika* which have still to be fully explored.

Although, as I mention above, the task of editing and revising a dictionary is the stuff of which many students' (in the broad sense of the term) dreams are made, there comes a time when even the editor's agenda becomes apparent. As the dictionary does enjoy such a well-defined autobiographical slant, I have endeavoured to remain as true to the original Panorama version as I have thought practical, and have tried to make my work as transparent or unobtrusive as possible. Few of the slang items included in the first edition have been expunged, and some amendments have inevitably been required to prepare the volume for British and other English-speaking users (as opposed to the speakers of American English addressed in the original). For instance, although the original Panorama edition contained English translations, many of these were rather stilted or vaguely expressed. Indeed, they tended to be 'politically correct' and lacked the bluntness or crudeness conveyed in the original Russian. The present work therefore includes British slang equivalents, many crude or vulgar, and is constructed on the basis that, if living language is to be properly researched, then one must give proper stylistic equivalents. To do otherwise would only serve to mislead or allow social prejudice to govern linguistic practice. This principle also applies to vulgarisms which have been added in the second edition to contextualize the many references UFO made in the original volume to euphemisms replacing vulgar language.

In addition, this second edition provides translations of all information given in Russian, where headings only were translated in the original version, and it contains more grammatical information for ease of use by non-native Russian speakers. There is now, for example, more information regarding aspect and gender: those verbs whose aspect was not stated in the first edition are now qualified as either perfective or imperfective (or, where appropriate, bi-aspectual). Indication of the gender of nouns has also been added. Similarly, instructions concerning use of the dictionary have been altered to suit the format of the present edition, although other introductory comments made by the original compiler have remained unaltered.

Finally, the present edition differs from the original UFO version in that over 200 new items have been added. This vocabulary, based on the editor's own research experience of nonstandard Russian, has been drawn from contemporary Russian journals and field-work, and thus provides what one hopes will be a clear illustration of actual usage, whilst still hopefully respecting the work of the original. All new sources—as well as other references consulted in the editing process—are indicated in a supplementary bibliography at the end of the volume.

To end this introduction, one important question: for whom has this dictionary been compiled and edited? Well, although it does contain much vocabulary specific to certain Russian social groups, and although it does have an autobiographical profile, the present volume is not so specific as to introduce readers to the kind of vocabulary they will never encounter. Far from it. Indeed, although it does contain some weird and wonderful expressions taken from the various contributing jargons, it is not so far removed from the language of everyday Russia as to be esoteric or arcane. Rather, it provides an insight into the kind of vocabulary which is *regularly* used both by the members of the relevant groups *and* by those who belong to the mainstream social collective. In fact, it is worth noting that much of Russian criminal and youth jargon, for instance, is known and, where appropriate, used by the wider Russian-speaking public. Therefore, it is hoped that this volume, the first Russian-English dictionary of sociolectal Russian to be published in the United Kingdom, will be of use to a wide range of readers, including those who wish to know more about the living Russian language, such as teachers, students, linguists, translators, those interested in Russian society and culture, those wishing to spend some time in Russia for whatever reason, or those who are simply curious about nonstandard Russian.

I would like to express my appreciation to the following people, who have contributed to the preparation of this volume in various ways: to Dr James Muckle (Bramcote Press) for his support in initiating and realizing the project; to Professor Terence Wade (University of Strathclyde) for specialist advice; to Dima and his colleagues from the State Pedagogical Institute of Novosibirsk, for the honesty and enthusiasm with which they answered my many queries on youth slang; to the University of Portsmouth, for the technical and other support they provided for the background research; and to Ruth, for her immeasurable patience. Any errors are, of course, the responsibility of the editor.

James D. Davie
Portsmouth, 1997

How to Use the Dictionary

All entries are listed in alphabetical order. Head words are given in bold and, unless precluded by alternative usage, in the nominative case. Information regarding transitivity, aspect, gender, number or genitive forms is indicated in italics.

The following abbreviated forms are used in the dictionary:

acc.	accusative case.
adj.	adjective.
adv.	adverb.
coll.	collective noun.
dat.	dative case.
dial.	dialectal (regional) form.
esp.	especially
f.	feminine gender.
gen.	genitive case.
impers.	impersonal phrase.
impf.	imperfective aspect.
indec.	indeclinable.
inst.	instrumental case.
interj.	interjection.
lit.	literal meaning
m.	masculine gender.
m.,f.	noun used as either masculine or feminine (common gender).
n.	neuter gender.
pf.	perfective aspect.
phr.	noun or verbal phrase, normally followed by the aspect of the verb involved.
pl.	plural.
pred.	predicate.
prep.	prepositional case.
sing.	singular
v.i.	intransitive verb.
v.t.	transitive verb.

Nouns

Nouns are indicated in the singular form or, when there is no singular, in the plural form (e.g. ба́шли).

Adjectives

Adjectives are provided in the masculine singular form. Plural forms are indicated where adjectives are more frequently used in the plural. Where appropriate, the use of adjectives as nouns is indicated (e.g. *adj. used as m. noun*).

Number

Number is indicated for plural-only nouns or in instances where a noun may have variation in reference (e.g. a singular noun for definition 1, but a collective noun for definition 2): менту́ра *coll.f.* the fuzz, the filth, pigs; *sing.f.* cop, pig, policeman. Otherwise, items provided are in the singular.

Stress

In certain items there may occur variation in stress, for instance, жло́бство́ may be pronounced either жлобство́ or жло́бство.

Phrases

Certain phrases have been included in those entries where the appropriate noun is specified, for instance, жить на а́ске in the аск entry. In some entries, other forms of additional information may be given, for example, де́мбельский акко́рд in the entry де́мбельский. This may also be given at the foot of some entries as material for cross-referencing. Other phrases and expressions may be given as separate entries, for instance, мо́жно хоть раз в жи́зни споко́йно?

Aspect

Aspect is indicated for all verbs after information concerning transitivity. Where both verbs of any aspectual pair are known, the perfective aspect is indicated in square brackets in the entry pertaining to the *imperfective* verb.

In addition, the perfective verb is also indicated as the partner of the imperfective verb in a separate entry:

вдуть *pf.* of вдува́ть.

Examples are normally given in entries for the imperfective aspect:

аска́ть *v.t.* [*pf.* **аскну́ть**] 1. to busk, tap, ask (usually passers by). *Аска́ть идти́ стрёмно, круго́м менты́.* It was dodgy busking, cops all over the place. 2. to mooch, cadge (usually money) from someone. *На́до у циви́лов ха́вку аскну́ть.* We'll have to cadge some grub out of some civilians.

Where there is no aspectual partner indicated, examples accompany the verb given, regardless of aspect:

запога́нить *v.t.pf.* to prepare a drug. *му́льку запога́нить* to sort some ephedrine.

Additional Information

Many entries are qualified by additional information or discussion. The function of such additions is mainly to provide explanation of what are assumed to be little-known facts (particularly regarding the criminal world). In other cases, additional information on derivation, literal meaning or references to synonyms may be offered.

Variation in Nonstandard Russian

As nonstandard Russian is, by its very definition, not subject to the strict regulations which form standard Russian, there may occur a certain degree of variation in reference works devoted to nonstandard language. The entries included in this volume may therefore differ in varying degrees from those found in other reference works (e.g. grammatical number, definition of items).

The present dictionary also contains monetary units commonly used during the Soviet era, when UFO first encountered them. Although now irrelevant to today's Russia, where roubles are counted in thousands rather than tens, these denominations have been retained for reader interest.

А

a-a-a-a! *interj.* expression of moderate reproach, when spoken in a tender or sad tone; when spoken sharply, an expression of approval.
 • Used only by *Mit′ki* and their followers.

абза́ц *m.* 1. something great. Да, абза́ц ха́йры. По́лный Зи-Зи-Топ. Yes, great hair: really ZZ Top. 2. garbage. Что ты нацепи́ла како́й-то абза́ц? Why are you all done up in rubbish like that? Рекша́новский *Санкт-Петербу́рг* был круто́й. А э́тот фуфло́вый—абза́ц! Rekshanov's *St Petersburg* was magic, but that other worthless lot was garbage. 3. *interj.* hell, bugger (as expression of annoyance or irritation). Абза́ц! Наве́рное, батино́к с фазе́нды верну́лся. Damn! Dad must have come back from the cottage.
 • Lit. *paragraph.* Euphemism for *пизде́ц, the end, death.* Rekshanov ran a rock band in Leningrad in the early 1970s. ZZ Top refers to the American rock band.

абитурие́нт *m.* someone intending to emigrate. Я́шка у нас тепе́рь абитурие́нт. — А куда́ он поступа́ет? — В Изра́иль. Our Yashka's now going to emigrate. — Where's he going? — Israel.
 • Lit. *school-leaver, university entrant.*

а вот так! *phr.* an expression of triumph or satisfaction.
 • *Mit′ki.* See also **дык.**

автопило́т *m.* autopilot, automatic, auto. добира́ться [*pf.* добра́ться] на автопило́те, идти́ на автопило́те *impf.* to go home, find one's way home dead drunk. Добра́лся вчера́ на автопило́те до до́ма, хотя́ был в хла́мину. He got home yesterday on automatic, although he was out of his face. О, Лёха идёт на автопило́те. Oh, Alex is going home on auto.

а́втор *m.* boss, guvnor, gang leader, gang member of high status. Мла́дшие беспрекосло́вно подчиня́ются ста́ршим, рядовы́е чле́ны группиро́вок—а́вторам. The lesser members do what the senior ones tell them without question, the rank-and-file kowtow to the big shots. А́вторы нигде́ не рабо́тают, но проси́живают все дни в рестора́нах да разъезжа́ют на кра́сных автомоби́лях. The big boys don't work anywhere—they sit in bars all day and drive around in bright red cars.
 • Abbreviation of *авторите́т* (authority).

авторите́т *m.* guvnor, boss, someone with authority in the criminal underworld. У ка́ждого авторите́та своя́ брига́да с боевика́ми и де́вочками. Every big shot has his crew with hard men and molls.
  • Lit. *authority.*

адида́сы *f.pl.* (Adidas) trainers. Отку́да адида́сы? Всё отту́да. ВСЁ отту́да. Where did you get your trainers? I get everything abroad—EVERYTHING.

а́зер *m.* an Azeri. Взя́ли дере́вню, а там ра́неных а́зеров полно́. They took a village with wounded Azeris all over the place.

азиа́тка *f.* kind of Asian cannabis. Сорта́ анаши́—Чу́йка (Чу́йская доли́на), Манжу́рка, Краснода́рка, Азиа́тка, а Ди́чка—дикорасту́щая конопля́. Types of cannabis are Chuika, Manzhurka, Krasnodarka, Aziatka; Dichka is wild hemp.
  • Lit. *Asian.*

айзы́ *m.pl.* eyes. 'У фрэ́ндов айзы́ горя́т', 'My friends' eyes blaze' (line from a hippy song). **откры́ть айзы́** *pf.* [+ *dat.*] to open (someone's) eyes. Я усво́ил препо́данный ва́ми уро́к, сэ́ры, вы откры́ли мне айзы́, и я излечи́лся, сла́ва Бо́гу. I've learned the lesson you taught me, gentlemen, you have opened my eyes, and I am cured, thank God.

аква́риум *m.* 1. cell with a window in a police station; building with a lot of windows, hence the nickname of the main building of the military intelligence service, the GRU. 'Аква́риум' вое́нной разве́дки military intelligence aquarium. 2. famous St Petersburg rock group.
  • Lit. *aquarium.* The term (sense 1) is said to come from a novel by Viktor Suvorov.

аквариуми́ст *m.* fan of the *Aquarium* rock group. Веду́щий ТВ-програ́ммы *Взгляд:* 'Как вы отно́ситесь к тому́, что в Воро́неже аквариуми́сты и го́пники выясня́ют отноше́ния с по́мощью кулако́в?' A presenter on the television programme *Outlook* asks: 'What do you think about the way *Aquarium* fans and local yobs in Voronezh settle their differences with their fists?'

аку́стка *f.* acoustic guitar. Он там на аку́стке лаба́ет. He plays the guitar there.

а́лик *m.* alkie, drunkard. У шалма́на сплошь и ря́дом одни́ а́лики. There are nearly always alkies round that dive. Э́того а́лика во́все не А́ликом зову́т. They don't call that drunk 'Alec' because it's his name [but because he's a drunk].
  • See also *алка́ш, алкона́вт, кирю́ха, синега́л, синю́га.*

а́лики *m.pl.* alimony. На Украи́не купо́ны вво́дят. Пла́кали тепе́рь мои́ а́лики. They're bringing in coupons [i.e. tokens instead of real currency] in Ukraine. There goes my alimony.

алисома́н *m.* Alisoman: fan of the Moscow rock-group *Alisa.*

алисома́нка *f.* female fan of the group *Alisa.*

алка́ш *m.* alkie, drunkard. Алкаши́ пьют всё, что гори́т. Alcoholics drink anything that stings.
  • See also *а́лик, алкона́вт, кирю́ха, синега́л, синю́га.*

алкона́вт *m.* alkie, drunkard. Ты уже́ стал са́мым настоя́щим алкона́втом. You've already turned into a real alkie.
  • Combination of *алкого́ль (alcohol)* and *космона́вт (cosmonaut).* See also *а́лик, алка́ш, кирю́ха, синега́л, синю́га.*

аллёрик *m.* Wop, Itye, Italian. Смотрю́: за рулём типи́чный аллёрик—италья́шка лет пяти́десяти с га́ком. I look and see at the wheel a typical Wop—an Itye of about 50 or more.

амбре́лла *f.* umbrella. Измоча́лили амбре́ллу об асфа́льт. They wrecked the umbrella scraping it on the asphalt.

амёба *f.* 1. female biology teacher. Опя́ть амёба сейча́с зану́дит о па́рно- и непарнокопы́тных. О по́рно- и непорнокопы́тных! Again the old girl will go on about artiodactyls and non-artiodactyls...porno and non-pornodactyls, more like. 2. boring person.
  • Lit. *amoeba.*

аме́рикос *m.* yank, American.
  • See also *шта́тник.*

амора́лка *f.* amoral conduct.

анаша́ *f.* hash.

анаши́ст *m.* pot-smoker.

андеграу́нд *m.* variant of **андергра́унд**

андергра́унд *m.* underground, the underground music scene. Э́то называ́ется андергра́унд. Пятьдеся́т па́нков бьют урлу́ из трёх проходя́щих ми́мо го́пников. This is called the underground. Fifty punks beat up a yob from a group of three walking by.
  • Example taken from the techno magazine, *ПТЮЧ.*

андеграу́ндовый *adj.* variant of **андергра́ундовый**

андергра́ундовый *adj.* underground.

андро́повка *f.* Moscow vodka, the price of which was reduced under Andropov, General Secretary of the Communist Party of the USSR 1982-84. Снача́ла сто́ила 3.62 и́ли 4.12, пото́м ста́ла пята́к. а Андро́пов сбро́сил наза́д, вот и ста́ла *Андро́повка* называ́ться. First it cost 3 roubles 62 or 4 roubles 12, then it cost a fiver, but then Andropov put the price back down, so they called it Andropovka.

антидамби́ст *m.* member of the 'Damba' movement, which opposed the building of a dam near Leningrad on the Gulf of Finland. На очередно́м собра́нии зелёных оди́н из ли́деров антидамби́стов заяви́л о созда́нии Христиа́нского эколо-ги́ческого сою́за. At a routine meeting of the Greens one of the leaders announced the formation of a Christian ecology group.

апофеге́й *m.* variant of **апофиге́й**.

апофиге́й *m.* something farcical or idiotic, something difficult to grasp. Апофиге́ем (сомни́тельный неологи́зм, продик-то́ванный само́ю жи́знью) э́той скло́ки яви́лся сканда́л с та́нковым кооперати́вом АНТ. The most farcical thing (a dubious neologism, dictated by life itself) about that squabble was the scandal with the tank cooperative ANT.

• See also *апофеге́й*.

апофиги́зм *m.* indifference, couldn't-care-less attitude. Посла́нцы деся́тков, е́сли не со́тен предприя́тий изуча́ли о́пыт москвиче́й. А внедри́ли? Два-три... Что э́то? Боя́знь вы́сунуться? Апа́тия? Апофиги́зм? Delegates from dozens if not hundreds of enterprises came to see the experiences of the Muscovites. Did it have any effect? In two or three cases... Why so? Fear of standing out? Apathy? Sheer indifference?

аппара́т *m.* gear (equipment for a rock band or disco). Клёвый аппара́т у вас. Сейча́с все бы́вшие обзавели́сь клёвым аппара́том, Ки́нчев, наприме́р. А как игра́ли, так и игра́ют. Да́же ху́же. You've got great gear. Now all the old stylers've got themselves great equipment, Kinchev for example, but they play the same way as they always did. Worse, even.

а́ра *m.,f.* a Caucasian or Armenian. — Эй, а́ра! У вас что, все а́ры? — Нет, ты ту́рок! Hey, you—Armenian! Are you all Armenians, or what? — No, you're an Azeri!

• Lit. *macaw*.

арма́да *f.* the Soviet Army. О, а ты чего́ тут зависа́ешь? — От арма́ды кошу́. And what are you doing here? I'm dodging the army. Шип, ты же, вро́де, в а́рмии? — Да закоси́л я арма́ду! — Как э́то? — Сбежа́л из ча́сти. You're in the Army, aren't you, dick? No, I gave the forces a wide berth! How come? I did a runner from my unit.

арно́льд *m.* body-builder, strong man.

• From the name Arnold Schwarzenegger. See also *качо́к*, *шварценейгер*.

арши́н *m.* phial of prepared drug solution. Пол-арши́на уже́ себе́ вка́лываю. I'm already injecting half a phial.

• *Арши́н:* old Russian measurement of 28 inches/70 cm.

аск *m.* busking, tapping, mooching, sponging. Пошли со мной на аск! Come busking with me! **жить на áске** *impf.* to live by begging, busking, tapping. На áске жить надоéло. I'm fed up living on the scrounge.

аскáть *v.t.* [*pf.* **аскнýть**] 1. to busk, tap, ask (usually passers-by) for money. Аскáть идти стрёмно, кругóм менты́. It's dodgy busking, cops all over the place. 2. to mooch, cadge (usually money) from someone. Мóжно аскáть всё, что угóдно, но обы́чно тéрмин аск подразумевáет и́менно дéньги. You can cadge anything, but usually the term tap refers to money. Нáдо у цивилов хáвку аскнýть. We'll have to cadge some grub out of some civvies. 3. to interrogate. В ментóвке продержáли три часá. Все какýю-то лáжу аскáли. They kept me in the cop-shop for three hours and asked me all kinds of crap.

аскéр *m.* busker, often experienced at begging for money.

аскнýть *pf.* of **аскáть**.

астрáл: вы́йти в астрáл *pf.* 1. to get high, cosmic. Я с Богдáновым не удрúнченный, ни утóрченный не свяжýсь, рáзве тóлько словлю́ крéзу с глю́ками и в пóлный астрáл вы́йду. I won't have anything to do with Bogdanov if I'm pissed or high, but only if I go crazy, start seeing things and get really cosmic. 2. to go beyond the physical world, have an out-of-body experience.

асфáльтовая болéзнь *f.* injuries caused by falling down drunk. Вáся, что э́то у тебя́ на лицé, проявилась асфáльтовая болéзнь? Vasya, what's up with your face—drunk again? **асфáльтовой болéзнью болéть** *impf.* to fall down dead drunk. Ну, подýмаешь, поваля́лся немнóжко, асфáльтовой болéзнью болéл. Well, you think: I'm down on the deck, drunk again.

• Lit. *asphalt* or *pavement sickness.*

атáс *interj.* watch out! edgy! look out! heads up! Атáс! Чи́ра тáщится. Look out—there's a teacher coming! **стоя́ть на атáсе** to stand guard, be lookout.

• Also *отáс!*

атáсник *m.* look-out. Лех, а атáсник-то наш слиня́л. — Стремянýлся, навéрное. Alex, our lookout's bolted. Probably freaked out.

атáсный *adj.* brilliant, excellent, very funny. Ксю́ша уж в такóм прики́де атáсном хóдит: шля́па какáя-то дря́ная, штаны́ сплошь из заплáт, босикóм. Ksyusha's going around in some really mad gear: a rubbishy hat, trousers with patches all over, and barefoot.

афга́нец *m.* soldier involved in the invasion of Afghanistan (1979-89); Afghanistan vet. Афга́нцы то́же бы́ли у Бе́лого до́ма. There were also Afghan vets defending the White House [i.e. during the failed coup of 1991].
• Lit. *Afghan.*

афга́нка *f.* military cap worn by Soviet troops in Afghanistan. Я представля́ю себе́ удивле́ние коопера́торов, когда́ на сле́дующий день к магази́ну подкати́ли два Нисса́н-патро́ла и вооружённые лю́ди в афга́нках поста́вили всех лицо́м к стене́. I can just imagine the surprise of the cooperative workers when the next day two patrol jeeps rolled up and armed men in Afghan caps put them face up against the wall.
• Lit. *Afghan.*

афи́ша *f.* round or fat face. Эй, жи́рный, полу́чишь по афи́ше, сра́зу вся кра́ска сле́зет. Here, fat face, look out or I'll clock you one straight in the kisser and let all the colour out.
• Lit. *poster.*

ахча́ *f.* money, dosh. С ахчо́й сего́дня ла́жа, и за́втра, и послеза́втра, и, пожа́луй, всегда́. It's been crap today for money, and tomorrow and the day after, maybe for good.
• See also *ба́бки, ба́шли, грин, грю́ник, зелёные, капу́ста.*

Б

ба́бки *f.pl.* money, dosh, dough. А ба́бки на рестора́н у тебя́ есть? And do you have dosh for the restaurant? **отби́ть ба́бки** *pf.* to take money back by violence. **поста́вить на ба́бки** *pf.* to sue. И е́сли ты что́-то пообеща́ешь и не сде́лаешь, тебя́ поста́вят на неусто́йку, на ба́бки и сни́мут их с тебя́ без по́мощи зану́дного арбитра́жа. If you promise something and don't produce the goods, they'll make you pay compensation, sue you and take it off you without the need for tiresome arbitration.
• Lit. *knuckle-bones* (children's game). See also *ахча́, ба́шли, грин, грю́ник, зелёные, капу́ста.*

ба́бник *m.* womaniser, romeo, skirt-chaser, chick-man.

ба́бочка *f.* girl, chick, young woman. Эй, ба́бочки, подходи́те к казака́м! Hey, girls—come and meet the Cossacks!
• Lit. *butterfly.* See also *герла́, ги́рла, жа́ба, тёлка, чуви́ха.*

база́р *m.* 1. gassing, yakking, chatting, talk. 2. gang fight. **впряга́ться в база́ры** *impf.* to get into gang fights. Паца́н обя́зан в зо́не жить в одно́й из семе́й, а по́сле освобожде́ния впряга́ться в база́ры. A non-conforming

prisoner has to live in the clink in one of the prison families but, after release, take part in gang fights.
- Lit. *bazaar.*

базáрить *v.i.* [*pf.* **побазáрить**] to gas, yak, chat.
- Lit. *to squabble.*

байкáл *m.* weak tea. Как ты пьёшь э́тот байкáл? How can you drink that dish-water?
- From Lake Baikal.

бак *m.* backup file. Зачéм тебé стóлько бáков? Why have you got so many backups?
- Used mainly by computer hackers.

баклáн *m.* hoodlum, thug, mugger (who often asks or goes looking for trouble). Ну и паршúвая зóна, однú баклáны. A right lousy area this is—swarming with thugs.
- Lit. *cormorant.*

бáксы *m.pl.* bucks, dollars. В автóбусе началúсь жáркие дебáты: стáвили бáксы. Heated debates started in the bus: people bet money.
- See also *ахчá, бáбки, бáшли, грин, грю́ник, зелёные, капу́ста.* Example taken from the youth fanzine, *Ниоткуда.*

балдёж *m.* 1. a great time, high. 2. drinking session, binge. Собралúсь всем клáссом, вы́пили—в о́бщем, балдёж. The whole class got together, drank, a great time, really.

балдёжный *adj.* funny, brill. Балдёжная дéвушка попáлась. A brilliant girl came along.

балдéть *v.i.* [*pf.* **забалдéть, обалдéть**] to have a great time, get high, adore. Я балдéю под *Аксéпт*! I'm really into *Accept*!

банáн *m.* 1. poor mark (1 or 2 from 5 in the Russian marking system). 2. dick, cock, prick, penis.
- Lit. *banana.*

бáнда *f.* band, group. Что за бáнда сегóдня игрáет? What kind of band's playing today?
- See also *бэ́нд, бэ́нда, комáнда.*

бандáн *m.* bandana, usually worn by rockers and metal-heads. Собралúсь мы на тусóвку, я—в бандáне. We got together for a gig, me in my bandana.

бáнка *f.* (also **полбáнки**) a half-litre bottle of vodka. Взя́ли на вéчер водя́ры две бáнки—показáлось мáло. We took two half-litre bottles of vodka to the party—it wasn't enough. **раздавúть бáнку** *pf.* to drink a bottle (often vodka). Раздавúли бáнку на двоúх. We downed a bottle of voddy for two.
- Lit. *jar.* C.f. *поллúтра* (*half-litre*). See also *пузы́рь.*

бардáк *m.* hell, nightmare, mess.
- Lit. *brothel.*

барда́чный *adj.* hellish, nightmarish.

бары́га *m.* black marketeer, fence, supplier. По паца́нским поня́тиям челове́к, занима́ющийся ку́плей-прода́жей—бары́га. In criminal terms anyone who buys and sells on is a supplier.

батино́к *m.* dad.
   • C.f. Ukrainian *ба́тя* (*father*).

батл *m., f.* [*pl.* батлы́] half-litre bottle. У меня́ с собо́й два ба́тла ва́йна. I have two half-litres of plonk with me.
   • See also *баттл, ботл*.

ба́тон *m.* [*pl.* батона́] 1. shirt made of soft multicoloured fabric with many buttons. 2. a large round badge. 3. button.

баттл *m., f.* variant of батл. задри́нчить из ба́ттла to have a drink out of the bottle.

ба́тя *m.* (term of address) mate, mister, pal. 'Куда́ пое́дем, ба́тя?' спроси́л такси́ст. 'Where are we off to, then, mate?' asked the taxi-driver.

башка́ *f.* nut, head, noggin.
   • See also *бестолко́вка, ре́па, ты́ква, ча́йник*.

башлеви́к *m.* artist working solely for money.
   • Coined by the musician Alexander Gradsky; a play on *большеви́к* (*bolshevik*).

ба́шли *pl.* [*gen.* -е́й] dosh, dough, money. Ра́зве э́то ба́шли? You call that money?
   • See also *ахча́, ба́бки, грин, грю́ник, зелёные, капу́ста*.

башля́ть *v.i.* [*pf.* забашля́ть] to pay. Ско́лько же он ей башля́ет за все удово́льствия? How much does he pay her for all the fun?

бая́н *m.* hypodermic syringe.
   • *Lit. bayan*, a traditional Russian accordeon. See also *маши́на*.

беда́ *f.* 1. bad news. Ну—э́то вообще́ беда́! Well, is that bad news or what? 2. generic term for drugs. 3. pervitine.
   • *Lit. trouble.*

бёздник *m.* a birthday. Ты был у него́ на бёзднике? Were you at his birthday party? Мне э́ту фе́ньку на бёздник подари́ли. I got this bracelet for my birthday.
   • See also *бёзник*.

безмазня́к *m.* garbage, rubbish, something worthless. Э́та кры́мская трава́—тако́й безмазня́к! That Crimean grass is hopeless.

безма́зовый *adj.* worthless, bad, rubbish, hopeless. Како́й-то безма́зовый пипл собра́лся—никако́го ка́йфа от обще́ния. Some useless folk were there: no buzz from hanging out with them. Здесь сто́пить—ситуа́ция безма́зовая. Hitch-hiking here is hopeless.

безнáл *m.* automatic bank transfer.
- In the Soviet system the amount paid in a cashless transaction was larger than that paid in cash. See also *нáлик*.

бёзник *m.* variant of **бёздник**.

бéлое *adj. used as noun* amphetamines, psychedelics, any manufactured drugs. Покупáю тóлько бéлое—от негó кайф лéгче. I only buy the white stuff—you get an easier kick from it.
- Lit. *white.* Also *бéлая хúмия.*

Бéлый дом *m.* 1. the Russian Supreme Soviet main building, the White House, scene of demonstrations and armed resistance to authority (as in the coup of 1991). Éльцин вы́ступил с тáнка у Бéлого дóма. Yeltsin spoke from a tank in front of the White House. 2. local authority headquarters in several Russian cities.

беля́шка *f.* morphine. Я на беля́шку подсéл—тепéрь прихóдится медсестёр бомбúть. I got hooked on morphine: Now I have to con some out of nurses.

бенд *m.* band, group. Флóра—крáйне неудáчный бенд. *Flora* are a really unlucky band.
- See also *бэнд, бáнда, комáнда.* Example taken from the fanzine, *Штирлиц.*

берёза *f.* 1. the Komsomol's team of volunteers which helped the police, often working as infiltrators; a member of that team. Вчерá берёза опя́ть устрóила винтúлово. The volunteers set up a raid again yesterday. 2. a police station where the Komsomol volunteer squad is based. Задéржанных достáвили в берёзу. They took those arrested to the nick. **свúнтиться в берёзу** *pf.* to be arrested or detained by the Komsomol squad.
- The team's radio call-sign was *берёза* (*birch-tree*).

беспонтóвый *adj.* good-for-nothing, worthless. беспонтóвый чувáк a hopeless guy.

беспрайсóвник *m.* being broke, skint. У меня́ в э́том мéсяце беспрайсóвник—бывáет, нé на что сигарéт купúть. I'm skint this month: sometimes can't even pay for fags. Не аскáй на негó—он беспрайсóвник. Don't ask him to tap you: he's broke.

беспрайсóвый *adj.* 1. free. Концéрт был беспрайсóвый. The concert was free. 2. skint, broke. Пипл был весь беспрайсóвый. The folk here were broke.

беспредéл *m.* 1. lawlessness, overt breaking of rules. Не занимáйся беспредéлом. Don't go breaking the rules. **творúть беспредéл** *impf.* to break the rules (in a labour camp). 2. person who flouts rules or acts in a lawless manner. 3. ill-treatment (usually of prisoners or army recruits).
- Criminal argot. See also *беспредéльщик.*

беспреде́льничать *v.i.impf.* to act in a lawless manner, to disregard the law. Конча́й беспреде́льничать! Stop breaking the rules!

беспреде́льщик *m.* lawless person, one who breaks rules or the law. Э́тот беспреде́льщик да́же свои́м надое́л. That mad swine has even got on his own lot's wick.
  • See also *беспреде́л.*

бестолко́вка *f.* head, nut, noggin. А бестолко́вка тебе́ заче́м? То́лько шля́пу носи́ть? And what's your nut for, just putting your hat on?
  • Lit. *a senseless thing*: ironic. See also *башка́, ре́па, ты́ква, ча́йник.*

бесфлэто́вый *adj.* homeless, having no place to stay over, or space for a guest. Пипл весь бесфлэто́вый—ви́дно, придётся ночь провести́ на вокза́ле. No one has anywhere to stay over; looks like we'll have to rough it at the station.

би́кса *f.* tart, slag, slut, whore, slapper.

биологи́чка *f.* biology teacher, lecturer (female).

битло́вский *adj.* Beatles, relating to the Beatles.

битлома́н *m.* Beatles fan (male).

битлома́нка *f.* Beatles fan (female).

би́тник *m.* 1. beatnik. 2. street fighter, hard man. Би́тники сказа́ли, что бу́дут всех бить, но не ста́ли. The bullies said they would beat everyone up, but they didn't.
  • Sense 2: play on words involving the Russian verb *бить* (*to beat*) and *beatnik.*

битни́ческий *adj.* Beatnik, relating to Beatniks.

битни́чество *n.* the Beatnik way, being a Beatnik.

блева́ть *v.t.* [*pf.* **блевану́ть**] to puke, spew, give the technicolour yawn. А быва́ют таки́е моме́нты, что в тече́ние 3-4 неде́ль блева́ть от э́того всего́ хо́чется. And there are times during the three or four weeks when it all makes you want to puke.
  • Example taken from the techno magazine, *ПТЮЧ.*

блево́тина *f.* spew, puke, sickness, vomit.

блин *m.interj.* blast! sugar! Блин! Sugar! May be used parenthetically: Вот, блин, неуда́ча кака́я. What a damned mess!
  • Lit. *pancake;* used as euphemism for *бля́дь* (*whore*). See also *бля́ха-му́ха.*

блэк *m.* negro, black person. На́ши вчера́ блэ́ка гро́хнули. Our lot did in a black yesterday.

блюз *m.* blues, blues music.

блюзме́н *m.* blues fan, musician. Но остально́е тошнотво́рно ту́по. Взбредёт кому́-то ещё в го́лову испо́лнить блюз 'Я Не Козёл'? По-мо́ему, они́ не шу́тят. But the rest is sickeningly stupid. Will someone else get it into their head to do the 'I'm No Swine' blues? In my opinion, they aren't joking.

• Example taken from the fanzine *Rock Fuzz*.

блю́зовый *adj.* blues, relating to the blues.

блю́минг *m.* a tall guy. Э́тот блю́минг как попёр на меня́! That big guy really tore a strip off me.

• Lit. *blooming (mill)*.

бля́дский *adj.* 1. relating to whores. 2. bloody, damned.

блядь *f.* whore, slag, slapper.

бля́ха-му́ха *interj.* damn! sugar! Опя́ть, бля́ха-му́ха, биле́ты потеря́ли. We've lost the tickets again, sod it!

• See also *блин*.

бодя́жить *v.t.* [*pf.* **забодя́жить, разбодя́жить**] to make up a fix (for injection). Пойду́ на ку́хню дрянь бодя́жить. I'm going into the kitchen for a fix (of a second-rate drug).

боеви́к *m.* 1. action film, blockbuster. В 19 часо́в в програ́мме телеви́дения сове́тский боеви́к. There's a Soviet action film on TV at 7 p.m. 2. member of a (criminal) paramilitary group. Боевики́ 'Па́мяти' угрожа́ют журнали́стам. 'Pamyat' hard men threaten the press.

болту́н *m.* chatterbox, big mouth.

болту́шка *f.* ephedrine. Как пионе́р, на болту́шке сижу́. I'm on ephedrine like some kid.

• Lit. *mash, swill*.

бо́мба *f.* 1. 0.7 litre bottle of wine. 2. crib sheet for cheating at exams.

• Lit. *bomb*. 2. See also *шпо́ра*.

бомби́ть *v.t.impf.* to rob, swindle. Реши́ли бомби́ть путан во́зле казино́. We decided to rob the toms by the casino. Бомби́ть ха́ты тепе́рь ста́ло сложне́е. It's got more difficult to screw apartments now. **бомби́ть фирму́** to swindle or rob foreigners. Е́здили в центр бомби́ть фирму́. They would go into town to rob foreigners.

• Lit. *to bomb*.

бомж *m.* down-and-out, tramp, homeless person. У петербу́ргских бомже́й появи́лась со́бственная газе́та, кото́рая называ́ется На дне. The homeless of Petersburg have started their own paper called *The Lower Depths*.

• Abbreviation for *без определённого места жительства. На дне* refers to Gorky's play. See also *бомжи́на, бомжи́ха*.

бомжа́тник *m.* place where drifters sleep and eat, doss-house, drop-in centre. Теа́тр начина́ется с ве́шалки, а Москва́—с бомжа́тника. At the theatre the evening starts at the cloakroom; in Moscow, at the doss-house.

бомжева́ть *v.i.impf.* to be, live on the street, to be homeless.

бомжина *m.* homeless person, tramp (also mode of address). Крутóй бомжина—без вóдки не остáнется. A great tramp—he'll never be short of vodka.

• See also *бомж, бомжиха.*

бомжиха *f.* female tramp, down-and-out, bag lady, homeless person.

• See also *бомж, бомжина.*

борзéть *v.i.* [*pf.* оборзéть] to be cheeky, to act cocky. Что э́то у вас в рóте молоды́е борзéют? What's this about the young lot in your company acting up?

бóрзость *f.* cockiness, cheekiness, act designed to draw attention to oneself. Я из тебя́ бóрзость-то вытрясу́! Пóнял? I'll shake that cheek out of you, got it?

бóрзый *adj.* cheeky, cocky, insolent. Ишь ты какóй бóрзый! You've a real cheek, you have! You haven't got half a cheek!

бормотá *f.* cheap red wine, plonk.

• See also *бормотýха.*

бормотýха *f.* variant of **бормотá**. От бормотýхи головá боли́т. I've got a headache from that plonk.

бортанýть *v.t.pf.* 1. to give the knock back, reject, refuse. 2. to deceive, con, swindle, fool. А егó бортанýли, конéчно. They conned him, of course.

босс *m.* boss, boss-man, big shot, chief, guvnor.

ботáн *m.* bookworm, swot.

• See also *ботáник.*

ботáник *m.* variant of **ботáн**. Дéвочки егó не люби́ли, потомý что он был ботáник. The girls didn't like him because he was a swot.

• Lit. *botanist.*

ботл *m.* [*pl.* ботлы́] variant of **батл**.

брáзер *m.* brother. Мой брáзер совершéнно отупéл от учёбы. My brother went completely mad from studying.

• See also *брáйзер.*

брáйзер *m.* variant of **брáзер**.

брандспóйт *m.* dick, prick, penis. Вы́тащил брандспóйт и давáй забóр поливáть. He got his prick out and watered the fence.

• Lit. *fire-pump, water-cannon.*

брейк *m.* break-dancing.

• See also *брейк-дáнс.*

брейк-дáнс *m.* break-dancing.

• See also *брейк.*

брéйковый *adj.* break-dancing, relating to break-dancing.

бри́тиш *m.* [*pl.* бри́тиша́] Briton, brit. Мне оди́н бри́тиш дал жвáчку. A British bloke gave me a chewing-gum.

бритишо́вый *adj.* British. Джи́нсы бритишо́вые никто́ не ви́дел. No one's seen British jeans.

бритоголо́вый *adj. or used as noun* skinhead.

брод *m.* main street. Жил, был, рабо́тал, не уныва́л, вечера́ми гуля́л по бро́ду, как называ́ют в го́роде коро́тенькую у́лицу, собира́ющую по вечера́м бря́нскую общи́тельную молодёжь. He lived his life, worked, never was glum, in the evening walked along the main street, as they call the short street where the sociable young people of Bryansk meet.
 • Derived from *Broadway.*

брэндо́вый *adj.* brand new. брэндо́вый тру́зер new trousers.

буго́р *m.* 1. leader, boss, boss-man. Ты хоте́л ви́деть бугра́? Did you want to see the boss? 2. head of work brigade in labour camp. Паралле́льно с отрица́ловкой существу́ет друга́я эли́та, друга́я власть—активи́сты, подде́рживаемые администра́цией. Называ́ют их *бугра́ми* и́ли *рога́ми.* Alongside the non-cooperators, there's another élite, another source of authority—activists supported by the authorities. They're called the *bugry* or *roga.* 3. **е́хать за буго́р** *impf.* to go abroad. **за бугро́м** abroad. **из-за бугра́** from abroad.
 • Lit. *mound.* See also *por.*

бу́ндес *m.* [*pl.* бундеса́] German, Jerry, Germany. Бу́ндес предложи́л мне провести́ с ним ночь. A German proposed that we spend the night together.
 • From German *Bundesrepublik* (*Federal Republic*). See also *бу́ндэс.*

бу́ндесовый *adj.* German. Та́чку хочу́! Бу́ндесовую. Мерс хочу́! I want a car—a German one. I want a Merc!
 • See also *бундэсо́вый.*

бу́ндэс *m.* variant of **бу́ндес.**

бундэсо́вый *adj.* variant of **бу́ндесовый.** Э́тот реко́рд родно́й? Нет, бу́ндэсовая печа́тка. Is this record Russian? No, it's a German pressing.

буре́ть *v.i.* [*pf.* забуре́ть] to get pissed, sloshed, ratted, legless.
 • Lit. *to go brown.*

бу́рый *adj.* 1. drunk, high on drugs. Вы́шел из ба́ра соверше́нно бу́рый. He came out of the pub smashed out of his mind. Ну, ты бу́рый—на самого́ бугра́ бо́чку ка́тишь! Look, man, you're smashed. You'd even have a go at your own boss!

буха́рик *m.* piss-head, alkie, drunk. Ва́ся—про́сто ти́хий буха́рик, никому́ жить не меша́ет, Vasya's just a quiet drunk. He doesn't give anyone any trouble.
 • See also *а́лик, алка́ш, алкона́вт, кирю́ха синега́л, синю́га.*

буха́ть *v.i.* [*pf.* **бухну́ть**] to have a drink (alcohol). Мы с дружко́м сиди́м по-ти́хому, буха́ем. My mate and I just sit quietly and have a drink.

бухну́ть *pf.* of **буха́ть**.

бык *m.* popular guy. Э́тот бык постоя́нно в на́шем рестора́не пасётся. That guy's always eating in our restaurant.
* Lit. *bull, ox.*

быто́вка *f.* trouble.
* See also **бытову́ха.**

бытову́ха *f.* (everyday) problem, life. Дава́й тепе́рь поговори́м о бытову́хе. Хо́дишь ли, наприме́р, по магази́нам? Где достаёшь проду́кты, оде́жду? Now let's talk about life in general. Do you go shopping? Where do you get your groceries, clothes? 2. also **быто́вка.** Something other than professional crime that lands you in trouble. Я по бытову́хе в тюрьму́ попа́л, когда́ с сосе́дями пья́ный подра́лся. I landed in prison for fighting with the neighbours when I was drunk.

бы́чить (наро́д) *v.t.impf.* to get (people) going. Но что но́вого мо́жет сказа́ть нам рок сего́дня? Он хо́чет встряхну́ть люде́й, бы́чить наро́д? What can rock music say to us today that's new? Does it set out to shake people up, to get them going?

бэ́би *m.,f., indec.* baby, kid. У неё ско́ро бэ́би поя́вится, а от кого́—неизве́стно. She's going to have a kid soon, but whose it is no one knows.
* See also *бэ́бик, бэ́бис, бэ́йби.*

бэбиёнок *m.* kid, baby. Они́ реши́ли бэбиёнка завести́. They decided to try for a baby.
* Mixture of *бэ́би* and *ребёнок.* See also *бэ́бик, бэ́бис, бэ́йби.*

бэ́бис *m.* [*pl.* бэбиса́] baby. У нас бэ́бис тако́й клёвый! We've got a fab baby! С бэ́бисами забо́т мно́го. Babies are a lot of work.
* See also *бэ́би, бэ́йби.*

бэг *m.* bag. У меня́ в бэ́ге ботл. I've a half-litre bottle in my bag.

бэ́йби *m.,f.* variant of **бэ́би.**

бэк *m.* backside, buttocks. укури́ться в бэк *pf.* to become high, out of it (esp. from smoking drugs).
* See also *бэкса́йд.*

бэкса́йд *m.* buttocks, backside. Иди́ ты в бэкса́йд. Go to Hell!
* See also *бэк.*

бэнд *m.* variant of **бенд.**

В

важня́к *m.* investigator assigned to important cases. Гдлян вро́де важняко́м был. It appears Gdlyan was a top detective.

вайн *m.* wine, alcohol. затари́ться ва́йном в шо́пе to stock up with booze in the shop.

вайто́вый *adj.* white. вайто́вый тру́зер white trousers.

вали́ть *v.i.* [*pf.* **свали́ть**] to beat it, scarper, bolt, do one. Вали́м отсю́да по-бы́строму. Let's beat it sharp like. Услы́шав э́то, я сра́зу же свали́л. When I heard that I beat it straight away.
  • See also *слиня́ть, сма́тываться, смыва́ться.*

ван *m.* one-rouble note. Дай мне хотя́ бы ван. Give me just one rouble!
  • See also *вано́к.*

вано́к *m.* variant of **ван.**

варёный *adj.* bleached (used mainly of denim garment). па́рень, оде́тый в варёную ку́ртку a lad in a bleached jacket.
  • Lit. *boiled.*

вдува́ть *v.i.* [*pf.* **вду́нуть, вдуть**] to give a blow-back (blow hashish into someone else's mouth). Ты вдува́ть когда́-нибу́дь про́бовал? Have you ever tried a blow-back?
  • Lit. *to blow into.*

вду́нуть *pf.* of **вдува́ть.**

вдуть *pf.* of **вдува́ть.**

ве́ник *m.* prat, idiot, blockhead. Э́тот ве́ник вина́ до за́втра не доста́нет. That prat will never get any wine by tomorrow.
  • Lit. *brush, besom.*

вентану́ть *pf.* of **вента́ть.**

вента́ть *v.i.* [*pf.* **вентану́ть**] to go. Вчера́ вента́ли на се́йшен. We went to a gig yesterday.
  • Variant of вэнтать [*pf.* вэнтануть].

веня́к *m.* [*pl.* **веняки́, ве́нники**] vein (for injecting narcotics). Попили́л веняки́. He cut his veins with a blade. **полоска́ть ве́нники** *impf.* to cut one's veins, slash one's wrists.
  • See also *поко́цать, попи́сать ве́нники.*

верня́к *adv.* for sure, a sure thing. Да не обла́мывайся, верня́к биле́ты доста́нем. Don't get down, we'll get tickets for sure.

верта́к *m.* record-player. Купи́л верта́к, тепе́рь пласти́нки нужны́. I've bought a record player; all I need now is some records.
  • See also *верту́шка.*

верту́шка *f.* record-player. У э́той верту́шки звук кла́ссный. This record-player gives a really classy sound.
  • Lit. *turntable.* See also *верта́к.*

верховоди́ть *v.t. impf.* to run (the show).

ветера́н *m.* veteran, old hand, person who has been in the hippy or youth scene for some time.

вздро́гнуть *v.i.pf.* to have a drink, a jar. Ну, что, вздро́гнем? Well, shall we have a snifter?
  • Lit. *to start, wince, flinch.*

взрыва́ть *v.i.impf.* to light up a joint. Дава́й, Ма́ня, взрыва́й сама́. Go on, Manya, light up one yourself.
  • Lit. *to blow up.*

вида́к *m.* video.

ви́деть в гробу́ в бе́лых адида́сах *phr.impf.* a contemptuous remark about someone worthless. Почему́-то мне присни́лся Джо́ша, в гробу́ бы я его́ ви́дел в бе́лых адида́сах. For some reason I dreamed I saw Josh in his coffin in white trainers.

винт *m.* 1. detention, arrest. Ещё оди́н винт—и я то́чно обхайра́юсь, чтобы менто́в не привлека́ть. One more pick-up and I'll get my hair cut so that I don't attract the attention of the fuzz. 2. police raid. В про́шлый винт сорва́ли у меня́ с руки́ люби́мую фе́нечку, пода́рок одно́й герлы́, к кото́рой я на тра́ссе приколо́лся—её фе́нечка мне в любо́й моро́з ру́ку гре́ла. In the last raid they took from me my favourite friendship bracelet, a present from one girl I really got to like on the road—it would always warm my hand however sharp the frost. 3. cop(s), pig(s), filth, fuzz. Смотри́, сюда́ винт е́дет. Look out, the cops are on their way. 4. pervitine. Сейча́с пол-Москвы́ на винте́ сиди́т. Half Moscow's on pervitine these days. 5. computer hard disk. На винте́ ме́ста почти́ не оста́лось. There's hardly any space left on the hard disk.
  • Lit. *screw, spiral.* Sense 5: see also **хард**.

винтану́ть *pf.* of **винти́ть**.

винти́лово *n.* police raid. Вчера́ на Го́голях тако́е винти́лово бы́ло! There was one hell of a raid on Gogol (Street) last night!
  • See also *винт* (2).

винти́ть *v.t.* [*pf.* **винтану́ть, повинти́ть, свинти́ть**] to arrest, pick up, detain. То́лько мы скипа́ть собрали́сь, как прие́хал по́лис и всех винти́ть на́чал. Just as we were to beat it the police came and started arresting everybody. Меня́ чуть не свинти́ли, но я во́время слиня́л. I nearly got picked up, but I cleared off just in time.
  • Lit. *to screw up.*

винтово́й *adj.* 1. addict who uses a psychedelic drug. Чува́к винтово́й, всего́ стрема́ется. A guy on psychedelic stuff, he freaks out at everything. 2. used to describe the effect of a psychedelic drug. **винтово́й прихо́д** psychedelic rush, buzz.
  • Lit. *spiral.*

вка́лывать *v.i.impf.* to put in a shift, work like a dog. По во́семь часо́в на заво́де вка́лываю. I work like a dog eight hours at a time at the factory.

вкос *m.* high, state of euphoria. Покури́ли, вошли́ во вкос. We had a smoke and got happy.

вла́мывать *v.i.* [*pf.* **вломи́ть**] to beat up, give a doing. Втроём они́ мне здо́рово вломи́ли. The three of them gave me a real doing.

влом *m.* see лом.

вломина́дзе *f.* beating, scrap. Там така́я вломина́дзе была́! What a scrap it was!

вломи́ть *pf.* of вла́мывать.

вло́мно *adv.* in a depressed or down way.

вло́мность *f.* state of melancholy, the blues.

вма́зать *pf.* of вма́зывать.

вма́зка *f.* fix, dose of a drug. Джéфа ещё на вма́зку хва́тит. There's still enough ephedrine for one shot.

вма́зывание *n.* injection of drugs, shooting up.

вма́зывать *v.i.impf.* [*pf.* **вма́зать**] 1. to hit, strike, whack someone. Вмажь ему́, чтобы не борзе́л. Give him a clout to stop his cheek. 2. to inject a dose of a drug, shoot up. То́лько он меня́ вма́зал, у меня́ круто́й кайф пошёл. As soon as he gave me a shot I had a great trip. **вма́зываться** [*pf.* **вма́заться**] to shoot up, get a fix, inject. 3. to have a drink (alcohol). Хорошо́ вма́зал. I've had a good drink.
• Lit. *to cement in.*

вмонти́ровать *v.t.pf.* to have a drink (alcohol). На́до ещё гра́ммов две́сти вмонти́ровать. Let's have another couple of drinks, let's have another glass.

води́ла *m.* driver. Води́ла попа́лся неразгово́рчивый, всю доро́гу кури́л. We got a real surly driver; he smoked all the way.
• See also дра́йвер.

водя́ра *f.* vodka, voddy.

возника́ть *v.i.* [*pf.* **возни́кнуть**] to annoy, act up. Я его́ уда́рил, чтобы не вознику́л. I gave him a clout so that he wouldn't get on my nerves.
• Lit. *to arise.*

возни́кнуть *pf.* of возника́ть.

вок *m.* variant of ворк. Удо́бный вок—су́тки на рабо́те, трое до́ма. It's convenient work—one day on, three off.

волоку́ша *f.* a high. Хоро́шая волоку́ша от э́той травы́. You get a good high from this grass.
• See also та́ска.

волоса́тый *adj. used as noun* long-haired person, hippy. Я узна́л, что волоса́тых без по́вода забира́ют в мили́цию, где нере́дко избива́ют, оскорбля́ют, наси́льно стригу́т. I found out that they march off hippies to the police station for no reason, often beat them up, humiliate them and cut their hair by force. **волоса́тые ублю́дки** long-haired, hippy bastards. **волоса́тый флэт** hippy pad.

• Lit. *hairy*. An often affectionate hippy mode of address.

вольтану́тый *adj.* mad, mental. Совсе́м вольтану́тый чува́к, техни́ческий спирт пить собира́ется. The guy's right off his rocker, he's gonna drink industrial alcohol.

вольты́ *m.pl.* hallucinations. Вольты́ пошли́. He started seeing things.

ворк *m.* (regular) job. Пойду́ на ворк устра́иваться. I'm going to try to get a job.

• See also *вок*.

во́ркать *v.i.impf.* to work, be in work. Я ны́нче не во́ркаю. I'm out of work at present.

во́ркер *m.* (manual) worker. Во́ркеры тепе́рь бастова́ть научи́лись. The workers have now found out about going on strike.

воро́на *f.* girl, babe, bird. Кла́ссная воро́на в ла́йбе сиди́т. The classy bird's sitting in a foreign car.

• Lit. *crow*, a regional term. See also *куку́шка* (*cuckoo*), *ку́рица* (*chicken*).

воя́ка *m.* military man. Воя́ки перевози́ли на свои́х самолётах спирт. The servicemen used to transport alcohol in their planes.

впа́ривать *v.t.* [*pf.* **впа́рить**] to sell unscrupulously, palm off. Впа́рил я ему́ э́ту ша́пку из соба́ки. I palmed off that hat made of dog-fur on him.

впа́рить *pf.* of **впа́ривать**.

вписа́ть *pf.* of **впи́сывать**.

вписа́ться *pf.* of **впи́сываться**.

впи́ска *f.* flat, crash-pad, place to hang out. Со впи́ской вообще́ по́лный обло́м, весь пипл бесфлэто́вый—придётся до утра́ в паradняка́х тусова́ться. There's absolutely nowhere to stay over, no one's got a place sorted at all. We'll have to hang around in doorways till the morning. У меня́ в э́том го́роде ни одно́й впи́ски нет. I don't know a single place to stay in this town.

• Lit. *entry*.

впи́сывать *v.t.* [*pf.* **вписа́ть**] 1. to put someone up (temporarily). Он бо́льше не впи́сывает—у него́ ма́зер из о́тпуска верну́лась. He can't put anyone up any more—his old dear's come back from holiday. Я герло́в впи́сываю, а мэ́нов—нет.

I put birds up, not guys. 2. to help someone to get somewhere. Он вписа́л нас в по́езд. He got us onto the train.
• Lit. *to enter, insert.*

впи́сываться *v.i.* [*pf.* вписа́ться] 1. to stay at someone's place (temporarily). Мы вписа́лись на найт к клёвым циви́лам. We stayed the night with some great civvies. 2. to join, to get a good job. вписа́ться в экспеди́цию to join an expedition. вписа́ться в КамАЗ to get a job at KamAZ (motor works).

вре́зать *pf.* of вреза́ть.

вреза́ть *v.i.* [*pf.* вре́зать] 1. to have a drink. Вре́зали по чуть-чу́ть. We all had a wee drop to drink. 2. to punch, whack, clock. Я ему́ так вре́зал, что он тут же вы́рубился. I clocked him so hard he passed out on the spot.
• Lit. *to cut in.*

вруб *m.* [*pl.* вру́бы] getting the hang of something, getting into (enjoying) something. По́сле э́того у меня́ начался́ вруб в матема́тику. After that maths just clicked for me.
• Lit. *cut.*

вруба́ть *v.t.* [*pf.* вруби́ть] 1. to switch on. Вруби́ компью́тер. Turn the computer on. 2. to treat someone to something. Я её в кайф вруба́л, а она́ вруби́лася в секс. I tried to give her a high, but she got into sex.
• Lit. *to cut into.*

вруба́ться *v.i.* [*pf.* вруби́ться] 1. to be turned on. Здесь свет не вруба́ется—наве́рное, про́бки перегоре́ли. The light won't go on here—the fuses must have blown. 2. to dig, be into, get (understand). Я в дринк не вруба́юсь. I'm not into alcohol.
• Lit. *to cut into.* See also *въезжа́ть, прика́лываться, рюха́ть.*

вруби́ть *pf.* of вруба́ть.

вруби́ться *pf.* of вруба́ться.

всё пучко́м *phr.* everything's all right, okay.
• See also *всё пучо́к.*

всё пучо́к *phr.* everything's all right, okay.
• See also *всё пучко́м.*

всё тип-то́п *phr.* everything's fine, hunky dory.

всё хокке́й *phr.* everything's okay.

вски́нуться *v.i.pf.* to get done, dolled up. Иногда́ хо́чется вски́нуться для о́тдыха. Sometimes I want to get all done up to feel good.
• Lit. *to leap on.*

втере́ться *pf.* of втира́ться.

втира́ться *v.i.* [*pf.* втере́ться] to shoot up, to get a hit. Он втира́ется опиу́хой. He shoots up with opium.
• See also *гнать по ве́не, дви́гаться, коло́ться, тре́скаться, ширя́ться, шмы́гаться.*

вторя́к *m.* tea used twice. Э́то уже́ вторя́к ти́па *Бе́лых ноче́й.* This is used tea, like *White Nights.*

втре́скаться *pf.* of **тре́скаться.**

ву́ндеркинд *m.* smart or clever student, swot, clever-clogs.
  • See also *зубри́ла, первокла́ссник.*

въезжа́ть *v.i.* [*pf.* **въе́хать**] [в + *acc.*] 1. to get the picture, take something in. Что, совсе́м не въезжа́ешь в происходя́щее? What, can't you see what's going on? 2. to dig (understand) Бра́тки и сестрёнки, е́сли вы въезжа́ете в DEATH, GRIND, DOOM, INDUSTRY, дава́йте меня́ться кассе́тами. Brothers and sisters, if you're into Death, Grind, Doom and Industry, let's swap cassettes.
  • Lit. *to enter, drive into.* See also *вруба́ться, прика́лываться.* Second example taken from the rock fanzine, *Blitzkreeg.*

въе́хать *pf.* of **въезжа́ть.**

вы́воз в лес *m.* abducting a victim to extract information by torture. Есть да́же назва́ние э́тому: вы́воз в лес. Одного́ мы вывози́ли, что́бы он созна́лся в уби́йстве подéльника. There's even a name for this: 'taking them into the woods'. We did it to one guy to get him to confess to murdering an accomplice.
  • Criminal argot.

вы́дринчать *pf.* of **дри́нкать.**

вы́дрынкать *pf.* of **дры́нкать.**

выдрю́чиваться *v.i.* [*pf.* **вы́дрючиться**] to show off, grandstand, draw attention to oneself. Выдрю́чивается как чемпио́н. He shows off like a champion.
  • See also *козли́ть* (1).

вы́дрючиться *pf.* of **выдрю́чиваться.**

выпада́ть *v.i.impf.* [*pf.* **вы́пасть**] to drop out (of society).

вы́пасть *pf.* of **выпада́ть.**

вы́писать *pf.* of **выпи́сывать.**

выпи́сывать *v.t.* [*pf.* **вы́писать**] to kick, throw out. Нас вы́писали с флэ́та. They chucked us out of the flat. 2. to get hold of (often in a hurry). Дава́й вы́пишем ба́бочек. Let's get hold of some chicks.
  • Lit. *to copy out, subscribe.*

выруба́ть *v.t.* [*pf.* **вы́рубить**] 1. to turn off. Вы́руби свет—пора́ спать. Turn the light off, it's time to get some kip. 2. to knock someone out. Он его́ с пе́рвого уда́ра вы́рубил. He knocked him cold with one smack. 3. to get hold of. Где бы джéфа вы́рубить? Where could we get some ephedrine?
  • Lit. *to cut down, out.*

выруба́ться *v.i.* [*pf.* **вы́рубиться, отруби́ться**] 1. to be switched off. Свет вы́рубился. The light went off. 2. to pass

out from exhaustion, be shattered. **Я две ночи не спал—совсем вырубаюсь.** I haven't slept for two nights; I'm completely done in. 3. to be knocked out. **Этот каратист вырубился после первого удара дубинкой.** This karate guy went out at one blow from the club.
 • Lit. *to cut one's way out of.*

вырубить *pf.* of **вырубать.**

вырубиться *pf.* of **вырубаться.**

вытерка *f.* 1. note, paper with written message. 2. railway ticket. 3. (fake) prescription for drugs.
 • Criminal argot.

вышак *m.* death sentence.

вышибала *m.* bouncer.

вэнтать *v.i.* [*pf.* **вэнтануть**] see **вентать.**

Г

газометр *m.* arsehole, anus.
 • Punk terminology.

гайка заслабить *phr.pf.* to be scared stiff.
 • Punk terminology.

гасилово *n.* fight, beating. **Вчера любера пришли—такое гасилово было!** Yesterday hard men from Lyubertsy turned up: what a fight there was!

гасить *v.t.* [*pf.* **загасить**] to beat (to death), to do in. **Сидели мы на флэту, а тут вдруг этот торчок пришёл, обдолбанный в умат, и начал всех гасить.** We were sitting at the pad when all of a sudden that junkie appeared, out of his face on drugs, and started beating the hell out of everybody.
 • Lit. *to extinguish.*

гвоздить *v.t.* [*pf.* **изгваздать**] to beat, give a doing. **Если бы он стучал, его можно было бы гвоздить на законном основании.** If he'd squealed on us, we'd have every right to give him a real doing.
 • Lit. *to bang.*

география *f.* any Western currency except the US dollar, British pound or the Deutschmark.
 • Lit. *geography.* Used in Moscow street markets.

герла *f.* [*pl.* **герлы, гёрлы;** *gen./acc. pl.* **герлов, гёрл**] girl, chick, babe. **Второй час треплется с какой-то герлой по телефону.** That's over an hour he's been blathering to some girl on the phone. **герла покайфная** cool chick, real babe, stunner.

Герла́ пока́йфная, но уже́ вписа́лась. She's a real babe, but already spoken for.
- See also *ба́бочка, герлёнок, герлёныш, герли́ца, герлу́ха, герлу́шка, гирла́, жа́ба, пчела́, тёлка.*

герлёнок *m.* chick, babe.
- See also *ба́бочка, герла́, герлёныш, герли́ца, герлу́ха, герлу́шка, гирла́, жа́ба, пчела́, тёлка.*

герлёныш *m.* variant of **герлёнок**.

герли́ца *f.* variant of **герла́**.

герло́вый *adj.* girl's, chick's, woman's.

герлу́ха *f.* variant of **герла́**.

герлу́шка *f.* variant of **герла́**.

гешефт *m.* shady transaction, put-up job.
- German *Geschäft* (*business*).

гирла́ *f.* variant of **герла́**. Ба́бки и гирла́—вот и все его́ дела́. Money and his chick: that's all he's interested in.

глаза́ в ку́чку *phr.* 1. wide-eyed (with amazement). 2. pie-eyed, drunk.
- See also *глаза́ в пучо́к.*

глаза́ в пучо́к *phr.* 1. wide-eyed (with amazement). 2. pie-eyed, drunk.
- See also *глаза́ в ку́чку.*

глу́хо *adv.* very bad, lousy. С пра́йсом глу́хо, не на что и ча́ю попи́ть. I'm absolutely skint—I can't even afford a cup of tea.

глюк *m.* [*pl.* глю́ки] 1. hallucination. У тебя́ уже́ глю́ки пошли́. You're already hallucinating. 2. A fantasy, something unreal. Сиди́м мы на флэту́, и вдруг у меня́ глюк, что сейча́с по́лис придёт. We're sitting at the flat and all of a sudden it gets into my head that the pigs are coming. **лови́ть глю́ки** *impf.* to get stoned, see things. Е́сли мне в кайф лови́ть глю́ки и ничего́ не де́лать? So what if I'm quite happy to get stoned and do nothing?

глюка́лово *n.* hallucinations.

глюкова́ть *v.i.impf.* to hallucinate, see things.

глюкови́дный *adj.* illusory, imaginary. Подхо́дит ко мне мент глюкови́дный и кося́к предлага́ет. An imaginary copper walks up and offers me a joint.

глюкоге́н *m.* hallucinogenic drug.

глю́читься *v.i.* [*pf.* приглю́читься] to imagine, see, be a product of one's imagination. Глю́чится мне, что менты́ пришли́. I think the cops've come. А мне приглю́чилось, что ты ещё вчера́ скипну́л. But I thought you'd left yesterday.

глю́чный *adj.* hallucinatory, mad (looking as if caused by hallucinogenic drugs). Смотри́, како́й глю́чный прики́д. Look at that mad gear.

гнать *v.i.impf.* 1. to tell lies, tell an unlikely story. Ты, Máшa, кончáй гнать про ночнóе дежýрство вне óчереди. *Masha, stop fibbing about being on night duty out of turn.* 2. [на+ *acc.*] to knock, criticize, slate. Что ты всё врéмя на меня гóнишь? *Why are you always having a go at me?* **гнать телéги** *impf.*, **прогнáть телéгу** *pf.* to spin someone a line, talk crap. Ну, чувáк, ты и гóнишь телéги. *Come off it, mate, you're talking rubbish.* **гнать** [*pf.* **прогнáть**] **по вéне** *phr.* to shoot up, inject drugs.

• Lit. *to drive, hunt; to distil.* Synonyms for *гнáть по вéне*: see also *втирáться, двúгаться, колóться, трéскаться, ширяться, шмыгаться.*

гнилóй *adj.* rotten, lousy. гнилóй человéк a lousy guy.

гниляк *m.* 1. rotten, bad feature. В нём гниляка мнóго—кúнуть мóжет. *There's a lot that's rotten about him—he might con you.* Им чáсто поговорúть бывáет нé о чем, вот и начинáют срáвнивать Пúтер с Казáнью: где гниляк, где—ништяк. *They often talk about nothing much; they'll compare Petersburg and Kazan' and work out what is rubbish and what is cool.* В Казáни тусóвка—гниляк. *The Kazan' scene is rotten.*

говнó *n.* crap, shit, bullshit. **съесть с говнóм** *pf.* to give a bollocking, to eat (someone) for breakfast.

• *Съесть с говнóм:* Mit'ki term. A combination of *смешáть с говнóм* (*to mix with shit*) and *съесть с кáшей* (*to eat with porridge*).

говносóс *m.* swine, bastard. Ну и тусóвка, сплошнýе говносóсы! *What a crew, utter bastards.*

• Lit. *shit-sucker.* See also *говносóска.*

говносóска *f.* swine, bastard.

• See also *говносóс.*

годúтся *impf.* okay, that's fine, that'll do. Я вас бýду ждать у Триумфáльной áрки...в шесть? Годúтся. В шесть у áрки. *I'll wait for you at the Triumphal Arch...at six? Okay. Six at the Arch.*

• See also *гожó.*

гожó *adv.* okay. Две бутýлки хвáтит? Гожó. *Will two bottles do? Okay.*

• See also *годúтся.*

голúмый *adj.* real, pure, extremely. Этот мен—голúмая шúза! *That guy's a pure schizoid!*

голосá *m.pl.* Russian-language broadcasts from the West. Éсли голосá перестáнут слýшать в нарóде, то их всё равнó бýдут слýшать в 16-ом ГУ КГБ. *Even if everyone stops listening to foreign stations, section 16 of the KGB will still be listening to them.*

• Lit. *voices.*

голя́к *m.* lack, absence. С сигаре́тами у нас голя́к. We've no cigarettes—zilch!

го́нки *f.pl.* unlikely stories, lies. Сейча́с он придёт—опя́ть го́нки начну́тся. He'll be here in a minute—more tales of the fantastic!
• Lit. *races.*

го́нщик *m.* liar, teller of unlikely tales, storyteller. Он го́нщик стрёмный—всем говори́т, что с племя́нником Бре́жнева во́дку пил. He's a real storyteller—tells everyone he used to drink with Brezhnev's nephew.
• Lit. *racer.* See also *теле́жник.*

го́пник *m.* [*pl.* го́пники, *coll.* гопня́ра, гопота́] yob, lout, neanderthal. Э́то го́пники, они́ меша́ют мне жить. They're yobs—they won't leave me in peace. Та пу́блика, на кото́рую ты се́туешь—сопли́вая гопота́,—к нача́лу перестро́йки находи́лась ещё в несозна́тельном во́зрасте. That lot you're grumbling about—they're snotty scum—they weren't old enough to know when perestroika started.

гоп-сто́п *m.* mugging. Фари́да продемонстри́ровала отрабо́-танную те́хнику гоп-сто́па, в не́сколько секу́нд сорва́в с прохо́жей се́рьги, часы́, кольцо́, вы́потрошив су́мочку. Farida demonstrated a very refined technique of mugging: in a few seconds she'd grabbed earrings, a watch and a ring from a passing woman and gutted her bag at the same time.

горчи́чник *m.* 1. police officer. 2. (also **горчи́шник**) hundred-rouble note. Ста́рый горчи́шник подде́лать легко́. It's easy to forge an old hundred-rouble note.
• Lit. *mustard poultice.*

горчи́шник *m.* variant of **горчи́чник** (2).

горшо́к *m.* crash-helmet. На горшке́ рога́ приде́ланы, как у фаши́ста. He had horns fixed to his crash-helmet, like a fascist.
• Lit. *pot, chamber-pot.* See also *шлема́к.*

гражда́нка *f.* 1. civilian clothes. У капта́ра гражда́нку для самохо́дов пря́тали. Soldiers would keep civvy gear hidden in the stores for going awol. 2. civilian, civvy life. Уво́лившись из а́рмии при пе́рвой возмо́жности, он нигде́ на гражда́нке не находи́л себе́ досто́йного ме́ста. Once out of the army as fast as he could, he couldn't find a suitable place in civvy street.

гра́ндж *m.* grunge, grunge music, culture. Для тво́рчества мно́гих подо́бных по сти́лю FAITH NO MORE групп характе́рен при́нцип: «гра́ндж у́мер, да здра́вствует гра́ндж!» The principle of 'Grunge is dead, long live grunge' is typical of the art of many groups of the Faith No More style.
• Example from the fanzine, *Наш драйв.*

гранж *m.* variant of **грандж**.

гранч *m.* variant of **грандж**.

гребень беспонтовый *m.* someone easily exploited and cheated, a sucker. Этот гребень беспонтовый и с ваучерами пролетел—отдал за три штуки. That sucker even messed up with his (privatization) vouchers—he gave them away for three grand.

грейндж *m.* variant of **грандж**.

грелка *f.* bottle of vodka. Раньше на демонстрацию 7 ноября всегда грелку прихватишь. You would always take a bottle with you on the November seventh revolutionary parade.
* Lit. *hot-water bottle.*

грета *f.* (punk) girl. У Ника новая грета появилась. Nick's got a new woman.

грин *m.* [*pl.* **грины**] dollar bill, buck. яйца раскрашенные иностранцам за грины запаривать selling painted eggs to foreigners for dollars.

гроб *m.* civil defence. Все нормальные студенты гроб сачкуют. All normal students skip civil defence sessions.
* Student jargon, used ironically as the first two letters of each word in *гражданская оборона (civil defence)* form *гроб,* lit. *coffin.*

грохнуть *v.t.pf.* to kill, do in. Стучал он, за то и грохнули. He grassed, so they did him in.
* Lit *to crash (down).* See also *угрохать.*

гроши *m.pl.* 1. [stressed **гроши**] very little money. А заготовительные фирмы платят за продукцию гроши. State procurement firms pay their workers peanuts. 2. [stressed **гроши**] a month's wages. А гроши-то тебе какие платят? And what money do you get every month, then?

грудь: принимать [*pf.* **принять**] **на грудь** to drink, booze. И поменьше принимайте на грудь. And cut down a bit on the booze.

грузить *v.i.impf.* to talk nonsense, rubbish, to go on. Он грузит людям об этих ваучерах, а они всему верят. He goes on to people about those vouchers, and they believe the lot.
* Lit. *to load.* See also *лечить.*

групповик *m.* group sex, orgy.
* See also *групповуха.*

групповуха *f.* 1. group sex, orgy. кайф от групповухи a kick from group sex. 2. crime committed by a group.
* See also *групповик.*

грызло *n.* poppy heads, poppy straw (prepared for chewing for narcotic effect).

грюник *m.* buck, quid. Для тебя—тысяча баксов. Или, как говорят московские коллеги—таузенд грюников. То

you—a thousand bucks. Or as our friends in Moscow say, a thousand greenbacks.

• See also *ахча́, ба́ксы, ба́шли, грин, зелёные, капу́ста.*

гря́дка *f.* 1. table (in a restaurant). Официа́нт подвёл меня́ к гря́дке фирмаче́й. The waiter led me to a table usually reserved for foreigners. 2. **гря́дку обдерба́нить** to collect poppy heads.

• Lit. *ridge, edge.*

грязно́тик *m.* sleaze ball, dirty or dirty-minded person.

гря́зные *adj. used as pl.noun.* [often **гря́зными**] money, dirty money. Гря́зными выхо́дит в полу́чку ты́сяч со́рок, чи́стыми, коне́чно, ме́ньше. It works out at about 40,000 in dirty money, less in clean, of course.

гуж *m.* technical or vocational school. На́до идти́ в гуж. I have to go to college.

• Lit. *tug.*

гужи́ *f.pl.* students of a vocational college.

гусь *m.* a thing, a bee in one's bonnet. Не пристава́й к челове́ку—ви́дишь, гусь у него́. Don't annoy the man—look: he's got a real bee in his bonnet.

• Lit. *goose.*

Д

дабл *m.* loo, bog, toilet. Пойду́, поищу́, где здесь дабл. I'm going to look for the bog.

да́блиться *v.i.* [*pf.* **прода́блиться**] to shit, take a crap. Пойду́, поищу́, где прода́блиться. I'm going to look for somewhere to have a crap.

да ла́дно alright, then; okay, fine.

дальнобо́йщик *m.* long-distance lorry-driver.

дальня́к *m.* latrine at labour camp. На́до по́сле обе́да сходи́ть на дальня́к. After dinner I have to go to the latrine.

• From *да́льний (distant),* as latrines are often placed far from other quarters.

да́тский *adj.* relating to festivals, holidays or birthdays. Ра́ньше у нас бы́ли да́тские спекта́кли. We used to have special shows at holiday times.

да́тый *adj.* drunk, pie-eyed, legless.

• See also *подда́тый.*

да́ун *m.* 1. downer, depression, the blues. Ушёл в да́ун. He got very low. 2. shock.

дви́га *f.* dose of a drug for injection, shot, hit, fix.

дви́гаться *v.i.* [*pf.* **дви́нуться, задви́нуться**] to shoot up, inject. Коло́ться мо́жно и пеницилли́ном, а дви́гаться—

поня́тно чем. You can even inject penicillin, but you know what you shoot up with.

• Lit. *to move, get going*. See also *втира́ться, коло́ться, тре́скаться, ширя́ться, шмы́гаться.*

движо́к *m.* 1. hypodermic syringe. 2. car passing along the road. Каки́е то́лько движки́ че́рез мой перекрёсток не проезжа́ют! The cars that pass my crossing!

• Lit. *slide*.

дви́нутый *adj.* crazy, loopy, mental, mad.

• Lit. *moved*. See also *завёрнутый*

дви́нуться *v.i.pf.* 1. to go crazy, nuts. 2. *pf.* of **дви́гаться**.

• Lit. *to move, get going*. See also *крезану́ться.*

дво́ечник *m.* idiot, dunce, dumb-dumb (student who gets grades of 2 from the five-point marking system).

дво́йка *f.* a two, an unsatisfactory grade of two given at school or university (from five, with five the maximum mark).

дед *m.* [*pl.* **деды́**] barrack-room senior, army bully-boy (soldier in the last year or 100 days in the army, often involved in army brutality).

• Lit. *grandfather*. See also *де́душка.*

дедова́ть *v.i.impf.* to rule the roost, be demob-happy, act as if release were approaching.

де́душка *m.* variant of **дед**.

• Lit. *grandfather*.

де́ка *f.* tape-deck. Де́ка джапэно́вая, со вся́кими примо́чками. A Japanese tape-deck with all kinds of gadgets.

делово́й *adj. used as noun.* smart Alec. Éсли ты тако́й делово́й, то свали́, пока́ по ча́йнику не да́ли. If you're so smart then you'll get out of here before someone clocks you one in the face.

• Lit. *business(-like)*.

де́мбель *m.* 1. demob-time. 2. soldier about to be demobilized.

де́мбельский *adj.* demob, relating to demobilization. Приходи́лось разрисо́вывать де́душкам де́мбельские альбо́мы. We had to draw all over the leaving albums of the soldiers being demobbed. **де́мбельский акко́рд** the last job a soldier has to do before leaving the army (usually construction or repair work). Вся́кий де́душка зна́ет—есть де́мбельский акко́рд, то есть сро́чное зада́ние, вы́полнив кото́рое, мо́жно сме́ло гла́дить пара́дку. Every serviceman on the point of demob knows that there's one urgent job he has to complete, and that after that he can iron his dress uniform knowing it's just about all over.

демократиза́тор *m.* rubber police truncheon (introduced during Gorbachev's 'democratization' policy). Разма́хивая демократи-за́торами, спецна́зовцы ста́ли разгоня́ть демонстра́нтов.

Brandishing their batons, the special police started dispersing the demonstrators.

деморо́сс *m.* member of the Democratic Russia Party.

демшиза́ *coll.f.* people who like going on demonstrations. Вся демшиза́ тепе́рь к Анти́лову переметну́лась. All the demo-crowd have gone over to Antilov.

• A blend of *демокра́т* and *ши́за.*

депресня́к *m.* downer, depression. У меня́ сплошны́е депресняки́. I'm depressed as hell.

• See also *депресу́ха.*

депресова́ть *v.i.impf.* to be on a downer, to feel low. Ну что ты депресу́ешь из-за таки́х пустяко́в? Why get down over such nonsense?

депресу́ха *f.* downer, depression.

• See also *депресня́к.*

дерба́н *m.* 1. field of cannabis or poppies. 2. collection of opium poppies.

дерба́нить *v.t.* [*pf.* **надерба́нить, обдерба́нить**] to collect poppies, cut poppy heads. В Ла́твии ма́ки дерба́нить мо́жно пря́мо на у́лице. In Latvia you can pick poppies straight off the streets. 2. to get (buy). Я тут карто́шечки надерба́нил. I managed to buy spuds here.

дербяно́й *adj.* wooden.

• See also *дербя́ный.*

дербя́ный *adj.* wooden.

• By analogy with *деревя́нный.* See also *дербяно́й.*

деревя́нный *adj. used as noun* derogatory nickname for the rouble, wooden (by analogy with gold, silver, paper currency). Кида́ли иностра́нцев на зелёные, бары́г—на деревя́нные. They conned foreigners out of dollars, and sellers out of roubles.

дёрнуть *v.i.pf.* to take a puff, drag, draw (of a cigarette). Герла́, дай дёрнуть! Give me a drag, love!

• Lit. *to pull.*

деса́нтик *m.* ten-copeck coin.

• Lit. *paratrooper.*

десанту́ра *coll.f.* parachute-troops, or former airborne troops.

десятю́нчик *m.* variant of **деса́нтик.**

джа *f.* cannabis. Гру́ппа *Джа́-дивижн* выступа́ет под фла́гом растафа́ри и воспева́ет траву́ с Яма́йки. The group *Ja-Division* appears under the banner of Rastafari and waxes lyrical about grass from Jamaica.

• From *ganjah,* Jamaican marijuana.

джаз *m.* jazz.

джаз- *in compounds* **джаз-гру́ппа** jazz group. **джаз-ба́нда, джаз-бенд** jazz band.

джазме́н *m.* jazz fan, musician.

джа́зовый *adj.* jazz, relating to jazz.

джангл *m.* jungle (music).

джа́пан *m.* [*pl.* джапэна́] a Jap, Japanese. Повора́чиваюсь—стои́т пе́редо мной тако́й симпати́чный джа́пан лет пяти́десяти. I turned round and saw such a nice Japanese of about 50.

джа́панский *adj.* Japanese. Ля́лька зале́зла ко мне в су́мку и доста́ла отту́да паке́т с нату́ра́льными джа́панскими кроссо́вками на липу́чках. The girl put her hand in my bag and took out a bag of Japanese running shoes with velcro.

джапэно́вый *adj.* variant of **джа́панский**.

джа-экпре́сс *m.* blow-back (blowing drug smoke into someone else's mouth).
  • See also *вдува́ть, парово́з.*

джеф *m.* 1. liquid drug from ephedrine. Где бы дже́фа вы́рубить? Where could we get some ephedrine? 2. ephedrone.
  • See also *сопле́вич, сопли́вчик.*

джордж *m.* [*pl.* джорджи́] a Georgian. Пришли́ джорджи́ с на́йфами. Some Georgians with blades appeared.

джорджо́вый *adj.* Georgian.

дзен *m.* Zen philosophy. У него́ шиза́—во́ркеров в дзэн вруба́ть. He's got this crazy idea in his head about turning the workers onto Zen.

дзэн *m.* variant of **дзен**.

дина́ма *f.* variant of **дина́мо**.

динами́зм *m.* constant letting-down. Меня́ зафа́кал его́ динами́зм. I got pissed off with his unreliability.
  • Lit. *dynamism.*

дина́мик *m.* supporter of the Moscow Dynamo football club. По́сле ма́тча начало́сь мочи́лово с дина́миками. After the match there was a scuffle with Dynamo fans.
  • Lit. *loudspeaker.*

динами́ст *m.* unreliable person, let-down.
  • See also *дина́мщик.*

дина́мить *v.t.* [*pf.* продина́мить] 1. to break one's word, let down. Он обеща́л коробо́к травы́, но уже́ тре́тий ме́сяц меня́ дина́мит. He promised me some grass, but that's already three months he's let me down. 2. to con. А мо́жет, лу́чше его́ продина́мим? Maybe it's better to con him?

дина́мо *n. indec.* 1. scam. 2. someone who stands you up. Ну, ты дина́мо! Я тебя́ уже́ час жду. A right let-down you are—I've

already been waiting an hour! **крути́ть дина́мо** *impf.* Дина́мо крути́ть взду́мала? Were you going to let me down?
- Lit. *dynamo.* See also *дина́ма.*

дина́мщик *m.* unreliable person, let-down. Он стра́шный дина́мщик. He's really unreliable.
- See also *динами́ст.*

диске́та *f.* computer diskette. Дай па́ру диске́т. Give me a couple of disks.

ди́чка *f.* wild cannabis.

догна́ться *pf.* of **догоня́ться.**

догоня́ться *v.i.* [*pf.* **догна́ться**] 1. to inject a second shot. По-мо́ему, пора́ догоня́ться. I think it's time for another hit. 2. to drink alcohol after drugs. Догна́лись бормоту́хой. We chased the gear with some cheap plonk.

дозня́к *m.* shot, fix (one dose). Я себе́ дозня́к наби́л до трёх ку́бов. I gave myself a massive shot, up to 3 c.c.

доро́га *f.* tracks, scars caused by injecting. С таки́ми доро́гами ско́рую вызыва́ть без ма́зы. With marks like that there's no point in calling out the ambulance.
- See also *доро́жка.*

доро́жка *f.* variant of **доро́га.**

доска́ *f.* 1. woman with small breasts. Доска́, два соска́. She has a really flat chest, just two nipples. 2. religious icon. Е́здили по деревня́м за доска́ми—у стару́х покупа́ли задёшево. We went round the villages looking for icons and picked some up cheap from old women. 3. **свой в до́ску** trustworthy, loyal, sound person. Ты его́ не стесня́йся—он па́рень свой в до́ску. Don't shy from him—he's a sound guy.
- Lit. *board.*

достава́ть *v.t.* [*pf.* **доста́ть**] to pick on, pester, bug someone. Жена́ меня́ достава́ла из-за де́нег. My wife's been nagging me about money. С утра́ на уша́х виси́т—всех доста́л. I've had him round my neck all day—everyone's fed up with him.
- Lit. *to get, touch.*

достав́учий *adj.* annoying, bugging.

доста́ть *pf.* of **достава́ть.**

доту́мкать *v.i.pf.* to get the point, click. Доту́мкал, заче́м парово́з пуска́ют? Do you see why people get blow-backs?

дофени́зм *m.* not giving a damn about anything, couldn't-care-less attitude. Оте́чественный дофени́зм воспи́тан Комсомо́лом. National apathy has been engendered by the Komsomol.
- See *фе́ня.*

дофени́ст *m.* apathetic or couldn't-care-less person. Э́тому дофени́сту ничего́ не дава́й. Don't give that bugger anything; he doesn't give a damn.

дошуру́пить *v.t.pf.* to understand, get, twig. Ну, выкла́дывай, что дошуру́пила? Come on, spill the beans, what did you make of it?

драб *m.* a drug sold by gypsies.
  • Gypsy term for *grass*.

дра́га *f.* pharmacy, drugstore. Пошёл бы в дра́гу, да тёрки нет. I'd go to the chemist's, but I haven't got a (fake) prescription.
  • See also *дра́гстор, дра́гстэр.*

дра́гстор *m.* pharmacy, chemist's shop. В э́том дра́гсторе маши́ны не продаю́тся. They don't sell hypodermics in this chemist's.
  • See also *дра́гстэр, дра́га.*

дра́гстэр *m.* variant of **дра́гстор.**

драйв *m.* drive, energy, pzazz. сыгра́ть с больши́м дра́йвом to play with great energy.

дра́йвер *m.* [*pl.* драйвера́, дра́йверы] 1. car (hitch-hiking). Засто́пили дра́йвер ти́па Во́лга. We hitched a lift in a Volga. 2. driver. Нам на тра́ссе клёвый дра́йвер попа́лся. This great guy gave us a lift.

дра́йвный *adj.* buzzing, full of pzazz, energy.
  • See also *драйво́вый.*

драйво́вый *adj.* full of go, pzazz, energy, buzzing.

дра́мер *m.* drummer.

драмс *m.* drums. А кто у них на дра́мсах? Who have they got on drums?
  • See also *дра́мсы́.*

драмси́ст *m.* variant of **дра́мер.**

дра́мсы́ *m.pl.* drums.
  • See also *драмс.*

дринк *m.* booze, alcohol. Я к дри́нку не прика́лываюсь. I don't touch booze.

дрикану́ть *pf.* of **дри́нкать, дринча́ть, дри́нчить, дры́нкать.**

дри́нкать *v.i., v.t.* [*pf.* дринкану́ть, вы́дринкать] to drink (alcohol), booze.

дри́нкач *m.* drunkard.
  • See also *дри́нкер.*

дри́нкер *m.* drunkard.
  • See also *дри́нкач.*

дринк-кома́нда *f.* a pack of drunkards. Вчера́ опя́ть э́та дринк-кома́нда завали́лась и устро́ила беспреде́л. That crowd of drunks turned up again yesterday and caused havoc.

дринч *m.* variant of **дринк.**

дринча́ть *v.i., v.t.impf.* variant of **дри́нкать**.

дри́нчить *v.i., v.t.impf.* variant of **дри́нкать**.

дринч-кома́нда *f.* variant of **дринк-кома́нда**.

дри́нчер *m.* variant of **дри́нкер**.

дриньк *m.* variant of **дринк**.

дрочи́ла *m.,f.* tosser, wanker, masturbator.
 • Vulgarism. See also *дрочи́ло*.

дрочи́ло *m.* wanker, tosser, toss-pot.
 • Vulgarism. See also *дрочи́ла*.

дро́чи́ть *v.t., v.i.* [*pf.* **подрочи́ть**] to wank, toss, jerk off, play with oneself.
 • Vulgarism.

дро́чка *f.* wanking, tossing, jacking off.
 • Vulgarism.

друг *m.* [*pl.* **друзья́**] mate, pal (a form of address). Ты, друг, вообще́ офиге́л. You're completely off your head, mate.

дрынд *m.* car. Купи́л дрынд америка́нский. I've bought an American car.

дрынк *m.* variant of **дринк**.

дры́нкать *v.i., v.t.* [*pf.* **вы́дрынкать**] variant of **дри́нкать**. После́днюю буты́лку вы́дрынкали. They drank the last bottle.

дрянь *f.* drugs, often of inferior quality, bogus gear. У Ма́ши всегда́ дрянь найдётся. Masha will always have some cheap gear on her.
 • Lit. *rubbish.*

дуба́к *m.* 1. frost. На у́лице тако́й дуба́к—под ми́нус со́рок! There's a hell of a frost outside: getting on for minus 40. 2. oaf, idiot, dolt. У нас старшина́ был тако́й дуба́к! Our sergeant major was an utter dolt.

дуби́зм *m.* stupidity. Он уво́лился из а́рмии, из боево́й ча́сти, и счита́л себя́ же́ртвой войсково́го дуби́зма и горбачёв-ской конве́рсии. He was discharged from active service, and considered himself a victim of military lunacy and Gorbachev's economic reforms.

дурдо́м *m.* psychiatric hospital, nuthouse, loony bin. Лёг отдохну́ть в дурдо́м. I went to the mental hospital for a rest. Там тако́й дурдо́м. That place is a such a madhouse.

дури́лка карто́нная *f.* friend, pal: a friendly mode of address.
 • Used by Mit'ki (lit. *cardboard idiot*).

дурь *f.* any drug which is smoked. Дурь кла́ссная, бы́стро цепля́ет. Great stuff—takes effect straight away. **дурь жена́тая** joint, spliff.
 • Lit. *stupidity.*

дух *m.* [*pl.* **ду́хи**] 1. native of Central Asia. Ду́хи пошли́ в ата́ку на рассве́те. The Asians went into the attack at dawn. 2. young

army recruit, scum, scumbag, new boy (new recruit, bullied by everyone in the barrack-room).
- (1) See also душма́н. (2) Army jargon. See also дед, де́мбель, слон, фаза́н, черпа́к.

душма́н *m.* 1. native of Central Asia. А росси́йские солда́ты привы́чно имену́ют таджи́ков душма́нами. Russian soldiers usually refer to Tadzhiks as *dushmans.* 2. young army recruit.
- Borrowed from Afghan *dushman* (*enemy*); was used by Soviet press to refer to anti-Soviet fighters in Afghanistan. See also дух.

дык *interj.* exclamation of confirmation, pleasure, surprise, pain, etc. Дык ёлы-па́лы! Damn!
- Used by Mit′ki. See also *а вот так!*

дыра́ *f.* 1. needle mark. С таки́ми ды́рами в менто́вку лу́чше не попада́ть. With marks on your arm like that you'd better not end up at the cop-shop. 2. hole, lousy place. Охо́та тебе́ жить в тако́й дыре́! What makes you want to live in such a dump?

ды́рка *f.* 1. see дыра́ (1). 2. tart, slapper. Е́сли я алка́ш, то ты про́сто ды́рка! If I'm an alkie, you're nothing but a tart!

дю *pron.* mode of address (to a stranger). Эй, дю! Hey, you!
- German *du* (*you*).

дя́дька *m.* boy, young man; mode of address to a boy. Де́вушки тепе́рь называ́ют ю́ношей дя́дьки, а те их—пчёлы. Girls these days call boys uncles and they call them bees.

Е, Ё

еба́ло *n.* gob, kisser, cake-hole.
- Vulgarism.

ёбаный *adj.* fucking, damned.
- Vulgarism.

еба́ть *v.t.impf.* [*pf.* вы́ебать, отъеба́ть] to fuck, shag, screw. Ёб твою́ мать. Fuck off, go fuck yourself, go and get fucked.
- Vulgarism. *еба́ть:* ебу́, -ёт; past: ёб/еба́л, ебла́/еба́ла.

еба́ться *v.i.impf.* to screw, fuck (each other), have a fuck, shag.
- Vulgarism.

ёкалэмэнэ *interj.* euphemism for *fuck your mother.*
- Formed like *блин* (q.v.) by using the first letter of a taboo word and several extra letters in alphabetical order.

ёлки-па́лки *interj.* sugar! damn! hell!

ело́вый *adj.* yellow. Ело́вые трузера́—э́то кру́то. Yellow trousers—cool!

ёлы-па́лы *interj.* damn, hell.

Ж

жа́ба *f.* girl, girlfriend
 • Lit. *toad.* Term used by punks.

желе́зная тра́сса *f.* a good road for hitch-hiking.

желе́зно *adv.* sure, for sure. Я сказа́л, встре́тимся,—зна́чит, желе́зно. I said we'd meet, and I mean it.

жид *m.* jew-boy.

жлоб *m.* [*pl.* **жлобы́**] 1. boor, lout, yob, rude person (usually male). 2. greedy person, miser.
 • From Yiddish.

жло́бский *adj.* rude, boorish. жло́бские шу́точки rude jokes.

жло́бство *n.* yobbishness, boorishness.

жлобьё *coll.n.* a crowd of yobs.
 • See also *жлоб.*

жмот *m.* miser, tight git.

жмур *m.* dead person, stiff. Ро́дственники жму́ра отстегну́ли ла́бухам по со́тне. The relatives of the deceased gave the musicians a hundred each. **жму́ра лаба́ть** *impf.* to play at a funeral. Когда́ был без рабо́ты, приходи́лось и жму́ра лаба́ть. When I was unemployed I used to have to play at funerals.

жо́па *f.* arse, ass, backside, bum. пья́ный в жо́пу pissed as a fart. Иди́ в жо́пу! Piss off! Fuck off!
 • Vulgarism.

жо́пник *m.* arse-bandit, shirt-lifter, queer, poof, bender.
 • Vulgarism.

жук *m.* 1. hit man, person employed to kill someone. И тот жук, что вса́дит перо́ в стукача́ с превели́ким свои́м блатны́м удово́льствием, тут же, родно́й, на вышша́к и отпра́вится. And the hit man is a guy who'll stick a knife into a grass with the greatest of criminal pleasure, mate, and will get the death sentence there and then. 2. person who knows the ins-and-outs of the criminal underworld.
 • Lit. *beetle.*

З

забалде́ть *v.i.pf.* to get high, to be out of it. Вы́пил две табле́тки, но забалде́ть не смог. I took two tabs, but they had no effect.

забашля́ть *pf.* of **башля́ть**.

забива́ние *n.* rolling a joint.

забива́ть [*pf.* **заби́ть**] **кося́к** *phr.* to roll a joint.
   • Also *заколáчивать кося́к.* See also *кося́к.*

забива́ть [*pf.* **заби́ть**] [на + *acc.*] to forget or ignore something. Забéй на э́ту исто́рию! Forget the whole thing! **забива́ть** [*pf.* **заби́ть**] **на всё** to forget all your troubles. Отдохни́, забéй на всё! Relax, forget it all!

забира́ть [*pf.* **забра́ть**] **в а́рмию** 1. to conscript, call up into the army. Не случа́йно ча́ще говоря́т *забра́ли в а́рмию*, чем *призва́ли*. It's no coincidence that you more often hear people say they were *called up* than *recruited*. 2. to be picked up (by the police).

заби́ть *pf.* of **забива́ть**.

заби́ться *v.i.pf.* to make an appointment, arrange to meet. Заби́лись на шесть часо́в вéчера. We agreed to meet at six in the evening.
   • Lit. *to get into.*

забодя́жить *pf.* of **бодя́жить**.

забо́йный *adj.* great, fab, first-rate. забо́йный фильм a terrific film.

за буго́р, за бугро́м see **буго́р**.

забурéть *v.i.pf.* to gain influence.

завали́ть *v.t.pf.* to fail (exam)
   • Lit. *to block up.*

завёрнутый *adj* 1. [на + *prep.*] obsessed (with something). 2. crazy, mad.
   • Lit. *wrapped (up).* See also *дви́нутый, задви́нутый.*

заверну́ться *pf.* of **завора́чиваться**.

завéситься *v.i.pf.* to hang oneself. А Ги́тлер завéсился и́ли застрели́лся? Did Hitler hang himself or shoot himself?

зависáлово *n.* obsession, problem, concern. У меня́ зависáлово насчёт э́тих дéнег. I've got a problem about that money.

зависáть *v.i.* [*pf.* **зави́снуть**] 1. to be attracted by, fancy [на + *prep.*]. Он на э́той герлé зави́с. He fancies that girl. 2. to lose all sense of time, wait for ages. Приéхал на флэт занайта́ть и зави́с надо́лго. He came to the flat to spend the night and hung around waiting for ages.
   • Lit. *to hover.*

зави́снуть *pf.* of **зависáть**.

завора́чиваться *v.i.* [*pf.* **заверну́ться**] 1. to be obsessed by [на + *prep.*]. Он заверну́лся на дзен-будди́зме. He's gone mad on Zen Buddhism. 2. to go off your nut, round the bend.

заворо́т: попа́сть в заворо́т *phr.pf.* to end up in a spot, hot water, trouble.
- Lit. *to end up round a bend.* See also *в капка́не.*

завяза́ть *pf.* of **завя́зывать.**

завя́зка *f.* close relationship. У нас появи́лись завя́зки в престу́пном ми́ре. We've gained some connections in the criminal underworld.
- Lit. *string, band; opening.*

завя́зывать *v.i.* [*pf.* **завяза́ть**] to give up, chuck. Наве́рное с ки́ром завяза́л бы и на́чал пы́хать. He'd probably quit the drink and start smoking pot.
- Lit. *to tie up.*

загаси́ть *pf.* of **гаси́ть.**

заги́б *m.* unlikely story, tall tale, bullshit. Ну, э́то уж по́лный заги́б. That's just a pure cock-and-bull story.
- Lit. *fold.*

загиба́ть *v.t.* [*pf.* **загну́ть**] to talk bullshit, tell unlikely stories. Ну, уж э́то ты загну́л. Come on, you made that up.
- Lit. *to fold, bend.*

загну́ть *pf.* of **загиба́ть.**

загру́зки *f.pl.* fibs, white lies. Я слу́шаю, как ты лю́дям загру́зки де́лаешь, и смею́сь. I hear the stories you tell people and I just laugh.
- Lit. *loads.* See also *зале́чки.*

задви́г *m.* mental disorder, turn. Е́сли бы не э́ти задви́ги, я не провёл бы три го́да в психу́шке. If it wasn't for these turns I'd never have spent three years in the crazy house.

задви́га *f.* girl on intravenous drugs.

задви́нутый *adj.* 1. way-out. задви́нутая му́зыка way-out music. 2. high on intravenous drugs. Он вчера́ задви́нутый был, стал по́лис в дзен вруба́ть—его́ и повинти́ли. He was high yesterday and started trying to convert some coppers to Zen, so they arrested him! 3. mad, crazy. Опя́ть э́тот задви́нутый пришёл. It's that nutter again.
- Lit. *pushed, bolted.* See also *завёрнутый, дви́нутый.*

задви́нуться *pf.* of **дви́гаться.**

задолба́ть *v.i.pf.* to bore someone out of his skull, to bore rigid. Существу́ет три сте́пени дебили́зма: деби́л, децибе́л, цеденба́л, а есть и четвёртая—задолба́л. Так вот, ты задолба́л! There's three degrees of lunacy: idiot, moron, screwball; and there's a fourth—boring git: and that's you—you've bored me stiff.
- The example is an intricate wordplay for which there is no easy translation. See also *затра́хать, зафа́кать.*

задри́нчить *v.i., v.t. pf.* А не задри́нчить ли нам? Shall we have a drink? Мы вчера́ так клёво ва́йна задри́нчили. We had such a great booze-up yesterday.
  • See also *дри́нчить.*

заеба́ть *v.t.pf.* to tire, wear out.

заеби́сь *interj.* variant of **зоеби́сь.**
  • Vulgarism.

закача́ешься *interj.* great! mental! brilliant!

заки́дывание *n.* pill-popping.

заки́дываться *v.i.* [*pf.* **заки́нуться**] to pop pills. Пе́ред се́йшеном на́до бы ци́клой заки́нуться. Before the concert we'll need to knock back some cyclodole. заки́нуться колёсами to swallow, take some tabs.
  • Lit. *to fall back.*

заки́нуться *pf.* of **заки́дываться.**

заки́сать *pf.* of **ки́сать.**

заки́саться *pf.* of **ки́саться.**

закла́дывать *v.i.* [*pf.* **заложи́ть**] 1. to inform, grass, rat on. 2. to drink alcohol. Он кру́то закла́дывает. He's a heavy drinker.
  • Lit. *to put behind, lay.* Also закла́дывать за га́лстук *to put away (drink).*

закола́чивать [*pf.* **заколоти́ть**] **кося́к** *phr.* to roll a joint. Она́ то́лько и уме́ет, что косяки́ закола́чивать. She only knows how to roll joints.
  • See also *забива́ть кося́к, кося́к.*

заколеба́ть *pf.* of **заколёбывать.**

заколёбывать *v.t.* [*pf.* **заколеба́ть**] to annoy, irritate. Заколеба́л ты меня́ свои́ми приди́рками. I'm really sick of your nagging.
  • *Колеба́ть* (lit. *to shake*).

заколоти́ть *pf.* of **закола́чивать.**

закомплексо́ванный *adj.* obsessively paranoid.
  • From *ко́мплекс неполноце́нности* (*inferiority complex*). See also зааци́кленный, комплексо́ванный.

законта́ченный *adj.* 1. contaminated, dirty. 2. a prisoner who has been in contact with the lowest-of-the-low in a labour camp. Е́сли опу́щенный воспо́льзуется веща́ми друго́го осуждённого, тот счита́ется 'законта́ченным' и до́лжен ли́бо смыть позо́р кро́вью петуха́, ли́бо призна́ть таковы́м и себя́. If one of the passive homosexuals uses the property of another prisoner, he's considered contaminated and has to expunge the disgrace with the blood of a queer, or else be considered one himself.

закоро́ты *pl.* stupid, senseless actions. У меня́ после́днее вре́мя каки́е-то стра́нные закоро́ты пошли́: вчера́ на рабо́ту идти́—в та́почках на у́лицу вы́шел. I've been doing some strange things recently. Yesterday I set off for work and saw that still had my slippers on.

закрыва́ть в ШИЗО́ (ПКТ) *v.t.* [*pf.* **закры́ть**] *phr.* to send to the psychiatric ward/punishment cells. За забо́ром нахо́дятся штрафны́е изоля́торы (ШИЗО́) и помеще́ния ка́мерного ти́па (ПКТ), куда́ закрыва́ют осуждённых за ра́зные посту́пки. Behind the wire they have the coolers and special cells where prisoners are confined for various offences.

• ШИЗО: *Штрафно́й изоля́тор* (isolation cell). ПКТ: *Помеще́ние ка́мерного ти́па* (cell).

закрыва́ться в ШИЗО́ (ПКТ) [*pf.* **закры́ться**] *phr.* to go to the punishment cells voluntarily. Петро́в на вре́мя бу́нта закры́лся в ШИЗО́, что́бы избежа́ть отве́тственности. During the riot Petrov had himself put in the cooler to avoid responsibility.

закры́ть в ШИЗО́ (ПКТ) *pf.* of **закрыва́ть в ШИЗО́ (ПКТ)**.

закры́ться в ШИЗО́ (ПКТ) *pf.* of **закрыва́ться в ШИЗО́**.

залета́ть *v.i.* [*pf.* **залете́ть**] to become pregnant (unintentionally). Ка́жется, я залете́ла, тепе́рь придётся тра́титься на або́рт. It seems I've got pregnant; I'll have to shell out for an abortion.

• Lit. *to fly beyond, into.*

залете́ть 1. *pf.* of **залета́ть. 2. залете́ть к бе́лым медве́дям** *phr.pf.* to be sentenced to a labour camp. Де́нег с меня́ не обло́мится, но зато́ подарю́ дорого́й сове́т: конча́й с Ка́реном, чтоб не залете́ть к бе́лым медведя́м. You won't get any money out of me, but I'll tell you this for nothing: break up with Karen, or you'll finish up in a camp.

• Lit. *to fly off to see the polar bears.*

зале́чки *f.pl.* white lies. Ты не зна́ешь его́ любо́вь к зале́чкам. You don't know his fondness for fibs.

• See also *загру́зки.*

зале́чник *m.* liar, fibber. Он стра́шный зале́чник. He's a real story-teller.

заложи́ть *pf.* of **закла́дывать**.

замасты́рить *pf.* of **масты́рить**.

замо́к *m.* second in command of a unit in the forces.

• A contraction of *замести́тель команди́ра взво́да*, the official abbreviation of which is *замкомвзво́да. Замо́к* lit. *lock.*

заморо́ка *f.* 1. disorientation after drug use. Заморо́ка пошла́. I'm out of it. 2. nonsense. Вся жизнь—одна́ заморо́ка. Life is just one big heap of nonsense.

заморочи́ть *v.t.pf.* to con, take in.

заморóчка *f.* something odd, strange. Ну вот, опя́ть он идёт со свои́ми заморóчками про Лао-цзе. Oh, look, here he comes again with his weird nonsense about Lao-Tse.

замочи́ть *pf.* of **мочи́ть.**

замути́ть *v.t.pf.* to cook up, brew, boil a strong tea used as a narcotic. Замути́-ка чайку́. Brew up some tea, will you.
• Lit. *to trouble.*

занайта́ть *v.i.pf.* to spend the night. Занайта́ли на тра́ссе. We slept on the road.
• See also *занайтовáть.*

занайтовáть *v.i.pf.* to spend the night.
• See also *занайтáть.*

зану́да *m.,f.* bore, boring git.

зану́дный *adj.* boring.

западлó *adv.* 1. humiliating, painful. Да́же послéднему из мужикóв западлó разговáривать с петухáми, рáзве что в слýчае осóбой нужды́ и непремéнно в грýбом, прикáзном тóне, с оскорблéниями и ругáнью. Even the lowest of the middle-ranking prisoners finds it very hard to speak to the queers, and even then does it only in extreme cases and always in a coarse, formal tone of voice, abusive and swearing. 2. *n.indec.* scumbag, scum.

запáривать *v.t.* [*pf.* **запáрить**] to sell.
• Lit. *to bake, stew.*

запáрить *pf.* of **запáривать.**

запи́л *m.* guitar solo. У Хéндрикса таки́е запи́лы! Hendrix has some really class solos.

запогáнить *v.t.pf.* to prepare a drug. мýльку запогáнить to sort some ephedrine.

запредéлиться *v.i.pf.* to go to the limit, to go as far as you can. Всё, я с э́тим запредéлился. That's enough, I've gone as far as I can with this.

зарáза *f.* cheap gear, inferior drugs. На э́том ры́нке зарáзу купи́ть прóще, чем картóшку. It's easier to buy the cheap stuff in this market than potatoes. 2. nuisance, pain (person).
• Lit. *infection.*

зарезáть *v.t.* [*pf.* **зарéзать**] to axe, demolish, chop (plan). На худсовéте прогрáмму зарéзали. The artistic committee chopped the programme.
• Lit. *to knife, kill.* See also *зарубúть.*

зарубúть *v.t.pf.* to demolish, chop (plan), to stop an article being published. Статья́ была́ готóва, но её заруби́л отвéтственный редáктор. The article was ready, but the editor-in-chief chopped it.

• Lit. *to kill.* See also *зарéзать.*

зарядúть *pf.* of **заряжáть.**

заряжáть *v.t.* [*pf.* **зарядúть**] to get a woman pregnant. Её рóдственники увéрены, что э́то ты её зарядúл,—так что придётся тебé женúться. Her family is sure it's you who got her pregnant, so you're going to have to get married.

• Lit. *to charge, load.*

засúтать *v.i.pf.* to sit for a while. Нáдо засúтать здесь, мóжет пипл подвáлит. We should sit here for a bit; maybe someone will come and join us.

заслúпать *pf.* of **слúпать.**

застебáть *pf.* of **стебáть.**

застóйные временá *n.pl.* the time of stagnation, i.e. the Brezhnev era. В концé застóйных времён он был молодым учёным в престúжном институ́те. At the end of the Brezhnev stagnation he was a young scholar in a prestigious institute. Also known as **застóльные временá.** В застóльные временá у всех под Нóвый год бы́ло шампáнское. In the time of stagnation everyone used to have champagne at New Year.

• *Застóльный (table-)* is a frivolous play on the word *застóйный (to do with stagnation).* The reference is to the many Soviet celebrations during the period of so-called *developed socialism.*

застóльные временá *n.pl.* see **застóйные временá.**

застóпить *pf.* of **стóпить.**

застремáть *pf.* of **стремáть.**

застремáться *pf.* of **стремáться.**

застэндовáть *pf.* of **стэндовáть.**

затáриваться *v.i.* [*pf.* **затáриться**] to provide the alcohol; to stock up with. Затáрились вáйном в шóпе. We stocked ourselves up with wine in the shop. Поéдем на овощебáзу рабóтать, апельсúнами затáримся. Let's go for a job at the greengrocery depot—we'll sort ourselves out with some oranges.

затáриться *pf.* of **затáриваться.**

заторчáть *pf.* of **торчáть.**

затрáхать *pf.* of **трáхать.**

• Euphemism for *заебáть.* See also *задолбáть, зафáкать.*

зафáкать *pf.* of **фáкать.**

• See also *задолбáть, затрáхать, зафáчить.*

зафáчить *pf.* of **фáчить.**

• See also *задолбáть, затрáхать, зафáкать.*

зафузóванный *adj.* fuzzy. зафузóванная гитáра fuzzy guitar (sound).

захабáрить *pf.* of **хабáрить.**

заха́вать *pf.* of ха́вать.

захи́дать *pf.* of хи́дать.

захомута́ть *pf.* of хомута́ть.

зацени́ть *v.t.pf.* to make the best of. Зацени́ плёночку! Try to do your best with the film!

зацепи́ть *pf.* of зацепля́ть.

зацепля́ть [*pf.* зацепи́ть] 1. *v.t.* to pick up, get. Приезжа́й и плёночку зацепи́. Come by and pick up the film. Е́сли бу́дет ма́за, зацепи́ где-нибудь ка́йфа. If you get the chance, pick up some gear somewhere. 2. *impers.* to feel the effects of alcohol or drugs, to be gone, out of it. Меня́ уже́ зацепи́ло. I've already lost it.
 • Lit. *to hook, catch.*

заци́кленный *adj.* obsessed.
 • See also *закомплексо́ванный.*

заци́кливаться *v.i.* [*pf.* заци́клиться] [на + *prep.*] 1. to be obsessed (with), neurotic (about). 2. to take cyclodole (tablets). На́до бы заци́клиться пе́ред се́йшеном. We should take some cyclodole before the concert.

заци́клиться *pf.* of заци́кливаться.

зачу́ханный *adj.* grotty, shabby. Все таки́е зачу́ханные, ру́чки двере́й в како́й-то смоле́, вокру́г пыль и грязь, секрета́рша под стать обстано́вке. Everything was so grotty—sticky door handles, dust and dirt everywhere, and a secretary to match the décor.

зашизо́ванный *adj.* 1. long-haired hippy. 2. schizo, mad, loopy.
 • See also *шизо́вый.*

защеми́ть *v.i.pf.* to put under pressure, make things difficult for. Плати́, ина́че защеми́м. Pay, or we'll make things tough for you.
 • Lit. *to pinch.*

зверь *m.* Caucasian (often serving as a soldier).
 • Lit. *beast, animal.*

звя́кать *v.i.* [*pf.* звя́кнуть] to ring up, to phone.
 • Lit. *to tinkle.*

звя́кнуть *pf.* of звя́кать.

здо́рово *adv.* well, great, brilliantly.

здоро́во *interj.* hi!

здра́вствуйте-пожа́луйста! *interj.* good grief! good God! Ну, здра́вствуйте-пожа́луйста, опя́ть купи́л не то, что проси́ла. Good God! He's gone and bought the wrong thing again.

зелёнка *coll.f.* dollar bills. У́ровни ра́зные—мо́жно гра́бить и раздева́ть, а мо́жно кида́ть на маши́ны, на кварти́ры, на зелёнку. There are different degrees of crime—you can rob and strip [cars], or you can con folk out of cars, flats or dollars.

зелёное *adj. used as n.noun* low-quality cannabis, ragweed.
- Lit. *green*. Named according to its colour.

зелёный *adj. used as m.noun* 1. dollar bill. 2. member of the Green environmental movement.
- Lit. *green*. 1. See also *ахчá, бáксы, бáшли, грин, грюóник, капýста*.

зéлень *coll.f.* variant of **зелёное**.

зёма *m.,f.* fellow town dweller, countryman, mate. Дай закурúть, зёма. Give me a fag, mate.

земéля *f.* variant of **зёма**.
- See also *зёма*.

зúпер *m.* [*pl.* зиперá] zip-fastener, zipper. трузерá на зúперах zip-up trousers.
- See also *зúппер*.

зúппер *m.* variant of **зúпер**.

зоебúсь *interj.* fucking great!
- Vulgarism. Also *заебúсь*.

зóна *f.* clink, inside, penal colony, compound. крáсная зóна labour camp dominated by prisoners connected with camp administration. В завúсимости от тогó, чьё влия́ние в колóнии преобладáет, зóны дéлятся на крáсные, úли сýчьи, и воровскúе. Крáсными чáще всегó бывáют колóнии усúленного режúма. Depending on whose influence predominates, labour camps are split into red or grasses or thieves. Strict régime camps are usually red ones.
- Lit. *zone, area*.

зубúло *n.* model 8 or 9 Zhiguli (car).
- Lit. *chisel*.

зубрúла *m.,f.* swot, nerd, brainbox, brainy git.
- See also *вýндеркинд*.

И

иглá *f.* needle, injecting, shooting up. Что касáется иглы́, то бы́ло óчень хорошó: бесконéчный покóй, ничегó не грызёт, и испы́тываешь рáйскую безмятéжность. As for the needle, it was really good: endless peace, nothing to grate you, a feeling of heavenly peace. **сидéть на иглé** *impf.* to shoot up, inject, use. **соскочúть с иглы́** *pf.* to stop shooting up. **спры́гнуть с иглы́** *pf.* to stop injecting.

игра́ть в Чапа́ева *phr.impf.* to push a rookie soldier's face into dirty water.
* Чапаев: Bolshevik cavalry commander who drowned in the river Ural in 1919.

изволо́хать *v.t.* to beat to a pulp. Пу́трин, тот вообще́ был сади́ст, дво́е тебя́ изволо́хают, а он подойдёт, пульс пощу́пает: 'Да,' ска́жет, 'части́т серде́чко-то.' Putrin was a real sadist: two people will beat you up, then he'll come along, feel your pulse and say: 'Yup, the old ticker's still going.'

изгва́здать *pf.* of **гвозди́ть.**

изме́на *f.* bad trip; negative reaction. Изме́на ка́тит. I've hit a bad trip. на изме́ну подсе́сть to be hooked on a bad trip.
* Lit. *treason, treachery*

измете́лить *pf.* of **мете́лить.**

индеани́ст *m.* member of a movement living a Native American lifestyle.

и́нди- *in compounds* indie. и́нди-клуб indie club.

и́ндия *f.* alternative, indie music. Сло́вом **и́ндия** называ́ют тепе́рь вся́кую му́зыку, схо́дную с за́падной сти́ля инденпе́ндент. The word *India* is now used to describe any music resembling western independent-style music.

индюки́ *m.pl.* 1. alternative music. 2. those who play alternative music.
* Lit. *turkeys.*

индюша́та *pl.* variant of **индюки́.**
* Lit. *turkey chicks.*

инома́рка *f.* foreign car.

интерде́вочка *f.* hard-currency prostitute.

ироке́з *m.* mohican, mohawk (punk hair-do). Го́да три наза́д я ходи́л с ироке́зом и була́вками. About three years ago I had a mohican and pins.

исто́рик *m.* male history teacher, lecturer.

италья́шка *m.* Italian, Wop, Itye.

и́тать *v.i.impf.* to eat.

иша́к *m.* an ИЖ motorcycle.
* Also the nickname of the I-16 light aircraft of the 1960s.

К

каба́к *m.* restaurant or café where alcohol is served. шара́шиться по кабака́м *impf.* to go pub-crawling (punk term).
* In older Russian, *a tavern* (often a grubby and disreputable one).

каблу́к *m.* 1. an ИЖ-2715 car. 2. быть у кого́-нибудь под каблуко́м to be under someone's thumb.
  • Lit. *heel.* See also *каблучо́к.*

каблучо́к *m.* variant of **каблу́к.**

кадр *m.* bloke, guy. Посмотри́ на э́того ка́дра в чёрных очка́х. Look at that guy in the black specs.
  • Lit. *frame.*

кайф *m.* 1. buzz, high, kick. У меня́ с э́той травы́ тако́й кайф начался́! I've started to get a real kick from that grass. 2. *interj., pred.* excellent, great, cool, mental. У меня́ три листа́ ци́клы есть.—Кайф! I've got three sheets of cyclodole.—Cool! 3. gear, drugs. Вчера́ таки́е стремаки́ бы́ли—нас повинти́ли, а у меня́ в бэ́ге кайф. We had really big problems yesterday—we got picked up by the police, and I had some gear in my bag. **кусо́к ка́йфа** bit of gear, portion of a drug (also 1: pleasure, fun. Да́йте мне мой кусо́к ка́йфа. Let me have my bit of fun). **тупо́й кайф** black rush. **вы́рубить кайф** *pf.* to provide, push drugs. **лови́ть** [*pf.* **слови́ть**] **кайф** to get stoned, high, out of it. Кайф ло́вит от одного́ за́паха. He's out of his face just on the smell. 4. booze, drink, alcohol. Сгоня́й в шоп за ка́йфом. Nip off down to the shop for some booze. **в кайф** cool, fab, great. **мне в кайф, по ка́йфу** I like it, it suits me. **кайфы́** *f.pl.* enjoyment, pleasure. **лома́ть кайф** [+ *dat.*] *impf.* to be a spoilsport, put a downer on.

кайфану́ть *pf.* of **кайфова́ть.**

кайфова́ть *v.i.* [*pf.* **кайфану́ть**] to have a good time, enjoy.

кайфо́во *adv.* excellent, excellently, cool.

кайфо́вый *adj.* cool, great, fab, sound. **кайфо́вая му́зыка** fab music.

кайфоло́м *m.* kill-joy, spoil-sport.
  • See also *кайфоло́мщик.*

кайфоло́мщик *m.* kill-joy, spoil-sport.
  • See also *кайфоло́м.*

кайфы́ *f.pl.* see **кайф.**

калга́н *m.* head.
  • From the Tatar for *pot.*

кале́чная *f.* chemist's shop, drugstore.
  • See also *ка́лька.*

ка́лики *m.pl.* pills.

ка́лька *f.* drugstore, chemist's shop.
  • Lit. *tracing-paper, calque.* See also *кале́чная.*

ка́мать *v.i.* [*pf.* **прика́мать**] to come. Ка́май сюда́! Come here!

кана́ть *v.i.* [*pf.* **прокана́ть, скана́ть**] 1. to pass for. Я за твоего́ бра́та не прокана́ю. I'll never pass for your brother. 2. to get out. Кана́й отсю́да! Get out of here! Beat it!

ка́нтри *f.indec.* 1. country cottage, dacha. Пое́хали на ка́нтри. They've gone off to their dacha. 2. *n.* country music.

кантро́вый *adj.* 1. rural, backward. 2. country (music).
  • 1. See also *колхо́зный*.

кантру́шник *m.* country bumpkin, yokel.

катру́шница *f.* country bumpkin, yokel.

кантры́ *m.pl.* country folk, yokels.

капка́н: в капка́не in a spot, a tough position. Поста́вили меня́ на счётчик, и я оказа́лся в капка́не. They turned the heat up on me, and I ended up in a jam.

каптёр *m.* soldier or labour camp prisoner in charge of supplies. Каптёр дедова́л, потому́ что был хозя́ином каптёрки, где деды́ могли́ выпива́ть. The supplies clerk ran the show because he was in charge of the stores where the long-service guys could drink.
  • From *каптена́риус* (*quartermaster sergeant*).

каптёрка *f.* supply room, store.

капу́ста *f.* money, dough, dosh. Капу́ста есть? Got any dosh?
  • Lit. *cabbage.* See also *ахча́, ба́бки, ба́шли, грин, грю́ники, зелёные.*

карда́н *m.* hand (when it is about to be shaken). Держи́ карда́н. Put it there!

карту́зник *m.* member of youth gang wearing Lenin caps.

карусе́ль *f.* partner-swopping party, swinging party.
  • Lit. *merry-go-round.*

ка́ссовый *adj.* box-office, hit. Фильм получи́лся ка́ссовый, принёс неплохо́й дохо́д. The film turned out to be a hit at the box-office; it brought in good receipts.

ката́ла *m.,f.* cardshark, card-sharp.

кати́ть *v.i.impf.* to happen to. Мне одни́ обло́мы ка́тят—всё вре́мя не везёт. I get nothing but let-downs—no luck at all.

кати́ть балло́н [на + *acc.*] *phr.impf.* to bad-mouth, slag, speak ill of. А что я на тебя́ балло́н кати́ла—извини́. Sorry if I bad-mouthed you.
  • See also *кати́ть бо́чку.*

кати́ть бо́чку [на + *acc.*] *phr.impf.* to bad-mouth, slag (off), speak ill of.
  • See also *кати́ть балло́н.*

Катманду́: пошёл ты в Катманду́ *phr.pf.* go to hell!

ка́тя *f.* hundred-rouble note. Говоря́т, что в середи́не 1980-х с центрово́й проститу́ткой мо́жно бы́ло договори́ться за ка́тю. They say that in the mid 1980s you could negotiate with a town-centre prostitute for a hundred.

ка́чаный *adj.* solid, well-built.

кача́ться *v.i.impf.* to work out, pump iron.
  • Lit. *to swing, rock, reel.*

качо́к *m.* [*pl.* **качки́**] bodybuilder. Мно́гие качки́ перешли́ на рабо́ту к паха́нам. Many fitness fanatics have gone over to work with the heavy mob.
  • See also *арно́льд, шварцене́йгер.*

каэспэ́шник *m.* someone who sings folk-songs, often by campfire.
  • From КСП (*Клуб самоде́ятельной пе́сни — folk ballad club*).

каэспэ́шница *f.* singer of folk-songs.

ква́сить *v.i.* [*pf.* **квасну́ть**] to have a drink (often cheap alcohol, medicine or perfume).
  • Lit. *to pickle.*

квасну́ть *pf.* of **ква́сить**.

квинома́н *m.* fan of the group *Queen*.

кент *m.* pal, mate, bloke, guy; also a form of address. Посмотри́ на э́того ке́нта, не из менто́вки ли он? Look at that guy—isn't he from the cop-shop?
  • See also *кенту́ха, кентя́ра.*

кентова́ться *v.i.impf.* to hang around with, be friends with. Нельзя́ кентова́ться с кем попа́ло. You shouldn't hang around with just anybody.

кенту́ха *m.* variant of **кент**.
  • See also *кент, кентя́ра.*

кентя́ра *m.* variant of **кент**.
  • See also *кент, кенту́ха.*

кероси́н *m.* booze, drink, alcohol.

кероси́нить *v.i.impf.* to have a drink, get drunk. Сейча́с на зарпла́ту мо́жно прожи́ть, е́сли не кероси́нить. You can now get by on your wages, if you don't spend it on booze.
  • See also *ква́сить.*

кероси́нщик *m.* wino.

кефи́рная отры́жка *f.* thickhead, dunce, dull person.
  • Punk term.

кида́ла *m.,f.* double crosser, someone who pays with forged money, con-artist.
  • See also *утю́г.*

кида́лово *n.* fast one, swindle, double-cross, con.

кида́ть *v.i.* [*pf.* **ки́нуть**] 1. [**на** + *acc.*] to con, swindle, cheat (out of something). Вчера́ одного́ ло́ха на кайф ки́нули—попроси́ли подожда́ть и ушли́ че́рез проходно́й подъе́зд. Yesterday we conned some gear out of some thickhead guy—we asked him to wait and then made off through the passage-way. Они́ ки́нули меня́ на кни́гу. They conned a book out of me. 2. to rob, hold up. ки́нуть апте́ку to rob a chemist's shop.
  • Lit. *to throw.*

кидня́к *m.* con, swindle, deception. Ребя́та выбежа́ли, напа́ли на не́гров, и тут я по́нял, что идёт не кидня́к, как мы догова́ривались, а настоя́щий грабёж. The lads ran out and set upon some black people; then I realised it wasn't a con as we'd agreed, but a full-scale robbery.

ки́ллер *m.* killer, hit-man. А к нему́ ки́ллера подосла́ли. They sent a hit-man to get him.

кима́рить *v.i.* [*pf.* **покима́рить**] to take a nap, to doze, sleep. Пойду́, покима́рю в каптёрке. I'll go and have forty winks in the stores.

кинд *m.* child.
   • From German *Kind* (*child*).

ки́ндэр *m.* [*pl.* **ки́ндэры**] child.
   • Transliteration of German *Kinder* (*children*). See also *кинд*.

кинома́н *m.* fan of the group *Kino*.

ки́нуть *pf.* of **кида́ть**.

ки́нуться *v.i.pf.* to commit suicide. Он в про́шлом году́ от беспробу́дного пья́нства ки́нулся. He did himself in last year out of unrestrained drunkenness.
   • Lit. *to throw oneself.*

ки́пиш *m.* noisy, exciting event; preparations for something exciting. 'Что у вас там за ки́пиш?' спроси́ла она́, услы́шав шум и гро́мкие голоса́ по телефо́ну. 'Have you got something good going on there?' she asked, hearing noise and loud voices over the phone.
   • Folk. See also *хи́пеж.*

кипишова́ть *v.i.impf.* to be excited.

кир *m.* alcohol, booze.

кирно́й *adj.* drunk, sozzled. Прихо́дит он домо́й кирно́й, а я его́ по ты́кве ска́лкой за таки́е дела́. He comes home drunk and I'll give him one on the nut with a rolling pin for it.

кирну́ть *pf.* of **киря́ть**.

кирю́ха *m.* drunkard, drinking buddy, pal. У магази́на одни́ кирю́хи, не у кого́ закури́ть попроси́ть. There was nothing but drunks by the shop—no one you could ask for a smoke.
   • See also *а́лик, алка́ш, алкона́вт, буха́рик, синега́л, синю́га.*

киря́ть *v.i.* [*pf.* **кирну́ть**] to drink, booze.

кис *m.* kiss.

ки́сать *v.t.* [*pf.* **заки́сать**] to kiss.

ки́саться *v.i.* [*pf.* **заки́саться**] to kiss.

ки́ски *f.pl.* triangle sunglasses (often worn by punks).

кислота́ *f.* acid, LSD.

кисло́тный *adj.* acid. Кисло́тные худо́жники украша́ют ма́ленький квадра́тник отде́льным рису́нком и́ли для карти́нки побо́льше испо́льзуют це́лый блок, кото́рый пото́м де́лится на отде́льные квадра́тники и расхо́дятся по рука́м как моза́ика. Acid artists decorate every small tab with a different illustration or use a whole block for a picture that's a bit bigger, which is then split into separate blocks and is distributed like a mosaic.

• Example taken from the techno magazine, *ПТЮЧ*.

ки́слый *adj. used as noun* acetic anhydride.

• Lit. *sour*, referring to the taste of the drug.

кишка́ *f.* thin person, someone who fights for food.

• Lit. *gut*. Criminal argot.

кишкопра́в *m.* dick, cock, penis.

• Punk term.

класс *m., often used as pred.* great, excellent. Ещё была́ клёвая афе́ра, э́то класс. There was also this great con, real class.

кла́ссно *adv.* class, classy.

кла́ссный *adj.* class, classy.

клёво *adv., interj.* excellent, cool, wicked.

клевота́ *f.* something excellent, great; coolness.

клёвый *adj.* neat, cool, sound, wicked. У тебя́ клёвые боти́нки. Cool boots you've got. Клёвый спо́соб познако́миться с круты́ми парня́ми. A neat way of getting to know cool guys (article title).

клевя́к *m.* excellent person or thing. клевя́к вещи́ца a groovy thing.

клику́ха *f.* nickname.

• From *кли́чка* (*nickname, name of an animal*).

клифт *m.* coat, jacket.

клозня́к *m.* variant of **клёуз**.

клоп *m.* bug. То́лько что постро́енное зда́ние посо́льства оказа́лось наби́то клопа́ми. The new embassy building turned out to be riddled with bugs.

• *Клоп* is also the zoological word for *bug*.

клóсес *m.* variant of **клёуз**.

клёуз *m.* clothes, gear. кла́ссный клёуз classy clothes.

• See also *клóсес, клёуза, клозня́к*.

клёуза *f.* variant of **клёуз**.

клю́ха *f.* adolescent hippy. Клю́хи собира́ются в Карма́не. Teenage hippies gather at the Pocket [a flight of steps on the Arbat in Moscow].

• Abbreviation of *Клуб люби́телей хи́ппи*. See also *пионе́р, клю́шка*.

клю́шка *f.* 1. as **клю́ха**. 2. girl. клёвая клю́шка a great bird.

коблу́ха *f.* lesbian, lesbo, lezzie, dyke (mainly in a labour camp). Коблу́хи начина́ют называ́ть себя́ мужски́ми имена́ми, говори́ть наро́чито гру́бым и ни́зким го́лосом, подража́ть

мужско́й похо́дке. The dykes are starting to give themselves men's names, speak deliberately in a coarse and deep voice, and try to walk like a man.
- Criminal argot. A feminization of *кобе́ль*, *male dog*.

ко́дло *n.* gang, crew, group.

коза́ *f.* 1. gesture made when heavy metal fans meet. Металли́сты приве́тственно вы́кинули на па́льцах козу́. The metal-heads warmly greeted each other with 'the sign'. 2. girl unfamiliar with street culture.
- Folk term. Lit. *she-goat*.

козёл *m.* 1. swine, bastard, scumbag. Козлы́, а не команди́ры. They're bastards, not commanders. 2. rat, grass, traitor. Э́тот козёл всех нас зало́жит мента́м. That traitor will shop us all in to the cops.
- Lit. *he-goat.*

козли́ть *v.i.impf.* 1. to grandstand, do a wheelie. 2. to rat on someone, to grass someone up.
- 1. See also *выдрю́чиваться.*

ко́ка *f.* coke, cocaine.
- See also *кокс, марафе́т.*

кокна́р *m.* dried poppy straw or other opium derivatives.
- See also *ку́кер, кукна́р, кухна́р.*

кокс *m.* cocaine, coke. Кокс ню́хать на́чали в Росси́и давно́. People started sniffing cocaine in Russia ages ago.
- See also *ко́ка, марафе́т.*

кол *m.* one rouble. Буты́лка во́дки ны́нче сто́ит 300 коло́в! A bottle of vodka now costs 300 roubles!
- Lit. *stake.*

колесо́ *n.* pill, tab.
- Lit. *wheel.* Mainly used in the plural *колёса.*

ко́лледж *m.* school, college. Сего́дня в ко́лледж не пойду́. I'm not going to lectures today.

колоти́ть кося́к *phr.impf.* to roll a joint.
- See also *забива́ть кося́к, кося́к.*

коло́ться *v.i.impf.* to inject (oneself).
- Lit. *to prick.* See also *втира́ться, гнать по ве́не, дви́гаться, тре́скаться, ширя́ться, шмы́гаться.*

колхо́зник *m.* 1. country bus. Снача́ла пое́дем на по́езде, пото́м на колхо́знике. First we'll go by train, then we'll catch the bus. 2. stupid or backward person, yokel, hick. Ты сам колхо́зник, и шу́тки у тебя́ колхо́зные. You're a real clod, and you tell stupid jokes.
- Lit. *collective farmer.*

колхо́зный *adj.* backward, unsophisticated. У э́того дурака́ и ю́мор колхо́зный! That idiot's even got a backward sense of humour.
  • See also *кантро́вый.*

ко́льщик *m.* stool-pigeon (prison).

кома́нда *f.* band, group, crew, team. Дубль-1—о́чень сла́бая кома́нда; де́вка поёт. Double-1's a very poor band—they have a girl on vocal. 2. crew, bunch of people. Не понра́вилась мне кома́нда у него́ на бёзднике. I didn't like the crew at his birthday.
  • See also *ба́нда, бенд, бэнд.*

команди́р *m.* skip, chief, boss (term of address to a person who has to pay). Команди́р, с тебя́ рубль за лобово́е и два за за́днее стекло́! Right, chief, that'll be a rouble for the front window and two for the back!
  • Lit. *commander.*

коммуни́здить *v.t.* [*pf.* **скоммуни́здить**] to steal, nick, swipe. Бу́дешь коммуни́здить—отпра́влю домо́й. If you start nicking things, I'll send you home. После́дний пиджа́к бомжи́ скоммуни́здили. The tramps took my last jacket.
  • A mixture of *коммуни́зм* and the vulgar *пи́здить to steal.* See also *пионе́рить.*

комо́к *m.* commercial stall, shop.

компаси́ровать мозги́ *phr.impf.* to talk garbage, crap.
  • Based on the humorous idiomatic phrase *компости́ровать мозги́* lit. *to punch one's brain* (i.e. punch a hole in it, as with a bus ticket), *to bullshit.*

комплексо́ванный *adj.* variant of **закомплексо́ванный**. Когда́ не понима́ют и не хотя́т понима́ть друго́го, его́ волне́ний, трево́г, увлече́ний и пристра́стий, говоря́т: 'Он весь комплексо́ван, он заци́клился', и ду́мают, что де́ло сде́лали, определи́ли суть челове́ка. When people don't want to understand someone else, his worries, fears, pleasures and passions, they say 'He's fixated, he's obsessed', and they think they've settled the matter and summed him up.

компо́т *m.* poppy-heads boiled with sugar.
  • Lit. *stewed fruit.*

коне́ц *m.* cock, dick, penis. Вы́лез он го́лый, коне́ц болта́ется. He crawled out naked, with his prick wobbling about.
  • Lit. *end.* See also *прик.*

ко́ни *m.pl.* 1. the TsSKA (Soviet Army) football team. 2. TsSKA fans.
  • Lit. *horses.* ЦСКА stands for Центра́льный спорти́вный клуб а́рмии, Central Army Sporting Club.

конта́чить *v.i.impf.* to keep in touch, associate with. Я с ним уже́ полго́да не конта́чу. I haven't had anything to do with him for six months now.

конто́ра *f.* 1. gang, crew. 2. the KGB (the Soviet security police). Шли го́ды, конто́ра меня́ла свои́ вы́вески. Я́году смени́л Ежо́в, Ежо́ва сверг Бе́рия, прогреме́ла война́, ушли́ в забве́ние стра́шные проце́ссы. Years passed and the KGB changed its faces. Yezhov took over from Yagoda, Beria overthrew Yezhov, war broke out and the fearsome trials were forgotten.

• Lit. *office.* КГБ stands for *Комите́т госуда́рственной безопа́сности* (*Committee of State Security*). However, these initials were ironically reinterpreted as *Конто́ра глубо́кого буре́ния* (*Office of Profound Probing*).

конто́рский *adj. used as noun* member of a gang or of the KGB.

ко́нус: на ко́нус *m.* pure, dead, really. Запу́ганный на ко́нус молодо́й начина́ет в карау́лке полива́ть из автома́та паха́нов. Scared stiff, the rookie soldier on guard starts gunning down the ring-leaders.

• Lit. *cone.*

коня́вые *pl. adj. used as noun*; see **ко́ни**.

копа́ть люде́й *phr.impf.* to rob graves for jewellery, etc. Споко́йным и ро́вным го́лосом он расска́зывает о том, как копа́ет люде́й. In a calm, even tone of voice he talks of how he digs up graves.

кора́бль *m.* small matchbox filled with grass (drug). Не взять ли нам на ры́нке кора́бль? Shouldn't we get a box of stuff at the market?

• Lit. *ship.*

ко́реш *m.* mate, pal, buddy.

ко́рка *f.* funny or odd story. Тут така́я ко́рка была́—я же из а́рмии неда́вно пришёл, а до э́того мой родно́й брат (мы с ним вне́шне о́чень похо́жи), ви́дно, что́-то напорта́чил. Иду́ к ста́нции, а тут—толпа́. Не сла́бо меня́ отде́лали. Then a really funny thing happened. I'd just recently come out of the army, but before that my brother (he and I are look really like each other) had apparently botched something up. I went to the station and a whole gang of locals was there. They didn't half duff me up.

• Lit. *peel, rind, crust.*

корое́д *m.* child, kid, nipper.

короно́вка *f.* initiation ceremony into higher criminal circles. Всё ча́ще верхово́дить в зо́нах беру́тся самозва́нцы, никогда́ не проходи́вшие короно́вку, и и́менно они́, не зна́я зако́на, творя́т са́мый чёрный беспреде́л. More and more often in the camps, would-be big guns start to call the shots, even though they haven't been initiated, and it's these people, the ones who don't know the law, who cause the worst aggro.

• Criminal argot; similar to the Russian word for *coronation* (**корона́ция**).

коси́ть *v.i.* [*pf.* **прокоси́ть**] to feign sickness or stupidity. **коси́ть под пси́ха** to make out you're off your trolley.
• Lit. *to mow, cut.*

костыли́ *m.pl.* legs.
• Lit. *crutches.*

ко́стя пересту́кин *m.* grass, informer. В фойе́ рабо́тали: вы́ставка митько́в, видеомультфи́льмы и ко́сти пересту́кины. In the foyer there was an exhibition of Mit'ki, video-cartoons and informers.

косу́ха *f.* 1. black leather coat, often covered in zips and worn by heavy metal fans. Всё, от плака́тов и газе́т, пласти́нок и ла́зерных ди́сков до футбо́лок, косу́х и музыка́льных инструме́нтов—в рок-магази́не. There is everything in the rock-shop, from posters, papers, records and laser-disks to football tops, leather coats and musical instruments. 2. grand, one thousand roubles.

кося́к *m.* joint, spliff. **забива́ть/заби́ть, закола́чивать/ заколоти́ть, прикола́чивать/приколоти́ть, колоти́ть** *(impf.),* **прибить** *(perf.)* **кося́к** to roll a joint. Заби́л кося́к я в пу́шку ту́го и ду́мал: угощу́ я дру́га! I rolled a joint quite nicely and thought, I'll treat my pal. У тебя́ штаке́т есть? Дава́й кося́к приколо́тим. Do you have you any fag paper? Come on, let's roll a joint.
• Lit. *door-post* or *slope.* See also **масты́рить**

котле́та *f.* tightly stuffed purse.
• Lit. *cutlet, chop.*

ко́цать *v.t.impf.* to cut (poppy-heads with a blade). **ко́цать веняки́** to cut one's veins.

кошма́р *m. often used as interj.* damn! What a nightmare!
• Lit. *nightmare.*

краб *m.* 1. palm of the hand (when shaking). Держи́ кра́ба! Shake! Let's shake! 2. sydnocarb, a psychostimulating drug.
• Lit. *crab.*

крабошлёп *m.* sailor.

кранты́ *pl.* [*gen.pl.* **кранто́в**] the end, curtains, doom. В оди́н прекра́сный день к Черему́хину влете́л Кузьми́н и заора́л, что е́сли так да́льше бу́дет, то ему́, Кузьмину́, приду́т кранты́ и тогда́ он тут всё разнесёт. One fine day Kuzmin came in to Cheremukhin, and bawled that if things went on like this then he'd be finished, and he'd spread the story around everywhere. Как он э́то сде́лает по́сле кранто́в, он не объясня́л, но, гля́дя в его́ бе́лые глаза́, Черему́хин пове́рил. How he would do this after it was curtains for him he did not say, but looking into his white eyes, Cheremukhin believed him.

краснода́рка *f.* type of cannabis.

креза́ *f.* 1. and **кре́зи-ха́ус, крэ́йзер** *m.* mad-house, loony-bin. Я два ме́сяца в крезе́ лежа́л. I was in the nut-house for two months. 2. mental disorder. Опя́ть у него́ креза́ начала́сь. He's gone bananas again. 3. and **крезэзу́ха** mental, absurd or unusual idea. 4. and **кре́зи** nutter, nut-job, loony. И заче́м ты с крезо́й связа́лась? How have you got tied up with that lunatic? **креза́ ка́тит, крэ́йза ка́тит** is going crazy. **слови́ть крезу́** *pf.* to go crazy.

• See also *кре́йза, кре́зи-хаус, крезо́вник, крезу́шник, кры́за, крэза́, крэ́зи, крэзу́ха, крэ́йза, крэ́йзи, крэ́йзихаус, крэйзу́ха.*

крезану́тый *adj.* mental, crazy, psychotic.

крезану́ться *v.i.pf.* to go crazy, round the bend, round the twist, off one's head. Ты что, крэйзану́лся? What's up with you—have you lost it or what?

• See also *дви́нуться* 1, *крэйзану́ться.*

кре́зи *m.* loony, nut-job, nutter.

• See also *креза́* 4.

кре́зи-хаус *m.* mad-house, loony-bin, funny farm.

• See also *крэ́йзи-хаус, крэ́йзи-хаус, креза́* 1.

крезо́вник *m.* 1. nutter, nut-job, loony. 2. nut-house, loony-bin.

• See also *крезу́шник, креза́* 1.

крезо́вый *adj.* 1. mental, great. крезо́вая му́зыка mental music. крезо́вый прики́д great gear. 2. schizo.

крезу́шник *m.* 1. nutter, nut-job, loony. 2. nut-house, loony-bin.

• See also *крезо́вник, креза́* 4.

кре́йза *f.* variant of **креза́**.

криво́й *adj.* mildly drunk, half-cut. Он опя́ть криво́й по го́роду шля́ется, и́щет, где бы доба́вить. He's wandering around the town half-cut again, looking for another drink.

• Lit. *crooked; one-eyed.*

крутизна́ *f.* coolness, cool. Молоды́е лю́ди быва́ют повы́шенной крутизны́, но попада́ются и подкру́ченные, то есть не о́чень кру́тые. You get some young people who are really cool, but there are also some pseuds, that is, they aren't really that cool.

• Lit. *steepness.* See also *кру́тость.*

крути́ть *v.t., v.i.impf.* to con, swindle, cheat, take in. **крути́ть ка́рты, крути́ть напёрстки** to gamble on the street, often involving swindling or cheating. С декабря́ крути́л ка́рты, напёрстки на каза́нском вокза́ле. Since December he's been card-sharping and playing thimblerig at the Kazan' station.

• Lit. *to twist. Напёрсток, напёрстки* involves guessing the correct location of an object hidden under one of several (usually three) thimbles.

крутня́к *m.* 1. serious state of affairs, tense situation. У меня́ сейча́с полоса́ сплошны́х крутняко́в. Just now I've got a barrel-load of problems. 2. and **круть** something excellent or powerful.
  • 2. See also *обса́д, убо́й, улёт.*

кру́то *adv.* 1. really, very. Кру́то перестрема́лись. We were scared stiff. Кру́то оттяну́лись. We had an excellent time. 2. coolly, excellently, to the nines. Кру́то прики́нулся. He was brilliantly done up, he dressed up really smart.
  • Lit. *steeply.* See also *круто́й.*

круто́й *adj.* 1. great, big, serious. Я не са́мый круто́й покло́нник Бейру́та. I'm not the biggest fan of the Beirut. круто́й обло́м a serious let-down, downer. круты́е раскла́ды a serious state of affairs. 2. smart, fab, cool, sound, wicked. круто́й мэн a cool dude. круты́е ребя́та great, rich, sound guys. Кру́че тебя́ то́лько я́йца, вы́ше тебя́ то́лько звёзды. You're the man! You're simply the best!
  • Lit. *steep, sudden, severe, drastic. Бейру́т* is the hippy name of a café in Pskov.

кру́тость *f.* coolness, cool.
  • See also *крутизна́.*

круть *f.* variant of **крутня́к** 2. У них му́зыка—круть! Their music's far out!
  • See also *крутня́к.*

кры́за *f.* variant of *креза́.*

кры́са *f.* 1. dog, hag, bow-wow (unattractive girl, often a term of address). Для чле́на мота́лки прести́жно гуля́ть с де́вочкой, с кры́сой же—про́сто опа́сно. It's good for a gang member to be seen with a girl, but with a bow-wow—it's just dodgy. 2. and **крыся́тник** *m.* someone who steals from fellow gang members or prisoners. Кры́са по паца́нским поня́тиям ху́же чем барь́га. In criminals' terms, a rat is worse than a fence. 3. punk term for girl.
  • Lit. *rat.* See also *крыся́тник.*

крыся́тник *m.* Someone who steals from fellow prisoners or gang members. Не свя́зывайся с ним, он—крыся́тник. Don't go near him, he's a thieving rat.
  • See also *кры́са 2.*

кры́тка *f.* jail, the clink, inside. Со́бственно тю́рьмы престу́пники называ́ют кры́тыми тю́рьмами и́ли по́просту кры́тками, а содержа́щихся там—'кры́тниками'. As a matter of fact, criminals call jails closed prisons or, in simpler terms, *krytki* and the inmates *krytniki.*
  • From *кры́тый* (lit. *sheltered*).

кры́тник *m.* jailbird, con, inmate of a jail.
  • From *кры́тка*.
кры́ша *f.* 1. head, nut, noggin. У тебя́ кры́ша не в поря́дке. You want your head seeing to. **кры́ша е́дет** *impf.* to lose it, go nuts, la-la. Сиди́т наркома́н обку́ренный, кры́ша у него́ е́дет, всего́ стрема́ется. There's this junkie sitting, doped up to his eyeballs, going to la-la-land and freaking out at everything. У неё кры́ша пое́хала. She's lost it, gone mad. **съезд кры́ши** *m.* downer, state of depression, being fed up. От ва́ших разбо́рок у меня́ съезд кры́ши начался́. Your aggro has got me down. 2. front, an apparently respectable cover for illegal activity. У нас появи́лось мно́го завя́зок в блатно́м ми́ре. Мы ста́ли волка́ми. Со свое́й кры́шей—челове́ком, кото́рый покрови́тельствовал нам. We gained lots of connections with the criminal world. We became criminal operatives. With our cover—a man who looked after us.
  • Lit. *roof.*
крэза́ *f.* variant of **креза́**. Крэза́ покати́ла у па́рня—у́лицу не мо́жет перейти́. The lad's going mad—he can't cross the street.
крэ́зи *m.* variant of **кре́зи**.
крэзу́ха *f.* crazy-house, nut house, loony bin.
  • See also *крейза́.*
крэ́йза *f.* variant of **креза́**.
крэйзану́ться *v.i.pf.* variant of **крезану́ться**.
крэ́йзи *m.* variant of **кре́зи**.
крэ́йзихаус *m.* variant of **кре́зи-хаус**.
крэ́йзи-хаус *m.* variant of **кре́зи-хаус**.
крэйзу́ха *f.* variant of **крэзу́ха**.
кси́ва *f.* passport or other document (often ID).
кси́вник *m.* small pouch or purse worn round the neck (sometimes for the **кси́ва**). А на кси́внике обы́чно рису́ют паци́фик. Usually people draw a pacifist logo on their pouch.
кся́вка *f.* punk teenager (usually female).
ку́кер *m.* variant of **кокна́р**.
ку́кла *f.* 1. wad of cash with genuine notes on the outside concealing plain paper within. Всучи́л клие́нту ку́клу. He palmed off a pile of dummy notes on a client. 2. dummy used in gun training for the police or armed forces; a condemned man acting as combat partner in these circumstances. Когда́ ведёшь уче́бный бой про́тив своего́ това́рища, то наперёд зна́ешь, что он тебя́ не убьёт. И он зна́ет, что ты его́ не убьёшь. Поэ́тому интере́с к уче́бному бо́ю теря́ется. А вот ку́кла тебя́ уби́ть мо́жет, но и тебя́ руга́ть не о́чень бу́дут, е́сли ты ку́кле рёбра перелома́ешь и́ли ше́ю. When you are doing

combat training with a comrade you know in advance that he isn't going to kill you and he knows you won't kill him. So the interest in the exercise gets lost. But you think a crim used for target practice can kill you, but no one's going to get on at you if you break his ribs or his neck.

• Lit. *doll, dummy*. See also *расстрельник:* It is known that men condemned to death were used in such training. These men were known as *гладиаторы* in the Cheka, *волонтёры* in the NKVD and *робинзоны* in Smersh, the counter-espionage department of the NKVD during the Second World War.

кукна́р *m.* variant of **кокна́р**.

куку́шка *f.* 1. secret apartment used by the KGB. Куку́шки испо́льзуются бы́вшими сотру́дниками КГБ в ча́стных це́лях. Safe houses are used by former KGB officials for their own private purposes. 2. *dial.* girl. Пойдём в центр, пои́щем куку́шек на́ ночь. Let's go into town and look for some birds for the night.

• Lit. *cuckoo*. See also *воро́на, ку́рица*.

кума́р *m.* withdrawal symptoms (from drugs). Раскума́рить— дать ка́йфа тому́, у кого́ кума́р. Helping out is when you give a bit of gear to someone with withdrawal symptoms.

кума́рить *v.t.impers.impf.* to crave drugs, need a hit. Там одного́ кума́рило кру́то—пришло́сь полдозняка́ отда́ть. There was one person there who was seriously desperate—we had to give him half a dose.

ку́мпол *m.* nut, head, noggin. настуча́ть по ку́мполу *pf.* to whack, give, belt someone on the nut.

• See also *башка́, ре́па, ты́ква*.

купи́ться *v.i.pf.* to be taken in, conned, to fall for. Как я мог на э́то купи́ться? How could I fall for that?

ку́рица *f.dial.* girl, chick. У них в Краснодре норма́льных де́вушек ку́рицами зову́т. In Krasnoyarsk they call good-looking women chicks.

• Lit. *chicken*. See also *воро́на, куку́шка*.

курсови́к *m.* term paper, student assignment. В день убийства Кара́ева он защища́л курсови́к. The day Karaev was murdered he was at a viva on his essay.

кусо́к *m.* a thousand roubles, grand. Ме́ньше пяти́ куско́в— ко́шка не ходи́. Less than five grand—there's no point.

• Lit. *piece, bit*. See also *штýка*.

кухна́р *m.* variant of **кукна́р**.

ку́чка: see **глаза́ в ку́чку**.

Л

лаба́з *m.* off-licence, offy; shop selling drink. Сгоня́й в лаба́з за спиртны́м. Nip off down to the off-licence for some drink.
• Lit. *warehouse.*

ла́бас *m.* Latvian. Ла́басы в а́рмии всегда́ в отли́чниках. In the army the Latvians are always among the best soldiers.

лаба́ть *v.i.* [*pf.* слаба́ть] to strum, busk, play music. В кабаке́ лаба́ю по вечера́м. I play in the pub in the evenings.

ла́бух *m.* musician.

лав *m.* love. Ты меня́ на физи́ческий лав не подпи́сывай. If it's physical love you're on about, don't include me.

ла́жа *f.* rubbish, garbage, crap. А ты в свобо́дное вре́мя чем занима́ешься? А ниче́м. Ну, быва́ет, в те́хникум зайду́...Там така́я ла́жа! What do you do in your spare time? Nothing. Well, sometimes I go in to college...But it's so rubbish there!

лажа́ть *v.i.impf.* to con, mislead, cheat. Музыка́нты открове́нно лажа́ли. The musicians openly deceived people.

лажо́вщик *m.* lousy so-and-so, no-good, hopeless person. А щас мно́гие к *Ла́сковому ма́ю* переки́нулись—ну, э́то лажо́вщики. But now lots of people have gone over to *Gentle May*—but they're just hopeless.

лажо́вый *adj.* rubbish, useless, lousy, rotten. Конце́рт был лажо́вый. The concert was crap.

ла́йба *f.* foreign car.
• Lit. *sailing-boat.* Once used for foreign lorries such as Volvos or Skodas. Now used for any car of good quality.

лайка́ть *v.t.impf.* to like. Я так Мака́ртни лайка́ю. I like McCartney so much.

лайф *m.* life. Без ка́йфа не́ту ла́йфа. No kicks, no life.

лапша́ *f.* talkative person, gab. Э́та лапша́ то́лько и мо́жет, что порожняки́ гоня́ть. All that windbag can do is blether. **лапшу́ ве́шать (на́ уши)** *impf.* to fool, take the mickey, rip out of someone, to take for a ride. Замолчи́, хоро́ш лапшу́-то на́ уши веша́ть! Shut up—don't think you can take me in!
• Lit. *noodles.*

лева́к *m.* black market goods.

левиса́ *m.pl.* Levis, jeans.

ле́вый *adj.* 1. unpleasant, nasty. ле́вые раскла́ды a poor state of affairs. Э́то всё ле́вые дела́. It's all such a bad mess. 2. bogus, fake, illegal. Как отличи́ть родны́е левиса́ от ле́вых. How to tell real Levis from fakes. 3. unknown. ле́вый мэн strange guy, stranger. 4. illegal, unofficial, stolen.
• Lit. *left.*

легáвка *f.* 1. police car. 2. cop shop, police station. Вчерá
залетéл в легáвку по пьянé. I ended up in the police station
yesterday for being drunk.

легáвый *adj. used as noun* pig, cop.
  • See also *лягáвый.*

лейбл *m.* trade mark, label, brand.
  • See also *лэйбл, лэ́йбэл.*

лекáрство *n.* dose, shot of drug or alcohol.
  • Lit. *medicine.*

ленúвец *m.* lazy student.
  • See also *лоботрáс, ло́дырь.*

лéсенка *f.* slow-releasing drug.
  • Lit. *stairs, ladder.*

летáть *v.i.impf.* to be mocked, abused (in armed forces). Как
говорúтся, 'Вы молоды́е, вам и летáть'. As they say, you're
new boys—so you're here to be laughed at. Пéрвые полго́да я,
конéчно, летáл, как и все молоды́е, зато́ послéднее—
дедовáл. The first six months I was the bottom of the barrel,
like all new recruits. However, in the last six months I called the
shots.
  • Lit. *to fly.*

лечúть *v.i.impf.* to talk rubbish, garbage. Лечú кому́-нибудь
друго́му. Go and talk rubbish to someone else.
  • Lit. *to treat.* See also *грузи́ть.*

лимитá *coll.f.* people with temporary permission to live and work
in a city, especially in Moscow and St. Petersburg. Смерть
лимитé. Death to those at the city limit! (graffito).

лимúтчик *m.* person without a residence permit for living in a city.

лимóн *m.* a million roubles.
  • Lit. *lemon.*

линя́ть *v.i.* [*pf.* слиня́ть] to scarper, beat it. Похо́же, нáдо
отсю́да линя́ть. Looks like we'd better get out of here.
  • Lit. *to moult.*

лист *m.* pack, sheet (drugs). Он вчерá лист циклы́ захáвал.
Yesterday he took a sheet of cyclodole.

литерáтор *m.* male literature teacher, lecturer.

литло́вый *adj.* little, small. Там прайс литло́вый. The price is
cheap there. 2. young. У неё есть брат литло́вый. She has a
little brother.

лифт *m.* tram. Замёрзли на остано́вке, покá лифт ждáли. They
all froze at the stop before the tram came.
  • Lit. *lift.*

лоботря́с *m.* lazy student, dunce.
  • See also *ленúвец, ло́дырь.*

лодырь *m.* lazy student, dunce, waster.

• See also *ленивец, лоботряс.*

лом *m.* [*pl.* ломы] 1. a lot, heap. В ответ на нашу прошлую передачу мы получили лом писем. We got a whole stack of letters in response to our last programme. 2. fed-up feeling, downer. У меня с утра лом—ничего делать не хочется. I've been feeling low all day—don't want to do a thing. 3. night queueing, jumping the queue to get tickets for touting. Студентом ходил по ночам в лом. When I was a student I used to go queueing at night. 4. в лом [+ *dat., nom.*] it's pointless to, it's too hard to, can't be bothered to. Мне в лом сейчас об этом рассуждать. I can't be bothered thinking about this right now.

• 3. From *ломать очередь* (*to jump the queue*).

ломак: в ломак *m.* too difficult for someone, beyond someone, over someone's head. Вообще такое дело надо бы проверить, но мне в ломак. I suppose I should check that kind of thing, but it's beyond me.

• See also *ломешник.*

ломануться *v.i.pf.* 1. to belt, whack, strike. 2. to really try.

ломать *v.t.impers.impf.* 1. to make fed up, depress. Меня с этих колёс второй день ломает. I've been feeling rotten from those tabs for a couple of days. Меня ломает об этом говорить. I hate talking about it. 2. to suffer from withdrawal.

• Lit. *to break.*

ломешник: в ломешник *m.* variant of **ломак.**

ломка *f.* [*pl.* ломки] 1. withdrawal symptoms, cold turkey. Алкоголики знают состояние похмелья, а наркоманы—так называемые ломки. Alcoholics know what a hangover is, and drug-addicts the so-called 'breaks'. 2. any state of depression. 3. con, swindle. ломка денег criminal cheating, a con (especially by gypsies). Цыгане занимаются ломкой денег так: подходит к вам цыганка и просит разменять деньги, потом говорит, что передумала, вы возвращаете ей её банкноту, но получаете назад гораздо меньше, чем давали. Gypsies con you like this—a gypsy woman comes and asks you to change a note, then she says she's changed her mind; you give her note back, but you get back less than you gave.

• Lit. *breaking.*

лонговый *adj.* long, tall. лонговый хайр long hair. лонговый мэн a tall bloke.

лопатник *m.* wallet.

лох *m.* 1. a badly dressed nobody, a state, tramp. Плохо одетых и ничего не представляющих собой школьники называют

ящерубо́гими, ло́хами. Badly dressed and unprepossessing people are called names like tramp and a state by school kids. 2. someone easy to deceive, simpleton. 3. country bumpkin.

лу́жа *f.* nickname for Luzhniki, a place in Moscow where bikers gather.

лук *m.* a look. **ки́нуть лук** *pf.* to look around, take a look.
- See also *пролу́кать*, similarly derived from *look.*

лу́кать *v.t.* [*pf.* **лу́кнуть, полука́ть**] to look, check out, look over.

луки́ч *m.* a Lenin monument, bust, portrait, etc. Там луки́ч ги́псовый стои́т. There's a plaster Lenin there. Э́тот никогда́ и не был худо́жником—портре́ты лукича́ писа́л. That one was never an artist—he used to paint Lenin.

лу́кнуть *pf.* of **лу́кать.**

лы́биться *v.i.impf.* to smile, grin, sneer. Како́й э́то рок?— лы́бились го́пники. 'Call that rock?' sneered the yobs.

лэ́йбл *m.* [*pl.* **лэ́йблы, лэйбола́**] label, brand.
- See also *лейбл, лэйбэл.*

лэ́йбэл *m.* label, brand. Трузера́ с лэ́йбэлом *Монта́на* trousers with the *Montana* label.
- See also *лейбл, лэйбэл.*

лю́бер *m.* [*pl.* **любера́, лю́беры**] hard men, boys from Lyubertsy.
- Lyubertsy is a town near Moscow, from where, during *perestroika* and after, gangs would go to terrorise westernizing young people (such as hippies, punks and the like).

ляга́вый *adj.* variant of **лега́вый.**

ля́лька *f.* girl, young woman.
- Folk. See also *герла́, ги́рла, жа́ба, тёлка.*

М

мавзоле́й *m.* shop selling alcohol with a long queue outside (i.e. resembling the Lenin mausoleum on Red Square in Soviet days). Кто от э́того в вы́игрыше—так э́то посети́тели мавзоле́я (так в наро́де называ́ют располо́женный ря́дом с Маяко́м в пристро́йке ви́нный магази́н). If anyone gains from that it's the patrons of the mausoleum (as people call the off-licence built next to the Beacon factory)
- Lit. *mausoleum.*

мажо́р *m.* rich kid, rich person, brat, spoilt kid. Мажо́р с круты́ми прэнта́ми, кото́рому всё мо́жно. A rich guy with great folks who can do anything.
- Lit. *major (key); good mood.*

мажо́рный *adj.* 1. rich; too rich for the place. в мажо́рном прики́де in cool gear. 2. relating to rich kids. мажо́рный пипл spoilt young people, hippies.
   • See also *мажо́рский.*

мажо́рский *adj.* variant of **мажо́рный**.

ма́за *f.* 1. chance. Есть ма́за вписа́ться на флэт. There's a chance of a place in a pad. Есть ма́за фа́кать водола́за. And there's a chance to fuck a four-eyes (hippy saying about pointless acts). 2. black-market job. Босс доверя́л мне бо́лее отве́тственные ма́зы. The boss gave me some more responsible jobs. **в ма́зу** just right, the very thing, just the job, just the ticket. Э́тот кси́вник мне о́чень в ма́зу. This pouch suits me—just the very thing. **без ма́зы** useless, hopeless, no use. Туда́ попа́сть без ма́зы. There's no point going there.

ма́зер *f.* mother. Ко мне вписа́ться нельзя́—ма́зер менто́в вы́зовет. You can't come and stay with me; mum would call the cops.

мазня́к: не в мазня́к *m.* worthless, no good.

майда́нник *m.* thief who operates on board a train. Никогда́ не был майда́нником, а тут пришло́сь в по́езде два чемода́на умыкну́ть. I'd never operated on a train, but then I had to nick a couple of suitcases.
   • Criminal argot.

мака́ка *f.* a *Minsk* motorcycle.
   • Lit. *macaque.*

малёвка *f.* note, message. Дошло́ до того́, что генера́лы престу́пного ми́ра спохвати́лись и разосла́ли по всем сле́дственным изоля́торам и коло́ниям малёвку—своего́ ро́да инструкти́вное письмо́: 'Прекрати́те производи́ть педера́стов—из них пото́м получа́ются 'пресс-ха́ты'. It got to the point where the leaders of the criminal world suddenly thought to send to all isolation cells and camps a message—a sort of letter of instruction, saying, 'Stop producing queers, as you later end up with press-huts'.
   • The term *пресс-ха́та* is used to describe cells where prisoners are put in with homosexuals.

мамбе́т *m.* half-wit, dunce, mug, someone easily cheated. Что скрыва́ть, жале́ла мамбе́тов, простако́в, кото́рых бу́дут на мои́х глаза́х обира́ть. Why conceal it?—I felt sorry for the dummies, the mugs that they'll be cleaning out before my very eyes.
   • Kazakh muggers' speech.

ма́ни *pl.indec.* money, dosh. Где ма́ни взять? Where can we get some dough?

манчжу́рка *f.* type of cannabis.

мара́зм *m.* 1. decay, crap. А когда́ про́сто де́ньги за счёт высо́кой цены́ забира́ют, а произво́дство свора́чивается, э́то како́й-то мара́зм. But when people amass money purely by charging high prices and industry declines, it's just crap. 2. boredom city, brain death.
  • Lit. *senility.*

марафе́т *m.* coke, cocaine.
  • See also *ко́ка, кокс.*

ма́рфа *f.* morphine.
  • See also *марфу́ша.*

марфу́ша *f.* variant of **ма́рфа.**

марцефа́ль *f.* 1. home-made ephedrine. 2. *interj.* Wow! Beauty!
  • Criminal argot. See also *марцифа́ль.*

марцифа́ль *f.* variant of **марцефа́ль.** Марцифа́ль, сказа́л он, разгля́дывая карти́нки в журна́ле. Wow! he said, looking at the pictures in the magazine.

ма́стер маши́нного дое́ния *m.phr.* speed trap.
  • Lit. *milking-machine operator.*

масты́рить *v.t.* [*pf.* замасты́рить] to roll a joint.
  • See also *закола́чивать, колоти́ть коса́к.*

масты́рка *f.* joint, spliff.
  • See also *коса́к.*

масть *f.* 1. drug mostly produced in former Soviet Asia (mainly cannabis). 2. rank-and-file prisoner in labour camp. Кро́ме основны́х масте́й есть ещё шестёрки—холу́и при вора́х ли́бо бугра́х, приду́рки—осуждённые, устро́ившиеся на непы́льные рабо́ты днева́льными, хлеборе́зами, библиоте́карями, че́рти—те, кто по́льзуется усто́йчивой репута́цией шута́ горо́хового. Apart from the basic rank and file there are skivvies—the gofers under the senior criminals or brigade leaders, mugs—prisoners who've fixed themselves up with cushy numbers, like orderlies, bread-cutters, librarians and jokers—men who have established a reputation as clowns.
  • Lit. *suit (at cards).*

ма́ся *f.* small young woman.

мате́ка *m.* maths teacher, lecturer.

матюга́льник *m.* loudspeaker, tannoy. Впереди́ шере́нги стоя́л мент и ора́л в матюга́льник. In front of the column there stood a policeman shouting into a loud-hailer.

маха́ться *v.i.* [*pf.* перемахну́ться, помаха́ться] to fight, scrap.

ма́хач *m.* street fight, brawl. Сра́зу по́сле ма́тча начался́ ма́хач ме́жду фана́тами. Right after the match a scrap started between the fans.

маховик *m.* young man whose fists have been enlarged by injecting chemicals such as paraffin.
• Lit. *fly-wheel.*

мачья надрать *phr.pf.* to collect poppy heads to make opium.

машина *f.* hypodermic syringe. Этой машиной плохо двигаться. You can't get a good hit with this syringe. **заправлять** [*pf.* **заправить**] **машину** to fill a syringe with a shot.
• Lit. *machine, car.* See also *баян.*

междусобойчик *m.* any private group of males making decisions, usually politicians; old boy network. Судьба страны решалась на партийных междусобойчиках. The fate of the country was decided at party cabals.

мейнстрим *m.* (the) mainstream, mainstream culture.
• See also *мэйнстрим.*

мент *m.* [*pl.* **менты**] pig, cop, copper. Когда одного полковника спросили, нравится ли ему название фильма *Авария—дочь мента,* он пожал плечами и выразил мнение, что *Авария— дочь милиционера* звучало бы куда приятнее. When one colonel was asked whether he liked the title of the film *Disaster, the Copper's Daughter,* he shrugged his shoulders and said he thought *Disaster, the Policeman's Daughter* would have sounded much nicer.
• A once dated term from criminal argot which has returned to modern slang. See also *мильт, мильтон, мусор* 1.

ментовка *f.* 1. the cops, filth, police. 2. police car. 3. cop shop, police station. Поосторожнее с этим человеком—он из ментовки. Be a bit more careful with that bloke—he's from the police-station.
• See also *мусорня.*

ментовский *adj.* police, relating to cops, pigs.

ментура *coll.f.* 1. the fuzz, the filth, pigs. Не отдашь бабки—сдам тебя в ментуру. If you don't hand the money over I'll report you to the fuzz. 2. *sing.f.* cop, pig, policeman.

месиво *n.* a massive beating, a real doing.
• Lit. *mash.*

месиловка *f.* fight, mass attack, especially by a gang of muggers.
• See also *месилово.*

месилово *n.* variant of **месиловка**.

месить *v.t.* [*pf.* **замесить**] to beat to a pulp, beat the hell out of, give someone a real doing.
• Lit. *to knead.* See also *мочить.*

место: пойти в одно место *phr.pf.* to leave for some unspecified reason (often to go to the toilet). Пойду в одно место. I'm going to see a man about a dog.
• Lit. *to go to a certain place.*

металл *m.* heavy metal music, metal.
- Lit. *metal.* See also *хэви-метал.*

металлист *m.* headbanger, metal head, heavy metal enthusiast.
- Lit. *metal-worker.* See also *металлюга.*

металлюга *m.* metal-head.

метелить *v.t.* [*pf.* **изметелить, отметелить**] to hit, beat.

метёлка *f.* girl, young woman.
- Lit. *little broom.* See also *герла, гирла, жаба, лялька, мочалка.*

милитарист *m.* military officer. Used also as a mode of address. Эй, милитарист, дай двадцать копеек. Hey, soldier, spare a few coppers, eh?

милитёр *m.* a hawk, or aggressive civilian who supported the Soviet invasion of Afghanistan. Оадовцы (питерские люберы) и милитёры устраивают у Сайгона 'разборки со всей этой гнилой кодлой'. The Oadovtsy (Petersburg hard-men) and the hawks are arranging to sort out 'all that rotten crew' at the Saigon.

мильт *m.* cop, copper, pig.
- See also *мент, мильтон, мусор.*

мильтон *m.* cop, copper, pig.
- See also *мент, мильт, мусор.*

мимо кассы *adv.* off target, irrelevant.

митёк *m.* [*pl.* **митьки**] follower of the movement created by Vladimir Shinkarev in the book *Mit'ki.* Участников движения предлагаю назвать митьками, по имени основателя и классического образца—Дмитрия Шагина. I suggest that we call members of the movement Mit'ki, after the name given by its founder and classical model—Dmitriy Shagin.

митинг *m.* appointment. У меня митинг на Пушке в шесть. I'm meeting someone at Pushkin Square at six. забивать [*pf.* забить] митинг to set up a meeting, make an appointment.
- Use of this term has significantly changed in recent years, from its Soviet meaning of a political mass-meeting to a much more informal gathering. See also *стрелка.*

митингнуться *pf.* of **митинговаться.**

митинговать *v.i.impf.* to meet, demonstrate. Хватит митинговать, пора работать. Enough demonstrating; time to work.

митинговаться *v.i.* [*pf.* **митингнуться, смитингнуться**] to meet with someone. Завтра смитингнёмся. We'll meet tomorrow.

митьки *m.pl.* see **митёк.**

митьковский *adj.* relating to the Mit'ki. Ты думаешь, к тельняшечке прирастает митьковская ментальность? Do you think the Mit'ki view of things is the same as the military one?
- See *митёк.*

мла́дший ро́кер вы́сшей ли́ги *m.phr.* a jocular way of addressing a young rocker: 'premier league rocker'.

моги́ла: брать [*pf.* **взять**] **моги́лу** *phr.* to rob a grave. Лу́чше всего́ брать моги́лу днём. It's best to rob graves in the daytime.

мо́дный *adj.* trendy, fashionable.

мо́жно хоть раз в жи́зни споко́йно? *phr.* Just for once, can't we have some peace?

мо́йка *f.* blade.
• Lit. *washing, washer.*

молодо́й *adj. used as m.noun* recruit, new boy, soldier in first year of service.
• Lit. *young.*

моне́ты *f.pl.* money, dough, dosh. На́до бы́ло моне́т раздобы́ть на прики́д и для пое́здки. We had to get money for gear and for the journey.
• Lit. *coins.* See also **ма́ни.**

мордоворо́т *m.* tough guy, hoodlum, hard-case. У тебя́ бы то́же га́йка засла́била, е́сли бы на тебя́ тако́й мордоворо́т попёр. You would be scared too if you came up against a hard-nut like that.

морко́вка *f.* prick, cock, penis.
• Lit. *carrot.*

мота́лка *f.* gang of muggers. Два́дцать проце́нтов мота́лок прили́чно вооружены́, как пра́вило, самоде́льным ору́жием. Twenty percent of gangs are pretty well armed, usually with home-made weapons.

мота́нг *m.* mugger from an organised gang. Мота́нги презира́ют лохо́в и ненави́дят пацифи́стов. Muggers despise stupid gits and hate pacifists.

мота́ться *v.i.impf.* to be involved in, run with a gang.

мото́р *m.* taxi, car. У вокза́ла всегда́ мото́ры стоя́т. There are always taxis waiting by the station.
• Lit. *engine, motor.*

мочáлка *f.* 1. an amusing young woman. 'Хочу́ я всех моча́лок застеба́ть'. 'I want to impress all the groovy chicks' (from a song by the group Aquarium). 2. tart, hussy.
• Lit. *loofah, mop.* See also **герла́, ги́рла, жа́ба, метёлка, тёлка.**

мочи́лово *n.* 1. thrashing, beating. 2. brawl, set-to, bust-up.

мочи́ть *v.t.* [*pf.* **замочи́ть**] 1. to beat, give a pasting, doing, going over. 2. to kill, do in. Е́сли мо́чат, то мо́гут и замочи́ть. If they beat you, they might even kill you. **мочи́ться** *v.i.impf.* to fight. Ви́жу: чуваки́ мо́чатся (мо́чат друг дру́га) пря́мо посреди пло́щади. I saw some blokes knocking lumps out of each other right in the middle of the square.

• Lit. *to soak, wet, steep.* The perfective *замочи́ть* usually means *to kill.* See also *меси́ть.*

мочка́ть *v.t.impf.* to drink alcohol.

муда́к *m.* stupid git.

мужи́к *m.* 1. bloke, guy, geezer, man; also a term of address. Слышь, мужи́к, покури́ть не оста́вишь? Listen, pal, won't you leave me a smoke? 2. middle-ranking prisoner in labour camp. По свиде́тельству режиссёра, в фи́льме о тюрьме́ охо́тно уча́ствовали во́ры, мужики́ снима́ться отка́зывались. According to the director, the senior crims willingly took part in the film about the prison, but the average criminals refused to be filmed.

• Lit. *peasant.* Criminal argot.

музо́н *m.* music.

му́лька *f.* ephedrine. Ты, как пионе́р, на му́льке торча́л? Were you doing ephedrine when you started?

• See also *марцефа́ль, му́ля.*

му́льтики *m.pl.* drug-induced hallucinations. Мне снача́ла торча́ть понра́вилось: как бу́дто смо́тришь цветны́е, о́чень краси́вые му́льтики. I liked being on drugs at first: it was like seeing beautiful coloured cartoons.

• Lit. *animated films, cartoons.*

му́ля *f.* 1. ephedrine. 2. zipper or other accessory worn by head-bangers. балахо́н мухо́вый, с му́лями a head-banger's coat with various bits and pieces.

• See also *му́лька.*

му́ра *f.* garbage, rubbish. Как ты то́лько мо́жешь э́ту му́ру слу́шать? Just how can you listen to that crap?

му́сарня *f.* variant of **му́сорня.**

му́сор *m.* [*pl.* мусора́] 1. filth, pig, policeman. 2. member or fan of the Moscow Dynamo football team.

• Lit. *garbage.* See also *мент* 1, *дина́мик* 2.

му́сорня *f.* cop-shop, police station.

• See also *менто́вка, му́сарня.*

муста́нг *m.* louse. У нас вся тусо́вка из Кры́ма муста́нгов привезла́. Our whole crew brought lice with them from the Crimea.

• Lit. *mustang.*

мусташа́ *m.pl.* moustache.

мухо́вый *adj.* heavy-metal, relating to a heavy metal coat.

• See also *му́ля* for an example.

мэйнстри́м *m.* variant of **мейнстри́м.**

мэн *m.* [*pl.* мэны́] dude, guy, bloke, man, lad.

мэно́вый *adj.* male; macho. мэно́вый прики́д men's gear.

мясно́й *adj. often used as m.noun* member or fan of the Spartak football team. Also a mode of address to a Moscow Spartak fan.

мя́со *n.* the Spartak football team or their fans.
  • The word *мя́со* is used to deface Spartak graffiti. The *meat* reference is said to relate pejoratively to the backing the club originally received from retail traders.

Н

нааска́ть *v.i.pf.* 1. to steal, shoplift. Пойду́ нааска́ю сигаре́т. I'll go and nick some cigarettes. 2. to scrounge, tap. Я нааска́л на ботл. I tapped money for a bottle.

навёрнутый *adj.* sophisticated. У Шу́льца навёрнутая му́зыка. Schultz has some complicated music.
  • Lit. *wound.*

навеселе́ *adv.* tipsy, half-cut. Пришёл домо́й навеселе́. He arrived home with a bit of a drink in him.

наворо́т *m.* complications, difficulties, problems. Меня́ э́ти его́ наворо́ты доста́ли. I'm brassed off at all these shenanigans of his. У нас на тра́ссе таки́е наворо́ты бы́ли. We had all sorts of hassle on the road.

наворо́ченный *adj.* 1. sophisticated, complicated. Де́ка наво-ро́ченная с примо́чками, идёт за четы́ре шту́ки. A tape-deck with all kinds of stuff—going for four grand. 2. well dressed.

на́глухо *adv.* really, big time, seriously.

надерба́нить *pf.* of дерба́нить.

надринча́ться *v.i.* to get sloshed, pie-eyed, legless, pissed.
  • See also *дринча́ть.*

наезжа́ть *v.i.* [*pf.* нае́хать] [на + *acc.*] to have a go at, to give someone a hard time. Ну, а рэ́кет на тебя́ наезжа́л? Well, did the racket lean on you?
  • Lit. *to run over, into.*

нае́сться *v.i.pf.* to get drunk, pie-eyed. Ты уже́ нае́лся? Нет, то́лько пи́ва попи́л. Are you drunk already? No, I've just had some beer.
  • Less crude than *нажра́ться.*

нае́хать *pf.* of наезжа́ть

нажира́ться *v.i.* [*pf.* нажра́ться] to get pissed, out of your face, tanked up. Мне надое́ло, что ты ка́ждый день нажира́ешься. I'm sick of the way you get pissed every day.
  • Lit. *to gorge oneself.*

нажра́тый *adj.* dead drunk, pissed. Ка́ждый пра́здник ты прихо́дишь домо́й с рабо́ты нажра́тый. Every holiday you come home from work legless.

нажра́ться *pf.* of **нажира́ться**.

найт *m.* night. Куда́ бы нам на найт вписа́ться? Where could we kip for the night?

найта́ть *v.i.impf.* to sleep (over). Мо́жешь э́то вре́мя найта́ть у меня́. You can spend the night at my place.
* See also *найтова́ть*.

найтова́ть *v.i.impf.* variant of **найта́ть**.

найф *m.* [*pl.* **найфы́**] knife. На нас напа́ла урла́ с найфа́ми. We were set upon by some yobs with knives.

нака́лывать *v.t.* [*pf.* **наколо́ть**] 1. [на + *acc.*] to beat something out of someone. Наколо́л я его́ на па́ру штук. I squeezed two grand out of him. 2. to target, mark out (the potential victim of a crime). Её отрави́л тот скрипа́ч, кото́рый наколо́л стару́ху в рестора́не. She was poisoned by that thief who marked out the old woman in the restaurant. 3. to cheat, con, trick.
* Lit. *to chop, prick.*

нака́чка *f.* 1. body-building. 2. telling-off, reprimand from the boss.

наклю́каться *pf.* of **наклю́киваться**.

наклю́квиться *v.i.pf.* to drink red wine. Пока́ жда́ли колхо́зника, успе́ли наклю́квиться, так что е́ле дое́хали. While we were waiting for the bus, we managed to have a drink, so we only just about got there.
* Refers to the colour of cranberry (*клю́ква*).

наклю́киваться *v.i.* [*pf.* **наклю́каться**] to get drunk. Да́же на сва́дьбе сы́на наклю́кался. He even got drunk at his son's wedding.

нако́лка *f.* scheme, plot, scam, swindle. Есть у меня́ нако́лка на па́ру тысчо́нок. I've got a way of making a couple of thousand.
* Lit. *headdress.*

наколо́ть *pf.* of **нака́лывать**.

накры́ться *v.i.pf.* to come to nothing, be lost. Креди́т накры́лся. The credit came to nothing.
* Lit. *to cover oneself.*

на́лик *m.* cash, ready money.
* Abbreviated form of *нали́чные де́ньги.*

намы́лить ше́ю *phr.pf.* to beat up, give a doing.

наперегонки́ с Мао Цзэду́ном *f.phr.* trying to outdo, put one over on.
* Lit. *trying to overtake Mao Zedong.*

напря́г *m.* dispute, hassle. У него́ с пэрэнта́ми напря́ги. He's at loggerheads with his parents. У меня́ на него́ напря́г. I want to pull him up about something, I've got a bone to pick with him. **в напря́г** it's a nuisance. В напря́г за ха́вкой идти́—дава́й лу́чше пы́хнем. It's a drag going out for food—let's just have a spliff.

напряга́ть *v.t.* [*pf.* **напря́чь**] to harass, hassle, bother, to give a hard time. Эта крезану́тая герла́ меня́ напряга́ет. That crazy bitch's giving me a hard time.
• Lit. *to strain.*

напряжёнка *f.* shortage. Напряжёнка с проду́ктами суще́ственно не отрази́тся на напряжёнку с се́ксом. Он был, есть и бу́дет при любы́х режи́мах. A shortage of groceries won't seriously be reflected in a shortage of sex. That was, is and always will be a feature of all régimes. 2. period of hard work, a long slog.

напря́жно *adv.* dangerous, dodgy. Напря́жно кайф сего́дня иска́ть. It's dodgy looking for a hit nowadays.

напря́жный *adj.* dodgy, tricky. Напря́жный разгово́р у нас получа́ется. We're getting into pretty tricky stuff (conversation).

напря́чь *pf.* of **напряга́ть**.

нарк *m.* junkie, druggie. В э́том подва́ле на́рки собира́ются. Junkies meet in this cellar.
• Abbreviated form of *наркома́н (drug user, addict).*

нарко́вый *adj.* pertaining to junkies, drug users. нарко́вый флэт a pad for addicts.

настуча́ть *pf.* of **стуча́ть**.

натре́скаться *v.i.pf.* 1. to get drunk. 2. to over-eat.

наха́вать *pf.* of **ха́вать**.

нацме́н *m.* man from any former (Soviet) national minority, especially Asian or Caucasian.
• Abbreviated form of *нацменьшинство́ (national minority).* See also *чу́рка.*

невкайфы́ *m.pl.* variant of **некайфы́**. Я уста́л от невкайфо́в. I'm fed up with all these hassles.

невру́б *m.* being totally confused or lost. У меня́ по́лный невру́б. I'm completely lost.

некайфы́ *m.pl.* trouble, problems, hassle, a jam. Опя́ть некайфы́ начали́сь. More trouble—again!
• See also *невкайфы́.*

не́куда: по са́мое не́куда *phr.* up to one's neck. Вли́пла я в э́то гря́зное де́ло по са́мое не́куда. I was in that dirty business right up to my neck.

нелега́лка *f.* illegal business. Он не осо́бенно хорошо́ понима́ет тех свои́х знако́мых, кото́рые, порабо́тав в нелега́лке, ушли́ тепе́рь в чи́стый би́знес, де́лают всё по зако́ну и я́кобы все о́чень дово́льны. He doesn't really understand those of his acquaintances who, after working illegally, have gone legit, do everything within the law and seem very happy with it.

не́мка *f.* female German teacher, lecturer.

• Lit. *German woman.*

непоня́тки *pl.* difficult position, trouble. Вы бу́дете до́лго пребыва́ть в непоня́тках, е́сли не смо́жете до́лжным о́бразом прокрути́ться. You'll stay in the fix you're in if you can't get out properly.

• From *непоня́тный,* lit. *incomprehensible.*

непру́ха *f.* run of bad luck (especially in gambling). Непру́ха начала́сь. I've hit a run of bad luck.

нетусо́вочный *adj.* 1. reference to people from a different group or *tusovka.* нетусо́вочный пипл people from a different group. 2. reference to a person who doesn't like parties or hanging around. нетусо́вочная герла́ square girl.

неуставня́к *m.* carry-on, funny business, irregularities (in the army). Ты у себя́ в ро́те неуставня́к прекрати́! Stop that mucking around in your company!

**нефор
ма́л** *m.* member of a non-official youth organisation, especially prominent in the mid to late 1980s.

нешу́точный *adj.* great, magic, cool. Е́сли молодо́й челове́к состоя́тельный, хорошо́ оде́тый, то о нём говоря́т: 'Ну, ты про́сто туз,' а та́кже 'круто́й' и́ли 'нешу́точный'. If a young man is well-off and well-dressed, people say, 'Well, you are the man,' or 'a cool guy' or 'a serious dude'.

• Lit. *serious.* See also *круто́й, прики́нутый, упако́ванный.*

ништя́к *m.* 1. cool, not bad. Всё ништя́к. Everything's cool, sound. Звуча́ние ништя́к! Sounds not bad at all! 3. soundness, everything being fine. Из пе́сни систе́много музыка́нта по про́звищу Па́па Лёша: 'Мой друг про́сто так не лю́бит напря́г. И ве́рит в Вели́кий Ништя́к.' There's a couple of lines in a song by the hippy musician nicknamed Papa Lesha: 'My friend doesn't like hassle. He believes in the Great State of Bliss.' **ништяки́** leftovers.

• Popularly held to derive from *ничего́* in the sense *quite well, OK, never mind.*

ништяко́вая *adj.* used as *f.noun* dive, cheap eating establishment where food is often given out free.

• See also *ништя́чная, ништя́чка.*

ништяко́во *adv.* good, sound, all right.

ништяко́вый *adj.* sound, all right. ништяко́вый се́йшен a sound gig.
 • See also *ништя́чный*.
ништя́чка *f.* variant of **ништяко́вая**.
ништя́чная *adj.* used as *f.noun* dive, cheap café.
 • See also *ништяко́вая, ништя́чка.*
ништя́чно *adv.* terrific. Ништя́чно съе́здили. We had a sound trip.
ништя́чный *adj.* pretty, nice, cool. ништя́чная фе́нька nice beads. Ништя́чный у тебя́ кси́вник. You've got a fab pouch there.
 • See also *ништя́ковый, ништяко́вая.*
ништячо́к *m.* 1. fag end, cigarette butt. 2. any food.
новоде́л *m.* old building reconstructed using new materials. Е́сли они́ и восстано́вят храм Христа́ Спаси́теля, то э́то всё же бу́дет новоде́л. If they even rebuild the Cathedral of Christ the Saviour, it'll still all be new materials.
 • The Moscow Cathedral referred to was destroyed on Stalin's orders, to the outrage of the population. It has now been rebuilt.
нога́: приде́лать но́ги *pf.* to pinch, nick, steal. Он спит до́ма и не запи́хивает под поду́шку пиджа́к с докуме́нтами, чтобы ему́ ненаро́ком не приде́лали но́ги. He sleeps at home and doesn't have to stick his jacket with his documents under the pillow so that no-one accidentally pinches them. **встать на́ ноги** *pf.* to get set up, to get on one's feet. Е́сли бы у меня́ была́ необходи́мая фурниту́ра, мы могли́ бы бы́стро встать на́ ноги—производи́ть небольши́ми па́ртиями недороги́е де́тские вещи́чки. If I had the right gear we could soon get ourselves set up—producing small batches of kids' things. **поста́вить на широ́кую но́гу** *pf.* to make progress. Усло́вия для рабо́ты прекра́сные, но на́ши фина́нсовые возмо́жности не позволя́ют поста́вить де́ло на бо́лее широ́кую но́гу. Working conditions are great, but our financial conditions don't allow us really to get on.
 • The final phrase is a blend of two standard expressions: *встать на́ ноги* (to get on your feet) and *жить на широ́кую но́гу* (to live in grand style).
нормалёк! *m., interj.* all right! По два рубля́ хва́тит? Нормалёк! Will two roubles each do? All right!
ностальги́ст *m.* someone reproducing fashions of the 1940s-60s. Сленг же ностальги́стов втори́чен. The slang used by nostalgists is second-hand.
ночна́я ба́бочка *f.* prostitute, hooker, tom. Пойма́ть ночны́х ба́бочек мо́жно у гости́ниц Интури́ст (Уголо́к), Росси́я (ра́шка, иногда́ её зову́т ря́шка), Ко́смос и в валю́тных рестора́нах. You can pick up a prostitute near the Intourist

(The Corner), Rossiya (Rashka; sometimes they call it Ryashka), and Cosmos hotels, and in hard-currency restaurants.
• Lit. *moth.*

O

оа́довец *m.* member of an extreme right-wing group called Отря́д акти́вного де́йствия. Моего́ фре́нда жесто́ко изби́ли оа́довцы. The Oadovites gave my friend a hell of a beating.
• Leningrad 1987. The name is an acronym of the initials of the group, whose members wore white gloves symbolic of cleaning the city of its filth.

обалдева́ть *v.i.* [*pf.* **обалде́ть**] 1. to get high, out of one's mind, stoned. Ты, что совсе́м обалде́л—не понима́ешь, что де́лаешь? Are you off your head—don't you understand what you're doing? 2. To have a great time, a hoot.

обалде́нно *adv.* brilliantly, excellently, stunningly. Ха́халь, коне́чно, хоро́ший—обалде́нно одева́ется. Of course, her fancy man is handsome—a real smart dresser.

обалде́ть *pf.* of **обалдева́ть**.

обдерба́нить *pf.* of **дерба́нить**.

обдо́лбанный *adj.* high, charged up, gone. Кро́ме того́, да́же на За́паде са́ми музыка́нты, как пра́вило, весьма́ скепти́чески относи́лись к тому́, что писа́ли про них журнали́сты, а для рядово́го англича́нина любо́й обдо́лбанный ма́лый с серьго́й и ироке́зом—то́же 'панк'. Moreover, even in the West, as a rule musicians were themselves very sceptical of what people wrote about them in the papers. And for the ordinary Brit, any guy who's high and with an earring and mohican is also a 'punk'.

обдолба́ться *v.i.pf.* to get high, stoned.

обезья́нник *m.* bench for detainees in a police-station.
• Lit. monkey-house. See also *аква́риум.*

оберну́ть де́ньги *phr.pf.* to charge or demand high interest for lending money, to be a loan shark. Взя́ли ссу́ду, за пе́рвый год успе́ли оберну́ть де́ньги, так что предприя́тие рабо́тает. They took out a loan and managed to charge high interest for the first year, so the concern works.
• Lit. *to wrap up the money.*

оби́женный *adj. used as noun* prisoner of low status, forced to endure all sorts of indignities in prison; scumbag.
• Lit. *offended.*

обку́ренный *adj.* stoned, out of it.
• Lit. *tobacco-stained, seasoned.* See also *уку́ренный.* See *кры́ша е́дет* for an example.

обла́мывать *v.i.* [*pf.* **обломáть**] 1. to bring down, put someone in a downer. Обла́мываешь ты меня́. You're getting me down. Он меня́ уже́ вчера́ обломáл. He already put me in a downer yesterday. 2. to spoil (something for someone).
• Lit. *to break off.*

обла́мываться *v.i.* [*pf.* **обломáться**] 1. to be in a downer, fed up. Он здóрово обла́мывался на э́том дéле. He was really down about that business. 2. to allow oneself to get stressed out, break down. 3. not to want to do something. Я чегó-то обломáлся идти́ на стрéлку. For some reason I wasn't really into going to the meeting.
• Lit. *to break off.*

облóм *m.* [*pl.* **облóмы**] 1. failure, crash-out. Со впи́ской облóм вы́шел. Turned out we had no luck with getting a pad for the night. 2. bummer, pain. Облóм хáвку готóвить. It's a pain cooking. 3. downer. Я уже́ мéсяц в облóме. I've been fed up for a month now.
• Lit. *break.*

облóманный *adj.* disappointed, gloomy, let down, out of sorts. Прихожу́ в Тури́ст—там все таки́е облóманные сидя́т. So I got to the Tourist hotel and there were a whole lot of fed-up people sitting around.
• Lit. *broken.*

обломáть *pf.* of **обла́мывать.**

обломáться *pf.* of **обла́мываться.**

обломи́ст *m.* bummer, square. Из-за э́того обломи́ста парáшливая тусóвка получи́лась. Thanks to that bum we had a bloody awful party.
• See also *облóмщик.*

обломи́ться *v.i.pf.* 1. to fail. Э́та затéя обломи́лась. That caper bombed. 2. and **обломáться** *pf.* to be down, desperate, fed up. обломи́ться от систéмы to get fed up of the hippy system. 3. to get out of. Мне-то с э́того ничегó не обломи́лось. I couldn't get anything out of that. 4. to get a roasting.
• The *Систéма* was traditionally a Soviet hippy network or brotherhood, but has since come to refer to a system incorporating a variety of traditionally subcultural groups.

облóмно *adv.* down, depressingly, gloomily.

облóмный *adj.* disappointing, gloomy.

обло́мов *m.* 1. pain, annoying person. 2. **быть в обло́мове**, to be fed up, bored. Не тро́гай меня́—я в обло́мове. Don't touch me—I'm fed up.
  • See also *обло́мово.*

обло́мово *n.* variant of **обло́мов.**

обло́мщик *m.* variant of **обломи́ст.** Твои́ пэрента́ таки́е обло́мщики. Your parents are such squares.

обмыва́ть *v.t.* [*pf.* **обмы́ть**] to christen, drink to, toast. Но́чью, когда́ отплыва́ли на теплохо́де, доста́ли буты́лку во́дки, что́бы обмы́ть э́то де́ло, оди́н поля́к сказа́л; 'Сейча́с не то вре́мя, что́бы пить во́дку'. At night, as they were sailing away on the ship, they got a bottle of vodka to drink to their departure, and a Pole said: 'Now's not the time for vodka'.
  • Lit. *to bathe, wash.*

обмы́ть *pf.* of **обмыва́ть.**

обнали́чивать *v.t.* [*pf.* **обнали́чить**] to withdraw money. А откры́л я все э́ти ла́вочки для того́, чтобы де́ньги не держа́ть до́ма в стекля́нных ба́нках, чтоб они́ в де́ле находи́лись, чтоб официа́льная чи́стая кры́ша была́ на вся́кий слу́чай и чтобы была́ всегда́ под руко́й возмо́жность обнали́чивать и отмыва́ть ба́бки. I opened all these shops so I didn't have to keep money at home in jars, so that it really was used, so there was an official clean front just in case, and so that I always had the chance to withdraw money and launder it.

обнали́чить *pf.* of **обнали́чивать.**

обожра́ться *v.i.pf.* to get dead drunk. Обожра́лся я до тако́й сте́пени, что на нога́х не стоя́л. I drank so much I couldn't stand.
  • Lit. *to guzzle, stuff oneself.*

оборзе́ть *v.i.* [*pf.* of **борзе́ть**] 1. to get really angry, blow one's top. 2. to get cocky, cheeky.

обса́д *m.* great, a gas. Портвяшо́к—по́лный обса́д. The port was dead good.
  • *Mit'ki* term. See also *крутня́к 2, убо́й, улёт.*

обсади́ться *v.i.pf.* variant of **обдолба́ться.**

обстеба́ть *pf.* of **стеба́ть.**

обторча́ться *pf.* variant of **обдолба́ться.**

обува́ть *v.t.* [*pf.* **обу́ть**] to rob, swindle. Вчера́ в ночь, к приме́ру, хорошо́ обу́ли одного́ чувака́ из Тамбо́ва. Last night, for example, they robbed a young dude from Tambov.
  • Lit. *to put on shoes.*

обуре́вший *adj.* 1. high, stoned, drunk. 2. insane, crazy, mad.

обуре́ть *v.i.pf.* to go crazy. Ты что, обуре́л, что ли? What's up with you—have you flipped or something?

обу́ть *pf.* of **обува́ть**.

обха́йранный *adj.* hippy with a short haircut. Он как жени́лся, так хо́дит обха́йранный. As soon as he got married he started going round with short hair.

обхайра́ть *v.t.pf.* to cut hair (very short). Обхайра́ли на су́тках. They cut all my hair when I did a short stretch.

• *Су́тки* refers to a short prison sentence (defined in days).

обхайра́ться *v.i.pf.* to have one's hair cut. Обхайра́лся на ле́то. I had my hair cut for the summer.

обшмона́ть *pf.* of **шмона́ть**.

общáга *f.* hostel, shared student accommodation, hall of residence.

общáк *m.* communal fund used by criminals, e.g. to help arrested offenders. Из э́тих де́нег где́-то ты́сяч две́сти отдава́ли на общáк. Of that money, they set aside about 200,000 for the kitty.

оглоу́шить *v.t.pf.* to surprise, startle, overwhelm. Он хоте́л оглоу́шить её э́той но́востью. He wanted to overwhelm her with this news.

окосе́ть *v.i.pf.* to become disoriented or giddy. Совсе́м мале́ц окосе́л от вы́хлопов. The lad got quite dizzy from the exhaust.

олдо́вость *f.* experience of being in the hippy scene.

олдо́вый *adj.* 1. experienced, of long standing (of a hippy). Весь олдо́вый пипл сиди́т по флэ́там. All the experienced hippies sit in their pads. 2. *adj.* good old. олдо́вый кси́вник a favourite old pouch.

опетуши́ть *v.t.pf.* (in prison) to make someone into a passive homosexual. Опетуши́ть мо́жно по-ра́зному, обли́ть мочо́й, заста́вить поцелова́ть пара́шу. You can make men into queers in various ways—piss on them, make them kiss the slops bucket.

• Criminal argot.

опиздене́ть *v.i.pf.* 1. to be worn out, exhausted. 2. to be really amazed, well fucking impressed.

• Vulgarism.

опиу́ха *f.* opium. Марго́, мо́жет, вма́жем опиу́хи? Margot, how about sharing some opium?

опроки́нуть *pf.* variant of **ки́нуть**.

опуска́ть *v.t.* [*pf.* **опусти́ть**] 1. to humiliate. Люде́й опуска́ют по пригово́ру воро́в за ра́зные грехи́: стука́чество, неупла́ту ка́рточного до́лга, неподчине́ние авторите́ту, за то, что на сле́дствии сдал поде́льников, что име́ет ро́дственников в правоохрани́тельных о́рганах. People are humiliated on the orders of the senior crims for various offences:

ratting, failing to pay gambling debts, insubordination against a guvnor, giving away accomplices during investigations, and for having relations in organisations connected with law and order. 2. (labour camps) to rape.

• Lit. *to lower.*

опусти́ть *pf.* of **опуска́ть.**

опу́щенный *adj. used as noun* badly maltreated person, scum, scum-bag. Есть, одна́ко, лю́ди, кото́рым прихо́дится гора́здо ху́же, чем работя́гам. Э́то петухи́, оби́женные, опу́щенные—те, из кого́ това́рищи по заключе́нию сде́лали пасси́вных гомосексуали́стов. There are, however, people who have it worse than the ordinary inmates. They are the scumbags, humiliated and bullied—those who have been made passive homosexuals by their fellow inmates.

• Lit. *downcast.* Criminal argot.

ортодо́кс *m.* new convert to the Orthodox Church.

• Lit. *conformist.*

оса́док: вы́пасть в оса́док *phr.pf.* to fall about laughing.

• See also *отпада́ть.*

отбомби́ться *v.i.pf.* to pass exams. Я в э́ту се́ссию на неде́лю ра́ньше суме́л отбомби́ться. I managed to pass everything in this lot of exams a week early.

• Lit. *to drop one's load of bombs.*

отвя́з *m.* entertainment (often hassle-free), relaxation. Рок привлёк э́ту пу́блику возмо́жностями отвя́за, но не мастерство́м. Rock attracted this audience with the chance to have a hassle-free good time, not because it was well played.

отвя́занный *adj.* independent, rebellious, unconventional. отвя́занная чуви́ха a chick with a mind of her own.

• Lit. *untied.*

отвяза́ться *pf.* of **отвя́зываться.**

отвя́зываться *v.i.* [*pf.* **отвяза́ться**] 1. to disregard the rules. 2. to have a good time, relax.

• Lit. *to come undone, untied.*

отде́лать *v.t.pf.* to beat up, give a doing. Не сла́бо меня́ отде́лали. They didn't half give me a kicking.

• Lit. *to put the final touches to.*

оте́ц *m.* mister, mate, pal; way of addressing a stranger. Оте́ц, дай закури́ть. Give us a light, mister.

• Lit. *father.* Folk.

отключка *f.* blackout (unconsciousness, often caused by alcohol). Здесь деру́тся сте́нка на сте́нку топора́ми и фи́нками, гро́бятся на́смерть на мотоци́клах, напива́ются до отклю́чки не́сколько раз в неде́лю. Here they pile in, fighting with axes and Finnish knives, kill themselves on motorbikes and drink themselves legless several times a week.

откоси́ть от а́рмии *phr.pf.* to escape or avoid military service. У него́ дво́е дете́й—вот и откоси́л от а́рмии. He has two kids, so he escaped military service.

откры́то-запрещённый *adj.* illegal but well-known. В отли́чие от большинства́ он пришёл туда́ из официа́льного би́знеса и не занима́ется откры́то-запрещёнными её ви́дами— ору́жием, нарко́тиками, кру́пными валю́тными опера́циями. Unlike most, he came here from legit business and doesn't concern himself with openly illegal operations: weapons, drugs, big currency deals.

отма́з *m.* excuse. Остава́лось лишь вы́брать кварти́рку для ограбле́ния и проду́мать дета́ли отма́за от подозре́ний со стороны́ уголо́вников. All he had to do was choose a flat to break into and think up the details of some excuse to escape suspicion from the criminals.
* See also *отма́зка.*

отма́заться *pf.* of **отма́зываться.**

отма́зка *f.* variant of **отма́з.**

отма́зывать *v.i.* [*pf.* **отма́зать**] to make excuses.

отма́зываться *v.i.* [*pf.* **отма́заться**] to escape punishment, to get away with. И ни ра́зу не попада́лись, а е́сли и случа́лось, то Ро́ме удава́лось отма́зываться—то он малоле́тний, то вро́де бы и не уча́ствовал. They were never caught, not once, but if they were, then Roma managed to get away with it: either he was a juvenile, or he just somehow didn't take part.

отмете́лить *pf.* of **мете́лить.**

отморо́женный *adj.* die-hard, hardened (criminal). Настоя́щей охра́ной любо́й серьёзной конто́ры занима́ются мафио́зные структу́ры. Там есть свои́ кома́нды, состоя́щие из от- моро́женных уголо́вников с автома́тами, кото́рые бу́дут стреля́ть в любо́го и ни перед чем не остано́вятся. The security of any serious outfit is looked after by mafia structures. They have their teams, consisting of hardened criminals with machine guns who will shoot at anyone and stop at nothing.
* Lit. *frostbitten.*

оторва́ться *pf.* of **отрыва́ться.**

отпа́д *m.* a scream, hoot, great (laugh); something brilliant. Ста́ло быть, он был из 'Па́мяти', в конце́ стал кулако́м стуча́ть и ора́ть: 'Доло́й рок-культу́ру, ура́ Столы́пину!'—отпа́д полне́йший, сил не́ было слу́шать. So, he was from 'Pamiat''. At the end he started thumping his fist and bawling 'Down with rock-culture, hooray for Stolypin!'—it was an absolute scream, you couldn't listen for laughing. **в отпа́де** great, sound (very impressed). Ну и прики́д—я в отпа́де. Your gear is just—Wow!

• See *Па́мять*: an extreme right-wing movement.

отпада́ть *v.i.* [*pf.* **отпа́сть**] 1. to be really amused. Он так передра́знивал Горбачёва, что все отпада́ли. He took off Gorbachev so well that everyone just fell about. 2. to be astonished. Я как уви́дел э́ту герлу́—так и отпа́л. When I saw that girl, I almost fainted.

• Lit. *to fall off.* See also *вы́пасть в оса́док.*

отпа́сть *pf.* of **отпада́ть**.

отписа́ть *pf.* of **отпи́сывать**.

отпи́сывать *v.t.* [*pf.* **отписа́ть**] to chuck out, chase, bomb out, knock back. Мы хоте́ли у него́ перенайта́ть, по он тепе́рь всех отпи́сывает. We wanted to kip at his place, but he's bombing everyone out these days. Я прико′о́лся к э́той герле́, но она́ меня́ отписа́ла. I fancied that girl, but she gave me the knock back.

• Lit. *to bequeath.*

отринга́ть *pf.* of **ринга́ть**.

отрица́ловка *f.* prisoners refusing to cooperate with the authorities. Так называ́емая отрица́ловка составля́ет о́коло 15 проце́нтов. The so-called awkward squad comprises about 15 percent.

• Criminal argot. See also *шерсть, отрица́лово.*

отрица́лово *n.* variant of **отрица́ловка**.

отруби́ться *pf.* of **выруба́ться**.

отрыва́ться *v.i.* [*pf.* **оторва́ться**] to let one's hair down, let go, relax. Мы в Крыму́ так клёво оторвали́сь. We really let go in the Crimea.

• Lit. *to be torn off.*

отрывно́й *adj.* wild, mental, crazy (lacking in restraint). Ско́ро все панко́вские отрывны́е гру́ппы соберу́тся в одно́м клу́бе. Soon all the mental punk groups will gather in one club.

• Lit. *perforated.*

отстёгивать *v.i.* [*pf.* **отстегну́ть**] to pay. Я ни на кого́ не клепа́ю, че́стно де́лаю де́ло, а на кого́ рабо́тать—мне всё равно́, лишь бы ба́бки отстёгивали. I slander no-one, go about my business honestly, and as for who I work for—it's all the same to me as long as they pay up the readies.

• Lit. *to unfasten.*

отстегну́ть *pf.* of **отстёгивать**.

отт́яг *m.* 1. wild party. 2. something great, wicked. Э́та гру́ппа— тако́й отт́яг! That group is pure great!

оття́гиваться *v.i.* [*pf.* **оттяну́ться**] to have a good time, to let one's hair down. Мы вчера́ на сэ́йшене так оттяну́лись! We had such a great time at the gig yesterday! **оттяну́ться в по́лный рост** to have a really excellent time.

отта́жник *m.* someone who has a great time, party-goer, raver.

отта́жно *adv.* brilliantly, with great excitement. Мы так отта́жно в Я́лту съе́здили. We had such a brilliant trip to Yalta.

отта́жный *adj.* exciting, great, sound. Фильм был отта́жный. The film was excellent.

оттяну́ться *pf.* of **оття́гиваться**.

отфа́чить *v.t.pf.* 1. to screw, con. 2. to fuck, screw.
   • Vulgarism.

отфейсова́ть *pf.* of **фейсова́ть**.

отходня́к *m.* cold turkey. Одни́—дви́гались, пы́хали, глота́ли колёса и пото́м му́чались в отходняке́. Some people shot up, smoked dope, took tabs and then suffered the after-effects.

отши́ться *v.i.pf.* to buy oneself out of a gang. Е́сли вы любо́й цено́й хоти́те не входи́ть в группиро́вку и́ли вы́йти из неё, что ж, мо́жете отши́ться. If you don't want to go in with a gang, or if you want to get out of one at any price, well then, you can buy yourself out.

отъе́хавший *adj.* out of it, wired to the moon, pissed, out of one's face. Е́сли де́вушка стра́нная и́ли вы́пившая, то о ней мо́гут сказа́ть отъе́хавшая. If a girl is strange or has a drink in her, people might say she's out of it.
   • See also *отвя́занный*.

отыме́ть *v.t.* 1. to screw, con. 2. to screw, shag.
   • See also *отфа́чить*.

офиге́ть *v.i.pf.* 1. to go screwball. 2. to be (well) impressed.

офиги́тельно *adv.* very, really, pure. Чёртова бриллиа́нтовая серёжка—сто́ила офиги́тельно до́рого. One hell of a diamond earring—cost a pure packet.

офонаре́ть *v.i.pf.* to go crazy, nuts, loopy. Ты что, офонаре́л? Have you gone nuts or something?

охра́на *f.* gang of racketeers. А ты слу́шай сюда́: до 30 проце́нтов чи́стой при́были почти́ с ка́ждой то́чки идёт охра́не. Про́ще, рэкети́рам. You just listen here—up to 30 percent clear profit from almost every joint goes to the protection gang. In simpler terms, to racketeers.
   • Lit. *guard, protection.*

охуева́ть *v.i.* [*pf.* **охуе́ть**] to be well fucking impressed.
   • Vulgarism.

охуе́ть *pf.* of **охуева́ть**.

очко́ *n.* 1. arse, ass, backside. Проигра́л—подставля́й очко́. You lose: time to kick ass. 2. [*pl.* **очки́**] toilet pan, bowl. Молоды́х в а́рмии заставля́ют дра́ить очко́ зубно́й щёткой. In the army they make recruits polish the bog with a toothbrush.
- Lit. *point* (in scoring a game).

П

па́лка: ки́нуть па́лку *phr.pf.* to have an orgasm, have sex. Я ей на́ ночь три па́лки ки́нул. I gave her three orgasms one night.

паль *f.* dope, grass, pot.

па́мятник *m.* member of the nationalist group Pamyat'. Па́мятники оби́делись на пре́ссу. The Pamyat' people were offended by the press.
- Lit. *monument*, derived from the movement's name Па́мять (*Memory*).

Па́мять *f.* Pamyat', a right-wing Russian social and political organisation.
- Lit. *Memory*.

пана́ма *f.* yarn, false tale, tall story. Это така́я пана́ма, тако́е безбо́жное враньё! It's a load of rubbish, godless lies!
- Lit. *panama hat.*

панк *m.* punk (person, style).

панк- *in compounds* punk. панк-му́зыка punk music. панк-движе́ние punk movement.

панко́вский *adj.* punk. Для сего́дняшних панко́вских ви́ршей характе́рен *Экспро́мт* Ге́йко Целко́вича: 'Поэ́зия—зага́дка для глухи́х. Ты блядь, но я ви́дал и не таки́х...' Geiko Tselkovich's *Impromptu* is characteristic of modern punk verse: 'Poetry is a riddle for the deaf. You're a slapper, but I haven't seen that kind...'

панк-ро́к *m.* punk rock. Панк-ро́к—не совсе́м му́зыка, э́то конце́пция. Punk rock is not so much music, more an idea.

панфу́рик *m.* variant of **фунфу́рик**.

пара́дка *f.* full military parade uniform.
- Abbreviated form of *пара́дная фо́рма*. See *де́мбельский акко́рд* for an example.

парадня́к *m.* front door, main entrance. Иеро́глифом тай парадня́к я укра́сил. I decorated the entrance with a Tai symbol.
- Example is a line from a hippy tanka.

пара́ша *f.* 1. slops, slops bucket, crap. 2. a lie.

пара́шливый *adj.* rubbish, lousy. пара́шливая тусо́вка a rotten party.

па́рент *m.* [*pl.* **парента́**] parent; *pl.* folks. У него́ парента́— круты́е совки́. His parents are real Soviets.
- See also *прэнта́, пэ́ренс, пэренса́, паренту́*

па́риться *v.i.impf.* to do a stretch, serve a sentence in prison. Мать па́рилась за кра́жу, а отца́ не знал. His mother was in prison for theft and he didn't know his father.
- Lit. *to steam*, as in a steam bath.

парово́з *n.* blow-back, blowing hashish smoke into someone else's mouth.
- Lit. *steam engine*. See also *джа-экспре́сс, парово́зик*.

парово́зик *m.* variant of **парово́з**. пусти́ть парово́зик to give a blow-back.
- See also *джа-экспре́сс, парово́з*.

партиза́н *m.* reservist, civilian called up for a short period.

пассажи́р *m.* client, buyer. Пассажи́р име́ется, а зна́чит, девятьсо́т ря́бчиков, счита́й, в карма́не. There is a buyer, which means 900 roubles in your pocket.
- Lit. *passenger*.

пасть *f.* gob, trap, mouth. Заткни́ пасть. Shut your trap.

пасы́фик *m.* variant of **паци́фик**.

паха́н *m.* 1. criminal ringleader, boss, guvnor. 2. someone trying to get authority especially by force, usurper.
- See *оби́женный* for an example.

паца́н *m.* criminal who is trustworthy and loyal to the criminal code.
- See also *паца́нка*.

паца́нка *f.* criminal loyal to the criminal code. Паца́нки деру́тся по-чёрному. The criminal chicks fight big time.
- See also *паца́н*.

паца́нский *adj.* criminal. паца́нские поня́тия street code, rules of street morality, honour among thieves. Практи́чески по паца́нским поня́тиям не живу́т—и́ми прикрыва́ются. They practically don't live by street rules, they're protected by them.

паци́фик *m.* peace sign, symbol of the peace movement. Обы́чно на кси́внике паци́фик рису́ют и́ли вышива́ют. People usually draw or embroider a peace sign on their hanging pouch.
- See also *пасы́фик*.

пе́нка *f.* laugh, good joke. Э́то была́ пе́нка! It was a scream!
- Lit. *skin*.

первокла́ссник *m.* brainbox, swot.
- See also *ву́ндеркинд, зубри́ла*.

передозня́к *m.* drugs overdose, OD. Он пое́хал на дерба́н и у́мер от передозняка́. He went out for some poppy and died of an overdose.

перекума́риться *v.i.pf.* 1. to take a drug to cure withdrawal symptoms. 2. to overcome withdrawal.

переломáться *v.i.pf.* to kick a drug habit, to chuck the gear.

перемахнýться *pf.* of махáться.

перенайтáть *v.i.pf.* to spend the night. Придётся перенайтáть на вокзáле. We'll have to kip overnight at the station.

> • See also *перенайтовáть.*

перенайтовáть *impf.* variant of перенайтáть.

пéрепись тушёнки *f.* Sixth Department of the KGB, dealing with financial fraud.

> • Lit. *inventory of canned meat.*

переплю́нуть с бороды́ на лы́сину *phr.pf.* to travel from Okhotnyy ryad to the Lenin Library on the Moscow metro.

> • Lit. *to spit from the beard to the bald patch.* The reference is to the old name for the first station: Marx Avenue.

перестремáть *v.t.pf.* to freak out, scare stiff.

перестремáться *v.i.pf.* to be really scared, freaked, scared out of one's wits.

перó *n.* knife, blade.

> • Lit. *feather.*

пéсня *f.* something great, brilliant. Э́то такáя пéсня! It's just so great!

> • Lit. *song.*

петрýшка *f.* fiver, five-rouble note. На трёх вокзáлах с жéнщинами свобóдного поведéния мóжно договори́ться за петрýшку и́ли, что сейчáс бóлее вы́годно,—за стакáн портвéйна. There are three railway stations where you can agree a price of five roubles with women of easy virtue; or a glass of port, which is more advantageous nowadays.

> • Lit. *parsley.*

петýх *m.* passive homosexual, poof, queer, gay-boy. Петухáм в зóне прихóдится горáздо хýже, чем работя́гам. In prison the queers have it far worse than the rank-and-file inmates.

> • Lit. *cockerel, rooster.*

печáтка *f.* production.

> • Lit. *signet.*

пи́дар *m.* poof, queer, gay-boy, arse-bandit.

пи́дорка *f.* uniform cap in labour camp.

пиздá *f.* hole, cunt, vagina. пиздá стáрая old bitch. Иди́ в пиздý! Go to fuck! Fuck off!

> • Vulgar.

пиздáто *adv.* fucking brilliantly.

> • Vulgar.

пиздáтый *adj.* fucking brilliant, excellent.

> • Vulgar.

пизде́ть *v.i.impf.* to talk crap, lie, bullshit.
  • *Пизде́ть: пизжу́, пизди́шь.*

пизде́ц *interj.* 1. (that's) the end. 2. shit! bollocks! hell!
  • Vulgarism.

пи́здить *v.t.* [*pf.* **спи́здить**] to nick, pinch, swipe, nab, steal.
  • See also *коммуни́здить.*

пи́леный *adj.* cut, scarred.
  • See also *попи́леный.*

пили́ть *v.t.* [*pf.* **попили́ть**] 1. to cut with a blade. попили́ть ве́нники to cut one's veins, do oneself in. 2. to screw, shag. Он её пи́лит? Is he shagging her?
  • 2. Vulgarism. Lit. *to saw.*

пили́ться *v.i.* [*pf.* **попили́ться**] 1. to cut one's veins, slit one's wrists. Пе́ли про како́го-то крезану́того мэ́на, ника́к ему́ не переки́нуться бы́ло, он и циани́стым ка́лием вма́зывался, и веняки́ ко́цал, и пили́лся—всё без ма́зы. They would sing about some crazy guy who had no way of deserting, and who injected potassium cyanide and slit his wrists—all to no good. 2. to shag (of a woman). Она́ уже́ с кем-нибу́дь пи́лится? Is she sleeping with anyone yet?
  • Meaning 2 is a vulgarism.

пинце́т *m.* something great, excellent. Посмотре́ли по ви́дику *Бульва́рное чти́во*—это пинце́т! We saw *Pulp Fiction* on video—it's fab!
  • Lit. *tweezers.*

пионе́р *m.* 1. kid, novice. 2. a new hippy.
  • The word was formerly used for members of the Soviet youth organization, the Pioneers.

пионе́рить *v.t.impf.* to pinch, nick, swipe, steal. Он ча́сто пионе́рил сигаре́ты у отца́. He often used to pinch fags from his father.
  • See also *коммуни́здить.*

пионе́рия *coll.f.* new hippies. На тусо́вке сего́дня то́лько пионе́рия, олдо́вых никого́ нет. There's only new hippies at the gig today; none of the old lot at all.

пипл *m.* [*pl.* **пиплы́**] 1. a hippy. 2. *coll.* hippies, folk.
  • Transliteration of *people.*

пиплёнок *m.* hippy kid (hippy's child).

пи́плики *m.pl.* hippies.
  • A pet name used mainly by girls.

пипло́вый *adj.* hippy, hippy's. пипло́вый прики́д hippy gear. пипло́вый наро́д hippy folk.

пи́сать *v.t.* [*pf.* **попи́сать**] 1. to cut with a blade. попи́сать ма́ковые голо́вки на гря́дке to cut poppy heads in a garden. 2. to piss.
  • Not to be confused with *писа́ть (to write).*

писи́шка *f.* personal computer, PC. Когда́ же в на́шей фи́рме писи́шки поя́вятся? When will we get PCs in this firm?

план *m.* 1. pot, dope. Что́-то у меня́ кры́ша ползёт. От чего́? От хоро́шего жи́зненного пла́на. Somehow my head's going all funny. What from? From good old dope. **пое́хать на план** *pf.* to go to an Asian (former Soviet) republic for cannabis. 2. joint, reefer.
  • Lit. *plan.*

планово́й *adj. used as m.noun* junkie, pot smoker.

пластили́н *m.* cannabis-based tar, mixed with dust into a kind of plasticine.
  • Lit. *plasticine.* See also *центря́к.*

плейс *m.* [*pl.* плейса́] place (to sit). На́до найти́ како́й-нибудь плейс. We'd better find somewhere to park our bums.

плотня́к *m.* dense musical sound. Хо́чется, что́бы звуча́л плотня́к на конце́ртах. You want there to be a really intense sound at the concerts.
  • Musicians' jargon.

повинти́ть *pf.* of **винти́ть.**

по́го *n.* pogo (dance).

пого́ны *m.pl.* police, pigs, cops.
  • Lit. *shoulder-strap.*

погране́ц *m.* [*pl.* погранцы́] (retired) frontier guard.
  • From *Пограни́чные войска́*, the troops responsible for frontier security.

подви́нуть зако́н *phr.pf.* to bend the law, rules. На собесе́довании спроси́л его́ па́ру раз и вскользь: не счита́ет ли он, что для де́ла лу́чше иногда́ зако́н подви́нуть? At the interview he was asked a couple of times in passing whether he thought it was good for business to bend the law sometimes.

подда́тый variant of **да́тый.**

подéльник *m.* accomplice.
  • See *опусти́ть* for example of usage.

подка́лывать *v.t.* [*pf.* подколо́ть] 1. to tell off, reprimand, give a roasting. 2. to play a trick on.
  • Lit. *to pin up.* See also *прика́лываться* 1 and *пристёбываться.*

подка́лываться *v.i.impf.* to occasionally inject small quantities of drugs (for fun).

подколо́ть *pf.* of **подка́лывать.**

подкру́ченный *adj.* putting on airs, trying to be important, being a pseud, wannabe. Молоды́е лю́ди быва́ют повы́шенной крутизны́, но попада́ются и подкру́ченные, то есть не о́чень круты́е. There are some young people who are real serious guys, but you come across people who try it on, that is, they're not very smart.

подкума́рить *v.t.pf.* 1. to give a dose of a drug to feel better. Подкума́рь дру́га. Pick your pal up with a shot. 2. to feel bad from a lack of drugs.

подку́риваться *v.i.impf.* to smoke cannabis. Да он не ширя́ется, а то́лько подку́ривается. No, he doesn't inject, he just smokes.

подма́хивать *v.i.impf.* 1. to get used to other people. А э́тот им подма́хивал—свой среди́ дедо́в, как же. But that guy could get on with them—in with the big shots, of course. 2. *v.t.* [*pf.* подмахну́ть] to sign hurriedly. Нача́льник подмахну́л заявле́ние, не гля́дя. The boss signed the statement without looking at it.

поднима́ться *v.i.* [*pf.* подня́ться] to go up in the world (in illegal business). С января́ на́чал поднима́ться, выходя́ в авторите́ты. Since January he's started to go up in the world, joining the big guns.
• Lit. *to go up.*

подня́ться *pf.* of **поднима́ться.**

подписа́ть *pf.* of **подпи́сывать.**

подпи́сывать *v.i.* [*pf.* подписа́ть] [на + *acc.*] 1. to pick up someone. подписа́ть герлу́ на фак to pick up a skirt for a shag. 2. to talk into. 3. to get something for free. Я подписа́л его́ на тэн. I got ten roubles out of him.
• Lit. *to sign.*

подре́зать *v.i.pf.* to drive or swerve a car very close to another vehicle, to cut up. Пое́хали на уголо́к, договори́лись прода́ть её за 200 рубле́й, а пото́м подре́зать клие́нта и девчо́нку забра́ть из такси́. We went to the Intourist hotel, agreed to sell the chick for 200 roubles, then cut up the client and take the girl out of the taxi.
• Lit. *to cut, clip.*

подсади́ть *v.t.pf.* to introduce someone to drugs. подсади́ть на иглу́ to get (someone) onto injecting.
• Lit. *to help to sit down.* See also подсе́сть.

подсе́сть *v.i.pf.* [на + *acc.*] to become addicted to. Он подсе́л на траву́. He got hooked on grass.
• Lit. *to sit near to.*

подфа́киваться *v.i.impf.* [к + *dat.*] to fool around (sexually). Ты к ней не подфа́кивайся. Don't you fool around with her.

подфа́кнуться *v.i.pf.* to have a one-night stand. Я на том флэту́ подфа́кнулся. I slept over in that pad.

пожа́рная кома́нда *f.* bully boys, gang which gets money back for loan sharks. Они́ обраща́ются в пожа́рные кома́нды, конто́ры по выкола́чиванию неусто́ек, с рабо́ты в кото́рой я чуть

бы́ло не на́чал свою́ комме́рцию. They go to the crews, outfits for extorting forfeits, from the place where I almost started my own business.
  • Lit. *fire brigade.*

позвоно́чник *m.* student who was admitted to university/college etc. not on merit but as a result of a telephone call by an influential parent or friend.
  • *Звоно́к* (*telephone call*).

покима́рить *pf.* of **кима́рить**.

поко́цанный *adj.* scratched. поко́цанный диск scratched record. поко́цанная плёночка scratched film.

поко́цать *v.t.pf.* to scratch, cut. Мою́ плёночку поко́цали. My film got cut. поко́цать ве́нники to slit, slash one's wrists.
  • See also *полоска́ть, попи́сать ве́нники.*

по́кет *m.* [*pl.* покета́] pocket.

полба́нки *f.* see **ба́нка** 1.

по́лис *m.* [*pl.* полиса́] 1. policeman, copper. Одна́жды стрёмный по́лис меня́ у Ра́ши взял. Once a dodgy copper picked me up near the Russia Hotel. 2. *coll.m.* the filth, police.

по́лный: в по́лный рост see **рост**.

полоса́тик *m.* prisoner in strict régime labour camp who wears a striped uniform. Обита́тели коло́ний осо́бого режи́ма но́сят не обы́чную, си́нюю и́ли чёрную, а полоса́тую спецоде́жду и зову́тся оттого́ не́жно-фамилья́рно полоса́тиками. The inmates of special régime camps don't wear an ordinary uniform, dark blue or black, but a striped special uniform, and because of that are affectionately known as stripeys.

полу́кать *pf.* of **лу́кать**.

получа́ть *v.i.* [*pf.* **получи́ть**] to get a doing, beating. Давно́ не получа́л? Haven't you had a doing for a while? получи́ть по́ уху *pf.* to get a beating, a clip round the ear.
  • Lit. *to receive.*

получи́ть *pf.* of **получа́ть**.

помаха́ться *pf.* of **маха́ться**.

помога́йка *f.* police patrol car. Два помо́щника лейтена́нта тесне́е сплоти́лись вокру́г Завадо́вского, ещё оди́н милиционе́р пойма́л соба́ку и сжал ей мо́рдочку ладо́нями, что́бы она́ не ла́яла, и все дви́нулись к помога́йкам. Two of the lieutenant's sidekicks came right up closer to Zavadovsky, another cop grabbed the dog and held its jaws to stop it barking, and they all moved off to the patrol cars.
  • ПМГ (*Патру́льная милице́йская гру́ппа*).

понт: брать/взять на понт *phr.* to con, trick, play someone for a fool. Следователь тебя на понт берёт. The detective is making a mug of you.

попере́ть *pf.* [на + *acc.*] to have a go at someone, to give someone abuse. Чего́ ты на него́ попёр? Why did you have a go at him?

попи́л *m.* slash mark on the wrists. Ви́дел у него́ попи́лы? Did you see his scars?

попи́ленный variant of **пи́леный.**

попи́ливать *v.t.impf.* to screw, shag (used of a man with a woman). Ты её попи́ливаешь? Are you screwing her?
• Vulgarism.

попили́ть *pf.* of **пили́ть.**

попили́ться *pf.* of **пили́ться.**

попи́сать *pf.* of **пи́сать.**

попи́сать ве́нники *phr.pf.* variant of **покоца́ть ве́нники.**

попс *m.* trendy, pop music. Заче́м митьку́ тако́й попс? Why does a Mityok need pop like that?

попса́ *coll.f.* 1. trendy (often snobbish) people. 2. *sing.f.* something naff, popular. Э́тот мой клип, коне́чно, попса́, но хоро́шая попса́. This video of mine is naff, but good naff!

попса́рь *m.* pop musician, pop fan, someone interested in or practising mainstream popular culture.

попсо́во *adv.* currently popular, the (in-)thing. Митьки́ одева́ются во что попа́ло, но ни в ко́ем слу́чае не попсо́во. Mit'ki wear anything, but never anything trendy.

попсо́вый *adj.* fashionable, trendy, in. Забеги́те на Тиши́нский ры́нок за острано́сыми бо́тами—попсо́вый вид обеспе́чен. Run down to the Tishinsky market and get some pointed boots and you're guaranteed to look trendy.

порнобо́й *m.* variant of **порногра́фия.**

порногра́фия *f.* 1. trash, crap, rubbish. Что э́то у тебя́ за порногра́фия? What's that rubbish you've got there? Ты смо́тришь э́ту порногра́фию, *Бога́тые то́же пла́чут*? Do you watch that crap *The Rich Also Cry*? Чего́ э́то ты тако́й порногра́фией заня́лся? How come you've got into that rubbish? 2. porn, pornography.

порну́ха 1. porn. 2. pornographic film.
• See also *порногра́фия.*

порожняки́: гоня́ть порожняки́ *phr.impf.* to chat, blether. Два часа́ гоня́ли порожняки́. They chatted away for two hours.
• Lit. *to chase empties* (i.e. empty railway waggons).

поря́дочный *adj.* pure, real, right. Ну, ты то́же су́ка поря́дочная! And a right bitch you are!
- Lit. *decent.* See also *хоро́ший.*

поси́тать *pf. of* **си́тать**

посла́ть *v.t.pf.* to tell someone off. Тебя́ сейча́с посла́ть и́ли по фа́ксу? Shall I tear a strip off you now or send you a fax?
- Lit. *to send.*

постеба́ться *pf. of* **стеба́ться.**

пост-па́нк *m.* post-punk. Те же ли́ца, та же му́зыка—пост-па́нк, но не хвата́ет им дра́йва. The same old faces, the same old music - post punk, but they don't have enough energy.
- Example from the magazine *ЭНСК.*

пост-панко́вский *adj.* post-punk, relating to post-punk.

потусова́ться *v.i.pf.* 1. to have a good time, party. 2. to hang around. Пойдём куда́-нибудь потусу́емся. Let's go somewhere to hang around.

пофа́рить *pf. of* **фа́рить.**

по́фиг *phr.* [+ *dat.*] unimportant, couldn't care less. Мне по́фиг! I couldn't give a damn!
- See also *по́фигу.*

пофиги́зм *m.* couldn't-care-less attitude, total apathy.

пофиги́ст *n.* a couldn't-care-less person, someone who couldn't give a damn, free spirit. А на́шим пофиги́стам на всё наплева́ть. Our free spirits couldn't care a damn about anything.

по́фигу *phr.* variant of **по́фиг.**

похиля́ть *v.i.pf.* to go.

по-чёрному *adv.* 1. seriously, big time, really. Ну, я от оби́ды и запила́ по-чёрному. Well, because of the resentment I started seriously hitting the bottle. 2. to have a mad rush. Зацепи́ло по-чёрному. I had one hell of a mad rush.

пра́вильный *adj.* used as noun (someone) with street cred(ibility).
- Lit. *correct.*

прайс *m.* 1. price, cost. Прайс-то како́й у э́тих часо́в? What does this watch cost, then? 2. the money for something. Дава́й ку́пим ва́йну.—А прайс у тебя́ есть? Let's buy some wine. Have you got any dough?

прайсова́ть *v.i.impf.* to tap, help out with money, support financially. Он прайсова́л всю тусо́вку. He gave dosh to the whole group.

прайсо́вый *adj.* 1. money, connected with money. прайсо́вый раскла́д money situation. 2. well-off. прайсо́вый мэн a guy with plenty of dough.

преде́л *m.* limit. Так поступа́ть нельзя́—э́то уже́ преде́л всего́! You can't act like that; that's just the limit!

пре́дка *f.* old dear.
 • See also *пре́док.*

пре́док *m.* [*pl.* **пре́дки**] dad, old man; *pl.* folks, parents.
 • Lit. *ancestor(s).* See also *пре́дка.*

преп *m.* teacher, lecturer.
 • Truncated form of *преподава́тель.* See also *пре́под.*

пре́под *m.* teacher, lecturer.
 • Truncated form of *преподава́тель.* See also *преп.*

пресс-ха́та *f.* a special prison cell full of homosexuals, used to pressurise (political) prisoners.

прибаба́х: с прибаба́хом *m.phr.* strange, eccentric, a screw loose, two sandwiches short of a picnic. Поэ́тому мы все каки́е-то немно́жко сумасше́дшие с прибаба́хом. Therefore we're all kind of a bit mad, weird.

приво́з *m.* abroad. де́ка с приво́за an imported tape-recorder.
 • Lit. *supply, import.*

приглю́читься *pf.* of глю́читься.

приду́рок *m.* 1. idiot, mug, stupid git. 2. prisoner who works for the administration, or who is employed in a library or educational section of a labour camp.
 • Criminal argot. See *масть* for an example of usage.

прик *m.* prick, cock, penis. Ни при́ка себе́! Great! Excellent!
 • See also *коне́ц.*

прика́лывать *v.t.* [*pf.* **приколо́ть**] to turn on, interest, attract. Э́та герла́ меня́ приколо́ла. That girl caught my eye.

прика́лываться *v.i.* [*pf.* **приколо́ться**] 1. to joke, kid. Не обраща́й внима́ния—он про́сто прика́лывается. Don't you pay any attention—he's only kidding. 2. to be into, enjoy, get into. Приколи́сь, кака́я герла́ клёвая! Take a look at her, what a babe! Я к аванга́рду прика́лываюсь. I'm into avant-garde. **приколо́ться к герле́** *pf.* to fall for, be attracted to a girl. Я к э́той герле́ приколо́лся. I really fancied that girl. **приколо́ться к дри́нку** *pf.* to take to drink, to hit the bottle.
 • See also *подка́лывать, пристёбываться, въезжа́ть, вруба́ться.*

прика́мать *pf.* of ка́мать.

прики́д *m.* gear, threads, clothing. По прики́ду мо́жно определи́ть, кто ты—панк и́ли металли́ст. You can tell by your gear what you are—a punk or a head-banger.

прики́нутый *adj.* done up, dolled up, dressed up.

прико́во *adv.* badly, crappily.
 • Euphemistic for the vulgarism *хуёво* (*worthless, lousy*).

прико́вый *adj.* ugly.
 • Euphemistic: see *прико́во.*

прикóл *m.* joke, prank, laugh, wild party. для прикóла for a laugh.

приколи́ст *m.* very amusing person, hoot, scream, gut laugh.
　• See also *прикóльщик.*

приколóть *pf. of* прикáлывать.

приколóться *pf.* of прикáлываться.

прикольнó *adv.* funnily, amusingly.

прикольнóй *adj.* variant of прикóльный.

прикóльный *adj.* funny, a scream.

прикóльщик *m.* amusing person, scream, gut laugh.
　• See also *приколи́ст.*

прикóрм *m.* supplies (of a gang). А банди́ты бы́ли у негó на прикóрме? And have thieves been at his supplies?
　• Lit. *bait.*

примóчка *f.* 1. distortion box, gadget. гитáра с примóчками a guitar with distortion boxes. 2. joke, trick, gag. Да, бáбка, знáем мы э́ти примóчки—я встáну, а ты ся́дешь. Yeah, grandma, we know those tricks—I get up, you take my seat.
　• Lit. *lotion.*

присéсть *v.i.pf.* to lose at cards. Он присéл вчерá на шесть кускóв. He blew six grand yesterday at cards.
　• Lit. *to sit down.*

пристебнýться *pf.* of пристёбываться.

пристёбываться *v.i.* [*pf.* пристебнýться] to play a joke. Кончáй ты к э́тим совкáм пристёбываться. Stop fooling around with those Sovs.
　• See also *подкáлывать, прикáлываться.*

приторчáть *v.i.pf.* to be thrilled, excited, have a great time, great laugh. Я с э́той шýтки приторчáл как есть. I had a great laugh at that joke.

прихвáты *m.pl.* bad points, little foibles. Он пáрень с прихвáтами. He's a guy with his bad points. У кáждого из нас свои́ прихвáты. We all have our little foibles.

прихóд *m.* 1. rush, start of a rush (early effects of a drug). 2. high, trip.
　• Lit. *arrival.*

приходнýться *v.i.pf.* to feel a drug rush, get high. Я впервы́е приходнýлся на прирóде под дéревом—э́то был такóй кайф. The first time I got high I was in the open air under a tree: it was so good. 2. to feel good.

проаскáть *v.i.* [*pf.* проаскнýть] to ask around. Пойди́, проаскни́, где весь пипл. Go and ask where everyone is.

проаскнýть *pf.* of проаскáть.

прога́р *m.* financial flop, failure. Для устро́йтелей э́тот фестива́ль означа́л то́лько фина́нсовый прога́р. This festival meant one thing only for the organisers—a financial disaster. **в прога́ре** in a hole, in a spot. По́сле ухо́да веду́щего исполни́теля мы оста́лись в прога́ре. After the principal performer left we were in a mess.
• From *прогоре́ть* (*to go bankrupt*).

прогна́ть по ве́не: see **гнать по ве́не.**

прого́н *m.* fib, lying, spreading false rumours. Э́ти прого́ны меня́ уже́ зафа́кали! I'm already pissed off with all these lies.
• Lit. *well-shaft.*

прода́блиться *pf.* of **да́блиться.**

продви́нутый *adj.* 1. advanced, avant-garde. Он продви́нутый мэн—ка́ждый год на Тибе́т к мона́хам е́дет. He's a clever guy—goes off every year to the monks in Tibet. 2. refined, high-class, way out there. 3. stoned, out of it, high on drugs.

продви́нуться *v.i.pf.* 1. to penetrate. 2. to inject a drug.

продина́мить *pf.* of **дина́мить.**

прокана́ть *pf.* of **кана́ть.**

проки́нуть *pf.* variant of **ки́нуть.**

прокоси́ть *v.i.pf.* 1. [под + *acc.*] to pass for someone. 2. to dodge, avoid. **прокоси́ть от а́рмии** to escape conscription, dodge the draft.
• See also *откоси́ть.*

прокрути́ться *v.i.pf.* to come out with a profit.
• See *непоня́тки* for an example of usage.

проле́т *m.* failure, flop.
• Lit. *flight.*

пролета́ть *v.i.* [*pf.* **пролете́ть**] to fail, flop.
• Lit. *to fly past* (i.e. and miss the target).

пролете́ть *pf.* of **пролета́ть.**

пролу́кать *v.i.* [*pf.* **пролу́кнуть**] to take a look, peep, shufty, to look around (for something). Пойди́ пролу́кай, что там происхо́дит. Go and take a peep what's going on there.

пролу́кнуть *pf.* of **пролу́кать.**

прома́зать *v.t.pf.* to inject someone. Придётся тебе́ её прома́зать, а то у меня́ не полу́чится. You'd better give her a hit—or else it won't work for me.
• Lit. *to oil.*

прома́заться *v.i.pf.* to shoot up, hit, score, inject (a drug). Мне ну́жно прома́заться. I need a hit.
• See *вма́зать* 1.

пропи́ска *f.* humiliating initiation ceremony (in prison cell). А пропи́ску тебе́ не де́лали? Haven't they christened you?
• Lit. *registration.*

прорюхáть *pf.* of **рюхáть**.

просачковáть *pf.* of **сачковáть**.

просекáть *v.t.* [*pf.* **просéчь**] to know, to work (something) out, to twig, dawn. Я просéк, почемý стóлько получáется. I've figured out why it comes to so much.

просéчь *pf.* of **просекáть**.

простебáть *pf.* of **стебáть**.

протрепáться *pf.* of **трепáться**.

протусовáться *v.i.pf.* to go for a walk, take a walk. Пойдём, протусýемся до магазúна. Come on, let's drift off down to the shop.

прохúдать *pf.* of **хúдать**.

прохилять *v.i.impf.* [за + *acc.*] to pass for someone or something.

прýха *f.* run of good luck. И вдруг пошлá мне такáя прýха. Suddenly my luck turned.

прэнсá *pl.m.* variant of **парентá**.

прэнтá *n.pl.* variant of **парентá**. Все пóняли, что éсли ты не мажóр с крутыми прэнтáми—лýчше в э́то дéло не совáться. Everyone realised that unless you're a rich kid with sound parents, you'd better not get mixed up in that business.

прэнсóвый *adj.* parents', relating to parents.
 • Variant of **пэрэнсóвый**.

прэнтóвый *adj.* parents', relating to parents.
 • Variant of **пэрэнсóвый**.

психýшка *f.* loony bin, nut house, funny farm, psychiatric hospital. Признáние, междунарóдное признáние, вóлей слýчая прихóдит к музыкáнту, что не мешáет емý, впрóчем, спúвшись совершéнно, оказáться в психýшке. Recognition, international recognition, comes to the musician by good fortune. That doesn't stop him from drinking himself into the madhouse, though.

пузы́рь *m.* bottle of vodka.
 • Lit. *bubble.*

пýнкер *m.* [*pl.* **пýнкеры, пункерá**] punk.
 • See also *панк.* Also a friendly mode of address.

пýнкерский *adj.* punk.

пýнкерша *f.* punk.
 • See also *панк, пýнкер.*

пупóк с моркóвкой! *m.* a punk's derogatory mode of address.
 • Lit. *navel with a carrot.*

пустúть по крýгу *phr.pf.* to gang rape, gang bang. Я хотéла сопротивляться, заплáкала, а он сказáл, что бýдет ещё хýже, что он привезёт ещё вóсемь человéк и пýстит меня по крýгу. I wanted to resist, and burst out crying, but he said it would be even worse, he'd fetch another eight men and pass me round.

• See also *карусель*.

путана *f.* prostitute, hooker, tom, tart, slapper.
   • Transliteration from Italian *puttana*.

пучок: глаза в пучок: see **глаза**.

пушка *f.* gun, rod, piece, revolver.
   • Lit. *cannon*.

Пушкин *m.* an imaginary person responsible for something (ironical). Напачкал, а убирать кто будет—Пушкин? You've stained it—and who's gonna clean it up, Pushkin?

пчела *f.* girl, young woman, bird.
   • Lit. *bee*. See also *герла, гирла, жаба, лялька, тёлка.*

пыль *f.* powdered drug, fine cannabis
   • Lit. *dust*.

пыхание *n.* a way of smoking opium, marijuana or hashish.

пыхать *v.t.* [*pf.* **пыхнуть**] to smoke opium, marijuana, hashish. Сначала пыхал траву, а теперь задвигаюсь. First I smoked grass, now I inject.
   • See also *пыхтеть*.

пыхнуть *pf.* of **пыхать**.

пыхтеть *v.i.impf.* variant of **пыхать**.
   • Lit. *to puff, pant*.

пэрэнс *m.* variant of **парента**.

пэрэнса *m.pl.* variant of **парента**.

пэрэнсовый *adj.* of parents, parental.

пэрэнсы *m.pl.* variant of **прэнса, пэрэнса**.

пэрэнт *m.* (*pl.* **пэрэнты, пэрэнта** or **прэнты**) variant of **парента**.

пэрэнтовый *adj.* variant of **пэрэнсовый**.

пятак *m.* nose, conk. Кончай борзеть, а то в пятак получишь. Stop your cheek or you'll get one on the face.
   • See also *рубильник, шнобель*.

пятая точка *f.* bum, bottom, buttocks.

пятихатка *f.* 500 roubles.

пятка *f.* tip, butt of a joint. В пятке больше кайфа. You get more kick out of the butt. **смять, снять пятку** *pf.* to roll the butt of a joint. **добивать** [*pf.* **добить**] **пятку** to smoke the butt of a joint. Теперь сама добивай пятку. Now smoke a butt yourself.
   • Lit. *heel*. See also *пяточка*.

пяточка *f.* variant of **пятка**.

Р

рабо́тать на апте́ку *phr.impf.* to bear the marks of a beating. Ну, смотри́, ку́рва, сорвала́,—всю красоту́ сотрём, на апте́ку рабо́тать бу́дешь. Look here, whore, you've ruined everything—we'll do in that pretty face of yours, you'll be marked for life.
• Lit. *to work for the pharmacy.*

разбодя́жить *pf.* of **бодя́жить.**

разбо́р *m.* quarrel, set-to, bust-up (among prisoners or gang members). Случи́лся конфли́кт ме́жду осуждёнными, заподо́зрили кого́-то в стука́чсстве и́ли кра́же у свои́х, кто кому́-то не заплати́л ка́рточный долг—за разбо́ром иду́т к паха́ну и его́ приближённым. A quarrel broke out among the convicts; they suspected someone of ratting or stealing from another prisoner, someone hadn't paid a gambling debt—they went to the chief and his sidekicks to sort it out.
• Lit. *sorting out, dismantling.* Criminal argot.

разбо́рка *f.* quarrel, dispute, bust-up, scene. Он соглаша́ется, но вско́ре возвраща́ется с друзья́ми и устра́ивает разбо́рку. He agrees, but soon comes back with his mates and starts a punch-up. Была́ ку́ча пи́сем, каки́е-то разбо́рки с же́нщинами, исте́рики-дра́мы—из меня́ пыта́лись сде́лать Алёна Дело́на. There was a pile of letters, some bust-ups with women, hysterical dramas—they tried to make me into some kind of Alain Delon hero figure. Почему́ суверените́т респу́блик начина́ется с национа́льных разбо́рок? Why does the sovereignty of the republics start with disagreements over nationality?
• Lit. *sorting out.*

развоня́ться *v.t.pf.* to go mental, berserk, hit the roof. Не тро́гай телефо́н—нача́льник опя́ть развоня́ется. Don't touch the phone—the boss will go berserk again.

раздева́ть *v.t.* [*pf.* **разде́ть**] to strip (a vehicle), remove tyres, radio, etc. Уже́ бы́ли при́быльные дела́: вскрыва́ть ваго́ны с холоди́льниками, наприме́р, и́ли телеви́зорами, и́ли раздева́ть маши́ны, стоя́щие на платфо́рме (желе́зная доро́га под бо́ком). They already had some nice little earners going: breaking into railway trucks for fridges, for instance, or tellies, or stripping cars parked on the platform (with the railway close by).
• Lit. *to undress.*

разде́ть *pf.* of **раздева́ть.**

разукра́сить *pf.* of **разукра́шивать.**

разукра́шивать *v.t.* [*pf.* **разукра́сить**] to beat, do someone over, leaving obvious injuries. Так могу́ и ли́чико разукра́сить! And I can paint your face a nice colour!
• Lit. *to decorate.*

ра́йска *f.* 0.33 litre bottle of vodka. Ра́йски, как утвержда́ют знато́ки, взба́лтываются не ху́же. As the connoisseurs say, Raiskas shake up no less well than anything else.
• Believed to derive from the name Raisa Gorbacheva.

райо́н *m.* 1. suburban youth gang. Ви́тя, райо́н тебя́ не забу́дет! Vitya, the gang won't forget you! (graffito). 2. you people, you lot (a folk mode of address). Алё, райо́н! Hi, you lot!
• Lit. *district.*

раке́тчик *m.* racketeer.
• A play on words: *раке́та* (*rocket*), *раке́тчик* (*rocket specialist*).

раска́чанный *adj.* often as *m.noun* (man) with big muscles, well-built bloke.

раскла́д *m.* [*often pl.* **раскла́ды**] situation, relationship. К нему́ на флэт идти́ без ма́зы. У него́ с пэрента́ми стрёмные раскла́ды. There's no point going to his place. He doesn't see eye to eye with his folks.

раскла́дываться *v.i.impf.* 1. to complain about (something). 2. to have it out with someone.

раскума́рить *v.t.pf.* to give a dose of a drug, fix.

раскума́риться *v.i.pf.* to take a drug to overcome withdrawal symptoms. На́до бы́ло переломаться, а я раскума́рился. I was meant to break the habit, but I took some more stuff.

расстре́льник *m.* someone condemned to death. Физи́чески кре́пких расстре́льников испо́льзуют в ка́честве ку́кол—объе́ктов для рукопа́шного бо́я. Physically strong condemned men are used as dummies—targets for hand-to-hand combat training.
• See *ку́кла* 2.

растама́н *m.* rasta, rastafarian, person interested in rasta music.

растамю́зик *m.* rasta, rasta music.

растусова́ться *v.i.pf.* to fall out.

реди́ска *f.* swine, bastard, bad guy (also a jocular way of addressing a friend). Ну ты, реди́ска, нехоро́ший челове́к. You're a swine, a really bad person!
• Lit. *radish.* Coined in the Soviet film *Джентльме́ны уда́чи.*

резиде́нт *m.* drug dealer, pusher. Сидя́т, ждут резиде́нта, кото́рый до́лжен принести́ нарко́тик. They're sitting waiting for the pusher who should be bringing drugs.
• Lit. *resident.*

резина *f.* car tyres.
• Lit. *rubber.*

рейв *m.* variant of **рэйв.**

ре́йвер *m.* variant of **рэ́йвер.**

реко́рд *m.* [*pl.* **рекорда́**] record. Этот реко́рд родно́й? Is this record an original copy?

ре́па *f.* head, noggin.
• Lit. *turnip.* See also *башка́, бестолко́вка, ты́ква, ча́йник.*

рерихну́вшийся *adj. used as m.noun* follower of Nicholas Roerich's ideas. Рерихну́вшиеся е́здят на Алта́й. The Roerichites go to the Altai.
• Coined by the Soviet press; unites the name of the painter and mystic, Roerich (1874-1947) and the past active participle form of the verb *рехну́ться* (*to go mad, crazy*).

ринг *m.* 1. telephone. А там ринг есть? Is there a phone there? 2. headband. Ринг у тебя́ клёвый. That's a cool headband you've got.

рингану́ть *pf.* of **ринга́ть.**

ринга́ть *v.i.* [*pf.* **рингану́ть, отринга́ть**] to phone, ring up, give a call, bell. Отринга́й мне сего́дня ве́чером/Рингани́ мне ве́чером. Give me a call this evening.

ринго́вать *impf.* variant of **ринга́ть.**

рингу́шник *m.* notebook with phone numbers, address book.

рог *m.* [*pl.* **ро́ги**] head of a work team in prison or labour camp. **рога́** *pl.* in various expressions. Че́рти и упира́ются рога́ми (рабо́тают и сопротивля́ются) и шеруди́т рога́ми (приме́рный эквивале́нт—раски́дывать мозга́ми). Им по нужде́ свире́по грозя́т: 'Смотри́, посшиба́ю тебе́ рога́!' The clowns both get stuck in (i.e. they work) and use their heads (approximate equivalent: to think something over). When necessary, they can be fiercely threatening: 'Watch it, or I'll give you a smack!' **встать на рога́** *phr.pf.* to get pissed, smashed, sozzled, very drunk. Вина́ взя́ли мно́го, так что к концу́ конце́рта музыка́нты вста́ли на рога́. They put away a lot of wine, so by the end of the concert the musicians were sloshed out of their minds.
• Lit. *horn.* Criminal argot.

родно́й *adj.* 1. original record (as opposed to a copy or re-release). Е́сли диск родно́й, он це́нится вы́ше, чем кака́я-нибудь югосла́вская перепеча́тка. If the record is an original, it's worth much more than some Yugoslavian re-pressing. 2. a derogatory street term of address.

• 1. See also *фирменный*. Lit. *own, native*.

рок *m*. rock. Éсли для пи́терского ро́ка э́та волна́ и но́вая, то по мировы́м станда́ртам её пора́ продава́ть со ски́дкой. If this is supposed to be new-wave Petersburg rock, then by world standards it's time to sell it at cut price.

• Example from *Rock Fuzz*.

рок- *in compounds:* рок-журнали́ст rock journalist. рок-поколе́ние the rock generation. рок-звезда́ rock star.

рокенро́лл *m*. variant of **рок-н-ро́лл**.

ро́кер *m*. 1. rock singer, fan, musician, biker. 2. and **роке́шник** rocker, biker.

роке́шник *m*. 1. mainstream rock number. 2. See **ро́кер** 2.

рок-н-ро́лл *m*. rock-n-roll.

• See also *рокенро́лл*.

рок-н-ро́лльный *adj*. rock-n-roll.

рост: в по́лный рост *m.phr*. like nobody's business, full swing. Оттяну́лись в по́лный рост. We had a bloody good time.

руби́льник *m*. big nose, conk, schnozzle.

• Lit. *knife-switch*. See also *пята́к, шно́бель*.

руби́ться *v.i.impf*. to struggle for, to try all out. Панк-ро́к—не совсе́м му́зыка, э́то конце́пция. Конце́пция как стеба́лово. И я э́то разделя́ю, и́бо глу́по, когда́ конце́пцию понима́ют как то, за что сле́дует руби́ться. Punk-rock is not so much music, more an idea. The idea as a laugh. And I share that view, because it's stupid to think of an idea as something you ought to fight for.

• Lit. *to fight*.

рубль *m*. 100 roubles. До́ллар на ры́нке сего́дня по четы́ре рубля́ идёт. The dollar's worth 400 roubles on the market today.

• Lit. *(one) rouble*.

руси́чка *f*. Russian teacher, lecturer (female)

ручни́к *m*. variant of **пластили́н**.

• Lit. *bench-hammer*. See also *центря́к*.

рыга́ловка *f*. cheap eating place, trough, dive. Студе́нты хо́дят обе́дать в рыга́ловке во́зле институ́та. The students go and eat in the dive near the college.

• From *рыга́ть* (*to belch, vomit*).

рэ́ггей *m*. reggae.

рэйв *m*. 1. rave (music, style, culture). Ра́ньше я бо́льше ходи́ла на вечери́нки—когда́ мо́да на рэйв то́лько начала́сь. Before I mostly went to parties, when rave had just become trendy. 2. rave (event). Всё э́то я узна́л из фла́ера, потому́ что на рэйв так и не попа́л. I found all that out from a flyer, as I didn't get to the rave.

• See also *рейв*. Examples from the techno magazine, *ПТЮЧ*.

рэйв- *in compounds:* **рэйв-му́зыка** rave music.

рэ́йвер *m.* raver, fan of the rave scene.

• See also *ре́йвер*.

рэ́йверский *adj.* rave, relating to raves or the rave scene.

рэп *m.* rap, rap music. Мы попыта́лись соедини́ть на́ши интере́сы: ввести́ немно́го гра́нжа и психоде́лии, места́ми как бы демонстри́ровать сам рэп. We tried to bring together our interests: to introduce a little bit of grunge and psychedelia, and in places to sort of demonstrate rap itself.

• Example from *ПТЮЧ*.

рэппо́вый *adj.* rap, relating to rap.

рэ́ппер *m.* rapper.

рюха́ть *v.i.* [*pf.* **прорюха́ть**] to understand, suss, see, get; to be knowledgeable. Как же я э́того не прорюха́л? How come I didn't suss that one out?

• Student slang. See also *вруба́ться*, *въезжа́ть*, *прика́лываться*, 2.

рюха́ч *m.* bright student, swot, brain-box. Э́тот рюха́ч уже́ отбомби́лся. That swot's already passed everything.

ря́бчик *m.* rouble. Пассажи́р есть—зна́чит, девятьсо́т ря́бчиков в карма́не. We've got a customer—that's 900 roubles in our pockets.

• Lit. *hazel-grouse.*

С

Сайго́н *m.* the Saigon café, once the favourite hang-out of Leningrad hippies, but closed by the authorities.

сайз *m.* size. Како́й у тебя́ сайз? What's your size? **в сайз** to fit well. Э́ти шу́зы мне не в сайз. These shoes don't fit me.

сайзы́ *m.pl.* boobs, large breasts. Клёвая герлу́шка—с сайза́ми. A real chick—with big boobs.

сакс *m.* sax, saxophone. Ми́шка забы́л свой сакс в метро́. Mishka left his sax in the metro.

• Abbreviation of *саксофо́н*.

салабо́н *m.* rookie, recent recruit; inexperienced person.

• See also *сыно́к*.

салпа́нка *f.* member of a female gang. Салпа́нки не́сколько раз в год меня́ют партнёров, име́ют на счету́ по деся́тку подпо́льных або́ртов и счита́ют свой о́браз жи́зни соверше́нно норма́льным. The girls change their partners several times a year, have dozens of illegal abortions and regard their way of life as completely normal.

• Jargon of Kazakh muggers.

салют *m.* solutan (drug).

самиздат *m.* bootleg alcohol, home brew. У меня с собой две бутылки самиздата. I've got too bottles of home brew.

• Abbreviation of самостоятельное издание произведений, lit. *independent edition of works*, usually referring to anti-Soviet underground literature.

самокат *m.* motorbike.

• Lit. *scooter*. Biker slang.

самопал *m.* home-made goods (particularly imitation jeans).

самопальный *adj.* referring to home-made goods sold as fakes. Цыгане продают самопальные шмотки. The gypsies sell home-made imitation gear.

самостроки *m.pl.* home-made jeans.

самострочный *adj.* home-made.

самоход *m.* awol, walkies, absent without leave. Рано тебе ещё в самоходы ходить. A bit early yet for you to go walkabout.

• Lit. *self-feed.*

сарай *m.* bus. Наш сарай ещё не ушёл? Has our bus not gone yet?

• Lit. *shed.*

сачкануть *pf.* of **сачковать**.

сачковать *v.t.* [*pf.* **сачкануть, просачковать**] to play truant, bunk off (school), throw a sickie, skive; to skip an appointment. Я сегодня работу просачковал—боюсь, уволят. I skipped work today; I'm scared I'll get the sack.

сачкодром *m.* a place to hang about, smoke (often in college building). Встретимся на сачкодроме. We'll meet at the hang-out.

сачок *m.* 1. a truant, skiver, person who bunks off, misses appointments. 2. person who goes to a **сачкодром**. 3. variant of **сачкодром**.

сблёвыш морковный *m.* worthless person, a nobody. Also a punk form of address.

свалить *pf.* of **валить**.

свинтить *pf.* of **винтить**.

свинчивание *n.* raid on a (hippy) party. Акция свинчивания происходит только с участием представителей органов охраны правопорядка. Raiding can only be carried out if representatives of organs of law and order take part.

свисток *m.* butt of a joint.

• Lit. *whistle.*

сгнить *v.i.pf.* 1. (of a person) to lose one's good qualities. Раньше был ништяк чувак, а теперь сгнил наглухо. He used to be a great bloke, but now he's really gone off. 2. to enjoy a good talk. Кто́-то прогна́л таку́ю телéгу—я сгнил на мéсте. Someone was telling such a tale; I had a great time.

• Lit. *to rot.*

сдава́ть *v.t.* [*pf.* **сдать**] to sell, flog. Я э́ти шузы́ ещё вчера́ сдал. I flogged off these shoes yesterday. 2. to sell (someone) out. Он нас сдал врага́м. He gave us away to the enemy.

• Lit. *to hand over.* 1. See also *толка́ть.*

сдать *pf.* of **сдава́ть**.

сда́ча: на сда́чу *f.* for sale. У тебя́ есть рекорда́ на сда́чу? Have you got any records for sale?

• Lit. *change, hand-over.*

сдвиг по фа́зе *m.* strange act, something crazy, odd. У меня́ сдвиг по фа́зе—вы́шел из авто́буса на остано́вку ра́ньше, чем на́до. I did something daft—I got off the bus a stop before I should have.

сдви́нуться *pf.* of **сдвига́ться**.

сдри́нчаться *v.i.pf.* to become an alcoholic, to take to the bottle.

седьмо́й батальо́н *m.* diagnosed psychopathy (as exemption from military service). Тебя́ же должны́ бы́ли о́сенью забра́ть в а́рмию.—А я в седьмо́й батальо́н попа́л. You should have been called up last autumn. —Yes, but I was classified psycho.

• Lit. *Seventh battalion*, from paragraph 7B of the list of medical exemptions from military service.

сéйшен *m.* sesh, gig, jam, concert or other event. Лаба́ли для администра́ции вся́кую ла́жу, оття́гиваясь на подпо́льных сéйшенах. We trotted out any old crap for the authorities, and were getting it on down at underground gigs.

• From English *session.* See also *сейшн, сэ́йшен, сэйшн.*

сейшн *m.* variant of **сéйшен**.

секрету́тка *f.* secretary having an affair with her boss. Шеф подари́л секрету́тке маши́ну. The boss gave his dolly-bird secretary a car.

• Combination of *секрета́рь* and *проститу́тка.*

секу́чий *adj.* clever, knowledgeable, clued-in. Э́тот па́рень о́чень секу́чий! This lad's very bright.

селява́ *phr.* variant of **селяви́**. Блин, опя́ть непру́ха. Что поде́лаешь, такова́ селява́. Damn! More bad luck! What can you do: c'est la vie.

• *Селява́* distorts the French phrase in order to rhyme with *такова́* in its Russian equivalent, *такова́ жизнь.*

селяви́ *phr.* C'est la vie, that's the way the cookie crumbles.

семёрка *f.* a VAZ-2107 car.

• See also *зуби́ло.*

се́но *n.* opium poppy straw. Пошли́ на ры́нок, там оди́н чёрный се́но сдаёт. Let's go to the market. There's a black guy who sells poppy straw there.
- Lit. *hay.* See also *гры́зло, ку́кер, кукна́р, соло́ма.*

сенс *m.* psychic, person claiming extra-sensory perception, clairvoyant.
- From *экстрасе́нс.*

сесть *v.i.pf.* [на + *acc.*] to become addicted to. Он сел на иглу́. He got hooked on junk, drugs.
- Lit. *to sit down.*

сечь *v.i.* 1. [в + *prep.*] to know about. Я секу́ в ма́рках. I know a lot about stamps. 2. *v.t.* to understand, get.
- Lit. *to cut.*

сиде́ть *v.i.impf.* [на + *prep.*] to use (a drug) regularly. Я сижу́ на винте́. I use pervitine.
- Lit. *to sit.*

си́ла: со стра́шной си́лой *f.phr.* like mad, big time, furiously. Они́ расхвата́ли биле́ты со стра́шной сило́й. They snapped up the tickets like mad.
- Lit. *with terrifying force.*

синега́л *m.* alkie, drunkard, wino. А вокру́г шалма́на синега́лы стоя́т. And hanging around the boozer there are winos.
- See also *а́лик, алка́ш, алкона́вт, буха́рик, кирю́ха.*

синте́тика *f.* drug made in back-street laboratories from cheap ingredients. Наряду́ с кустаря́ми синте́тику ста́ли производи́ть хорошо́ оснащённые подпо́льные лаборато́рии. Alongside the D.I.Y. merchants, well-equipped underground labs started manufacturing synthetic drugs.

синю́га *m.* alkie, wino, drunkard. Ду́маешь, прия́тно, когда́ подхо́дит к тебе́ здорове́нный синю́га и про́сит закури́ть. You think it's nice when a great big wino comes up and asks you for a light.
- See also *синега́л, синя́к.*

синя́к *m.* alkie, wino, drunkard.
- Lit. *bruise.* See also *синега́л, синю́га*

систе́ма *f.* the System; youth, particularly hippy network; people in the know.
- Lit. *the system.* The System initially comprised Soviet hippies, but later incorporated members of various subcultural youth groups.

систе́мный *adj.* member of the (former) Soviet hippy movement, network. Невозмо́жно перечи́слить многообра́зие люде́й, кото́рые счита́ют себя́ систе́мными. It's impossible to list the variety of people who think of themselves as part of the System.

си́тать *v.i.* [*pf.* **поси́тать**] to sit. Поси́таем здесь, мо́жет, кто́-нибудь подойдёт из свои́х. Let's sit here and perhaps some of our lot will come and join us.

ситуёвина *f.* a lousy situation, shit creek.
• Apparently coined by the musician Alexander Gradsky: a euphemistic blend of *ситуа́ция* (*situation*) and *хуёвина* (*crap, bullshit*).

скана́ть *pf.* of **кана́ть**.

скворца́ в ду́шу запусти́ть *phr.pf.* to beat up, do in. Я тебе́ сейча́с как запущу́ скворца́ в ду́шу, и пойдёшь отсю́да гопака́ пляса́ть! I'll give you such a doing in a minute, you'll be leaving to dance the hopak!
• Lit. *to let a starling into someone's soul.*

скейтборди́ст *m.* skateboarder.

ске́йтер *m.* skateboarder. Вчера́ ходи́л на тусо́вку ске́йтеров. Yesterday I went to a skateboarders' group.

скинхэ́д *m.* skinhead.

скинхэди́зм *m.* the skinhead ethic, way; being a skinhead.

скипа́ть *v.i.* [*pf.* **скипе́ть, скипну́ть**] to scarper, beat it, do one, get out. Вдруг ви́жу: наро́д с Сайга́ скипа́ет и всей тусо́вкой куда́-то вали́т. Suddenly I saw people from the Saigon scarpering, going off somewhere in a group.

скипе́ть *pf.* of **скипа́ть**.

скипну́ть *pf.* of **скипа́ть**.

скоммуни́здить *pf.* of **коммуни́здить**.

скрипа́ч *m.* thief.
• Lit. *violinist, fiddler.*

скры́сивший *adj. used as noun* someone who has stolen something within a gang. На мои́х глаза́х одна́жды скры́сившему о́бщие де́ньги отпи́ливали столо́вым ножо́м указа́тельный па́лец, пока́ он не призна́лся, где они́ лежа́т. I once saw them sawing off with a table knife the index finger of a thief who'd nicked the kitty until he would tell them where the money was.

скул *m.* school. Напьёмся и в скул не пойдём. We'll get drunk and stay away from school.

скуло́вый *adj.* school. скуло́вый фрэнд a school mate.

слаба́ть *pf.* of **лаба́ть**.

слеза́ть *v.i.* [*pf.* **слезть**] (с иглы́) to break the habit (drugs). Всё, я слеза́ю. That's it, I'm coming off the junk.
• Lit. *to come down.*

слезть *pf.* of **слеза́ть**.

сленг *m.* slang.

сле́нговый *adj.* slang.

слета́ть с эфи́ра [*pf.* **слете́ть**] *phr.* to be taken off the air. Кста́ти, слета́ют с эфи́ра и други́е переда́чи, так как

трансля́ция пойдёт сра́зу по всем програ́ммам ра́дио и телеви́дения. By the way, they're taking other programmes off too, as the coverage will run on all radio and television channels at once.
* Lit. *to fly off the air.*

слиня́ть *pf.* of **линя́ть**.
* See also *смыва́ться.*

сли́пать *v.i.* [*pf.* **засли́пать**] to sleep, have a nap. Сли́пали на флэту́ с гёрлами. They slept at the pad with some girls.

слон *m.* new recruit, member of the barrack room pecking order.
* Lit. *elephant.* See also дед, де́мбель, фаза́н, черпа́к.

смехуёвое пальтецо́ *n.* a punk's winter coat.
* A combination of *смех* (*laughter*) and *хуёвый* (*lousy, hopeless*).

смитингну́ться *pf.* of **митингова́ться**.

смок *m.* fag, cigarette, a smoke. Лажо́вый смок курю́. I've got a rotten fag here (passage from a hippy song). У тебя́ смок есть? You got a smoke?

смыва́ться *v.i.* [*pf.* **смы́ться**] to scarper, disappear, clear off.
* Lit. *to wash off.* See also *линя́ть, вали́ть.*

смы́ться *pf.* of **смыва́ться**.

снима́ть *v.t.* [*pf.* **снять**] to hit on, chat up, pull. снять тёлку to pull a bird (for a one-night stand).
* Lit. *to take off.*

снима́ться *v.i.* [*pf.* **сня́ться**] to be available, to be a free agent (of a girl).

снять *pf.* of **снима́ть**.

сня́ться *pf.* of **снима́ться**.

соба́ка: на соба́ках *f.phr.* to travel by train without paying a fare. Съе́здить в Пи́тер на соба́ках. To travel to Petersburg without a ticket.

совко́во *adv.* badly; of poor quality (i.e. typically Soviet).

совко́вый *adj.* 1. ninth-rate, as in Soviet days. Совсе́м совко́вый сэ́йшн вчера́ получи́лся. Yesterday there was a really lousy concert. 2. Soviet. Для борьбы́ с совко́вой уголо́вщиной МВД РФ бу́дет закупа́ть за́падную те́хнику. To defeat Soviet-style criminality, the Interior Ministry of the Russian Federation will be buying Western technology. Купи́л совко́вые шу́зы. I bought some Soviet shoes.

сово́к *m.* 1. Сово́к The Soviet Union. Слу́шай, ты вро́де не собира́лась остава́ться в Совке́ ещё на це́лый год? Listen, surely you aren't intending to stay in the Soviet Union another whole year, are you? 2. Soviet ideology, mind-set, etc. Э́тот фильм—тако́й сово́к! That film was typical Soviet crap! 3. [*pl.*

совки́] ordinary Soviet people. У него́ пэрента́—круты́е совки́. His parents are real Sovs.

• The derivation of this word is unclear; however, it is commonly regarded as a resemanticised form of *сово́к* (*shovel, dust-pan*) which also happens to resemble *сове́тский* (*Soviet*).

соло́ма *f.* poppy heads, poppy straw.

• Lit. *straw.*

сопле́вич *m.* sunoreph or ephedrine.

• See also *джеф, сопли́вчик.*

сопли́вчик *m.* variant of **сопле́вич.**

сопля́к *m.* snotty person, wimp.

спи́кать *v.i.impf.* to talk, speak.

• See also *спи́чить.*

спиногры́з *m.* kid, child, nipper. Ты уже́ обзавёлся спиногры́зами? You got any kids yet?

• Folk. Lit. *back-gnawer, nipper.*

спич *m.* talk. О чём спич, друзья́? What are we on about, folks?

спи́чить *v.i.impf.* to talk, speak.

• See also *спи́кать.*

спо́нсор *m.* man who keeps a mistress; fancy-man, sugar-daddy.

• Lit. *sponsor.*

спроси́ть *v.t.pf.* to rob, mug. Те, кто занима́ется ску́пкой валю́ты ли́бо зо́лота—фарцо́вщики—бары́ги са́мые ни́зкие. С таки́х люде́й по паца́нским поня́тиям мо́жно спроси́ть—потребова́ть ба́бки. Those who buy up currency or gold—speculators—are the lowest of the black marketeers. According to the criminal code, it's all right to rob or demand money from them.

• Lit. *to ask.* Criminal argot.

стано́к *m.* 1. bed. Ха́та была́, как и все ха́ты, предназна́ченные для свида́ния проститу́ток с клие́нтами: отде́льная, одноко́мнатная, почти́ без ме́бели, с большо́й и ни́зкой тахто́й, и́ли, как говоря́т, станко́м, журна́льным сто́ликом и обша́рпанным кре́слом. The place was like any other set up for prostitutes and their clients: separate, one room, almost unfurnished, with a big, low divan, or as they say, a work bench, a coffee table and a dilapidated armchair. 2. sexy body. Клёвый стано́к—я бы на тако́м порабо́тал но́чку. A cracking figure—I'd work over that all night. 3. sex pot, man-eater, highly-sexed woman.

• Lit. *lathe.*

стари́к *m.* soldier in the last period of his compulsory service.

• Lit. *old man.* For an example of usage see *молодо́й.*

старпёр *m.* old fogey, old git.

старша́чка *f.* leader of a gang of teenage girls, queen bee. Мла́дшие беспрекосло́вно повину́ются ка́ждому ж́есту, взгля́ду, кивку́ старша́чек. The younger ones obey without question every gesture, every glance, every nod of the leaders.
  • Kazakh muggers' argot.

стёб *m.* 1. fun, a laugh. У тебя́ превра́тное представле́ние о лёгком стёбе. You've got a weird idea of a bit of fun. 2. mickey-take, taking the rip. ра́ди стёба just for fun, for a laugh, kicks.

стеба́ло *n.* source of amusement, fun, mickey-take.
  • See also *стеба́лово*.

стеба́лово *n.* variant of **стеба́ло**.

стебану́ться *pf.* of **стеба́ться**.

стеба́ть *v.t.* [*pf.* **застеба́ть**] to take the mickey, take the rip, pull someone's leg, tease. Конча́й меня́ стеба́ть. Stop taking the mickey out of me. Застеба́л ты меня́ совсе́м. You've really taken the rip out of me.
  • See also *стеба́ться*.

стеба́ться *v.i.* [*pf.* **стебану́ться**, **постеба́ться**] 1. to make fun (of), poke fun at. Лю́бит челове́к постеба́ться. The guy likes poking fun. **стебану́ться** only: to go mad, crazy, round the bend, bonkers. 2. **стеба́ться** *v.i.* [*pf.* **постеба́ться**] to sleep with, screw, shag.

стёбно *adv.* funny, mental.
  • See also *стебо́во*.

стёбный *adj.* 1. funny. Э́то нельзя́ воспринима́ть всерьёз— всё же э́то соверше́нно стёбная пе́сня. You shouldn't take that seriously—after all it's a completely funny song. 2. sarky, ironic, mocking.
  • See also *стебо́вый*.

стебо́во *adv.* variant of **стёбно**.

стебо́вый *adj.* variant of **стёбный**.

стебо́к *m.* [*pl.* **стебки́**] funny person, joker, someone who likes to fool around.

стекло́ *n.* 1. ampoule with drug. 2. *coll.* empty bottles. Вот, стекло́ несу́ сдава́ть—накопи́лось за пра́здники. Right, I'm going to hand in the empties; they've mounted up over the holidays.
  • Lit. *glass.*

стенд *m.* hard-on, brickie, stiffy, erection.
  • See also *стэнд*.

сте́нка на сте́нку *f.phr.* wall-to-wall.
  • See *отклю́чка* for an example.

сте́рва *f.* bitch.
  • Lit. *carrion.*

стиля́га *m.* teddy boy.

стимуля́торщик *m.* addict who prefers psychedelic drugs.

сто́льник *m.* hundred-rouble note.
- From *сто* (*one hundred*).

сто́пить *v.t.* [*pf.* засто́пить] to hitch a lift, stop a car.

сто́пник *m.* road map.

сто́п: éхать сто́пом *phr.impf.* to hitch, hitch-hike. Доберёмся сто́пом. We'll hitch our way there.
- Truncated form of *автосто́п* (*hitch-hiking*).

сто́пщик *m.* hitch-hiker.

сторча́ться *v.i.pf.* 1. to completely lose it, become debilitated by drugs. 2. to die from drug use.

стра́шно *adv.* very, really. В Москве́ появи́лись стра́шно краси́вые лю́ди. Some really good-looking people have turned up in Moscow.
- Lit. *terribly.*

стрела́ *f.* appointment. забива́ть [*pf.* заби́ть] стрелу́/стре́лку *phr.* to arrange a meeting.
- Lit. *arrow.* See also *ми́тинг.*

стре́лка *f.* variant of **стрела́**.

стрём *m.* something suss or dodgy, strong feeling of fear, danger or dislike. быть на стрёме to be lookout, on guard. Алексе́й не теря́л созна́ния, и он запомина́л, что оста́вшийся на стрёме страж поря́дка с кем-то разгова́ривал. Andrei did not lose consciousness, and he remembered that the lookout who had stayed on watch was talking to someone.

стрема́к *m.* [*pl.* стремаки́] 1. source of worry, cause of anxiety. снима́ть [*pf.* снять] стремаки́ to pull oneself together, get a grip. Сними́ стремаки́, а то нас по́лис свинти́т на пе́рвом поворо́те. Get a grip on yourself or the police will arrest us at the first turn. 2. trouble, worry, hassle, aggro. У нас в Крыму́ таки́е стремаки́ бы́ли. We had such hassle in the Crimea. **стремаки́ накати́ли/пошли́** *pf.* the trouble's started, the shit has hit the fan.

стрема́лово *n.* frightening or dodgy situation.

стрема́ть *v.t.* [*pf.* застрема́ть] 1. to frighten, scare. 2. to hassle, trouble, give someone aggro.

стрема́ться *v.i.* [*pf.* застрема́ться] to be worried, scared stiff.
- See *кры́ша* for an example.

стрёмно *adv.* dodgy. Аска́ть идти́ стрёмно, круго́м менты́. It's dodgy going begging—cops all over the shop.

стрёмность *f.* paranoia, often about the (Soviet) system, feeling of threat.
- See also *стрёмопа́тия.*

стрёмный *adj.* 1. dodgy, dangerous, suss. Это стрёмное дéльце. It's a nasty business. Твоя мáтушка—óчень стрёмный человéк. Your mum's a very difficult person. 2. weird, strange. Он наскóлько стрёмный чувáк, что герлы́ от негó прóсто шарáхаются. He's such a spooky bloke, girls just keep away from him.

стрёмопáтия *f.* paranoia, often about the Soviet system.
 • See also *стрёмность*.

стрит *m.* street.

стритóвый *adj.* street. стритóвый поэ́т Мúша Красноштáн the street poet Misha Krasnoshtan.
 • Particularly used by hippies.

струнá *f.* hypodermic (needle).
 • Lit. *string*. See also *иглá, машúна*.

стýкануть *pf.* of **стучáть**.

стукáч *m.* informer, rat, grass, stool pigeon.

стукáчество *n.* (act of) informing, squealing, grassing.

стукáчка *f.* grass, rat, informer (female).

стусовáться *v.i.pf.* to meet, get to know. Мы с ним в Рúге стусовáлись. He and I met each other in Riga.

стучáть *v.i.* [*pf.* **стýкануть, настучáть**] to rat, squeal, grass, inform.
 • Lit. *to knock, tap, bang.* See *гвоздúть* for an example. See also *заклáдывать* 1, *сучúться*.

стэйтс *m.* [*pl.* **стэйтсá, стэ́йтсы**] Yank, American.

стэйтсóвый *adj.* American, Yank.

стэнд *m.* [*pl.* **стэндá, стэнды́**] hard-on, stiffy, brickie, erection. У меня́ на э́ту герлý стэндá. That girl really turns me on.

стэндáть *v.i.impf.* to stand.

стэндовáть *v.i.* [*pf.* **застэндовáть**] to get an erection, brickie, hard-on. Я застэндовáл в момéнт. I got a hard-on right up.

сульты́га *f.* home-made heroin.
 • See also *шня́га*.

сýпер *m.* [*pl.* **суперá**] 1. something fab, brilliant, excellent. 2. gang member aged 15-16.

сухáрь *m.* 1. criminal claiming high status. 2. someone who tries to pass for another.
 • Lit. *rusk*.

сухостóйчик *m.* motorcycle wheelie.
 • See also *выдрю́чиваться, козлúть*.

сучúться *v.i.* to rat, grass, inform. Глáвное не сучúться. The main thing is not to be a grass.
 • See also *заклáдывать* 1, *стучáть*.

сушня́к *m.* 1. sour wine. 2. dry throat as a result of drinking or drugs, drooth, thirst. Меня́ сушня́к заму́чил. My throat felt like cardboard from that booze.

сха́вать *pf.* of **ха́вать.**

сходня́к *m.* conference of high-ranking criminals, often secret. Ча́сто представи́телей воровско́й эли́ты называ́ют 'генера́лами престу́пного ми́ра', но по спо́собу комплектова́ния э́та ка́ста напомина́ет скоре́е акаде́мию нау́к: присво́ить воровско́е зва́ние име́ют пра́во то́лько други́е авторите́ты, собра́вшись на сходня́к. Representatives of the criminal élite are often called 'generals of the criminal world', but in composition this caste more resembles the Academy of Sciences: only other big-shots met in conclave can award the title of criminal.

счётчик: поста́вить на счётчик *phr.pf.* to impose a fine (by illegal means), turn the heat up on. Éсли он не вернёт де́ньги в срок, его́ поста́вят на счётчик. If he doesn't return the money on time they'll screw it out of him.

съём *m.* pick-up.
 • See also *съёмка.*

съёмка *f.* variant of **съём.**

сыно́к *m.* rookie, soldier in first year of service.
 • Lit. *sonny.*

сэ́йшен *m.* [*pl.* сэйшена́] variant of **се́йшен.**

сэ́йшн *m.* variant of **се́йшен.**

Т

табуре́тка *f.* scooter.
 • Lit. *stool.*

талóн: ка́цаный талóн *m.* punched token for a bus ride. Нека́цаный талóн—большóй стрём, ка́цаный талóнчик—клёвая отма́зка. An uncancelled ticket is well dodgy, a used one is a great excuse.
 • A reference to fare dodging on public transport, for which a hefty fine may be imposed.

тарч *m.* variant of **торч.**

таск *m.* a high (drug-induced).
 • See also *волоку́ша, кайф.*

та́ска *f.* variety of **таск.**

та́узенд *m.* thousand. С тебя́ та́узенд грю́ников, как говоря́т в Москве́. That'll be a thousand bucks from you, as they say in Moscow.
• Transliteration of German *tausend*.

та́чка *f.* car, wheels. В Герма́нии це́ны на та́чки значи́тельно вы́ше—воспо́льзуйтесь э́тим. In Germany cars cost a good deal more; take advantage of that. **заряди́ть та́чку** *pf.* to get a taxi. Заряди́ та́чку для де́вочек—им на́до домо́й е́хать. Grab a taxi for the girls; they have to go home.
• Lit. *wheelbarrow*.

тащи́ться *v.i.impf.* 1. to be high, out of it (on drugs or alcohol). Чи́ра та́щится. Хоте́л бы я посмотре́ть, как она́ та́щится, да и от чего́. На́до бы ей кося́к предложи́ть. Prof's out of it. I'd like to see how she does it, and on what. We should offer her a joint. 2. to do drugs. 3. to dig, be into. Я тащу́сь! I dig that! 4. to fancy, be mad about.

таю́ха *f.* (neck)tie.

теле́га *f.* tall tale, shaggy dog story, yarn, fib. Мне здесь така́я теле́га в го́лову пришла́. Then such a yarn came into my head.
• Lit. *cart*.

теле́жник *m.* story-teller, liar, teller of tall tales. Э́тот чува́к—ста́рый теле́жник. That guy's just an old story-teller.
• See also *го́нщик*.

тёлка *f.* skirt, bird, doll. Я объясни́л, что хочу́ снять двух тёлок для рабо́ты. I explained I wanted to pick up two chicks for some work.
• Lit. *heifer*. See also *герла́, ги́рла, жа́ба, пчела́*.

телогре́ечный ши́бздик *m.* a punk's schoolmate.

темнота́ *f.* 1. *coll.* tranquillizers. 2. dunce, simpleton, divvy.
• Lit. *darkness*.

темня́к *m.* obscure case to investigate. Сле́дователи не скры́ли, что де́ло—темня́к, то есть вряд ли бу́дет раскры́то. The cops made no secret of the fact that the matter was a total enigma, that it probably wouldn't be cleared up.

теневи́к *m.* spiv, black marketeer.

тёрка *f.* variation of **вы́терка**.

терпи́ла *m.,f.* victim of a crime (often robbery). Е́сли терпи́ла чу́вствует себя́ уве́ренно—споко́йно отвеча́ет, да́же улыба́ется,—то исхо́д в большинстве́ слу́чаев благоприя́тен для тако́го челове́ка. If the victim is sure of himself and answers calmly, even smiles, then in most cases the outcome is OK for him.

тётка *f.* girl, woman, missus (young).
• Lit. *aunt*.

тéхно *n.* techno (music, culture). *Собáки* бýдут игрáть индустриáльную мýзыку с нéкоторым уклóном в тéхно. The *Dogs* will be playing industrial music with a certain techno slant.
 • Example from *Я молодой.*

тéхно- *in compounds.* тèхно-движéние techno movement. тèхно-сцéна the techno scene.

тúкет *m.* [*pl.* тикетá] ticket. Ты тикетá на сéйшн достáл? Did you get tickets for the gig?

типогрáфия *f.* woman's genitalia.
 • Lit. *printing works.*

тип-тóп: всё тип-тóп. *phr.* Everything's hunky-dory.

ток *m.* chat, talk. серьёзный ток a serious talk. **продавúть ток** *pf.* to pretend to be a foreigner by speaking English, French, etc. Мы продавúли ток и нас впустúли. We spoke a foreign language, so they let us in.
 • Russian rendition of the English *talk*: not to be confused with its standard meaning, *current.* Dated slang. The ruse was necessary to obtain admittance to restaurants, discos, etc. from which Russians were excluded.

толкáть *v.t.* [*pf.* **толкнýть**] to sell, flog. Вáся зáпонки толкнýл ещё недéлю назáд. Vasya flogged the cufflinks a week ago now.
 • Lit. *to push, shove.* See also *сдавáть,* 1.

толкнýть *pf.* of **толкáть.**

толкýчка *f.* flea market.

толпá *f.* 1. gang, bunch of friends. Привéт, толпá! Hi, folks! 2. gathering of locals. Идý к стáнции, а тут—толпá. I'm on my way to the station, and then there were all these people.
 • Lit. *crowd.*

толчóк *m.* 1. toilet. 2. flea market.
 • Lit. *push, shove.*

тончáк *m.* brilliant idea.

тóрмоз *m.* dolt, foolish or incompetent person (esp. male). Ну, ты и тóрмоз. What a drip you are.
 • Lit. *brake.*

тормозúть *v.i.impf.* 1. to stall, stop. 2. to dither, act stupid. Ты тормозúшь! You're dithering.
 • Lit. *to brake.*

торпéда *f.* tough guy, hardman supporting and serving a top criminal. В кáждой колóнии отрицáловку возглавляет пахáн зóны. Сам он, разумéется, никогó не избивáет и не рéжет, для э́того при нём состоя́т подрýчные—торпéды. In every labour colony the awkward squad is run by a local baron. He, of course, doesn't beat up or cut anyone himself; he's got his assistants—his hardmen—to do that.
 • Lit. *torpedo.*

торч *m.* 1. high (mainly drug induced). 2. gear, junk, drugs. 3. drug use.
* See also *тарч*.

торча́ть *v.i.* [*pf.* **заторча́ть**] 1. to be high, out of one's face (often drug- or alcohol-induced). Он задви́нул два ку́ба и торчи́т. He's injected two c.c. and is well away. 3. to get a high from, really like. Я от неё заторча́л. She just sent me. 3. to use or be addicted to drugs. Я торчу́ на джёфе. I use ephedrone.
* Lit. *to stick out.*

торчко́вый *adj.* drug, addicts'. торчко́вый флэт pad where addicts hang out.

торчо́к *m.* junkie, addict.
* See *гаси́ть* for an example.

точня́к: всё точня́к *phr.* exactly what is expected; just it, the very thing.

трава́ *f.* pot, grass. Any cannabis-based drug. Спиртно́го нет—увели́чился спрос на траву́. There's no booze, so the demand for grass has increased. Ей-Бо́гу, в э́той смешно́й стране́ хлеб купи́ть трудне́е, чем тра́вку. God, in this crazy country it's harder to buy bread than grass.
* See also *тра́вка*.

тра́вка *f.* grass, weed. **тра́вка бо́жья** kingdom weed.
* See also *трава́*.

транк *m.* tranquillizers, tranks.
* Truncated form of *транквилиза́тор*. See also *транквил*.

транквил *m.* variant of **транк**

тра́сса *f.* 1. road, the road. Поёхали в Пи́тер по тра́ссе. We hit the road to Petersburg. 2. main road.
* Lit. *route.* Hitch-hiking term.

тра́ссник *m.* road map.

тра́ссовый *adj.* road, relating to items used during hitch-hiking. Да ты не стрема́йся—э́то мой тра́ссовый прики́д. Don't you worry there: this is my hitch-hiking gear.

тра́узера́ *m.pl.* trousers, slacks.
* See also *трузера́*.

трах *m.* sex, shag, screw. Как твои́ впечатле́ния от тра́ха с ним? What's he like in the sack?
* Vulgarism.

тра́хать *v.t.* [*pf.* **тра́хнуть**] to screw, shag. 2. [*pf.* **затра́хать**] to bore stiff, rigid, to annoy. Затра́хал ты меня́ свои́ми теле́гами. You've bored me to death with your fairy-stories.
* Vulgarism. Lit. *to bang, crash.* See also *тра́хаться*.

тра́хаться *v.i.* [*pf.* **тра́хнуться**] to shag, screw, sleep or have sex with.
* Vulgarism.

тра́хнуть *pf.* of **тра́хать**.

тра́хнуться *pf.* of **тра́хаться**.

трёп *m.* chat, babble, gassing.

трепа́ться *v.i.* [*pf.* **протрепа́ться**] to gas, yak, blether, chat.
- Lit. *to tear.*

трепа́ч *m.* 1. gasser, blether, bletherskite. 2. windbag, bigmouth, bullshitter.
- See also *трепло́.*

трепло́ *n.* 1. gasser, blether, bletherskite. 2. windbag, bigmouth, bullshitter.
- See also *трепа́ч.*

тре́скать *v.i. impf.* to booze, drink (alcohol)

тре́скаться *v.i.* [*pf.* **втре́скаться**] to inject, shoot up.
- Lit. *to crack.* See also *втира́ться, дви́гаться, коло́ться, ширя́ться, шмы́гаться.*

треш *m.* variant of **трэш**. 9-й ЭТА́Ж (г. Могилёв). Па́рни лю́бят 'треш'...Руби́лись ми́лые! Не да́ли отдохну́ть восьми-кла́ссникам у сце́ны. Ninth Floor (from the town of Mogilev). The lads like 'thrash'...They really gave it their all, the darlings. They didn't give the eighth-formers at the stage a chance to catch their breath.
- Example taken from *Окорок.*

трип-хо́п *m.* trip hop. Э́тим ле́том я мно́го занима́лся так называ́емым трип-хо́пом. This summer I did a lot of the so-called trip hop.
- Example taken from *ПТЮЧ.*

труба́ *f.* 1. long underground pedestrian passage or subway in a city. 2. *often interj.* the end, hell.
- Lit. *pipe, chimney.*

трузера́ *m.pl.* trousers, slacks.
- See also *траузера́.*

трусня́к *m.* underpants, boxers.

трусы́ *pl.* [*gen.pl.* **трусо́в**] shop.
- Lit. *underpants.* Punk term.

трэш *m.* thrash, thrash metal.
- See also *треш.*

трэ́шевый *adj.* thrash, relating to thrash metal.

трэ́шер *m.* thrash metal fan.

тря́пки *f.pl.* clothes, gear.
- Lit. *rags.*

тря́ска *f.* withdrawal symptoms.
- Lit. *shaking.*

туз *m.* the man, ace, or top-class person. Ну, ты про́сто туз! You are the man!
- Lit. *ace.*

тума́н: соли́ в тума́н! *pf.phr.* Clear off! Do one!

ту́рок *m.* an Armenian's contemptuous term for an Azeri. Тут наш нача́льник не вы́держал, вы́тащил нож, и отхря́пал ту́рку у́хо. Then our leader lost his temper, fetched out a knife and took the Azeri's ear off.

• Lit. *Turk.*

тусня́к *m.* variant of **тусо́вка.**

тусова́ться *v.i.impf.* 1. to hang around, knock around (with). Что-то в лом мне тусова́ться. Somehow I don't want to hang around. Я с ней два го́да тусова́лся в Литве́. I knocked around with her for two years in Lithuania. 2. to be into the youth scene. 3. to party, to have fun, have a good laugh, go out with your friends. Ты по дела́м в Пи́тер е́дешь? Нет, тусова́ться. Are you off to Petersburg on business? No, I'm going out with some friends.

тусо́вка *f.* 1. party, gig, do, get-together. У хиппо́в сего́дня мо́щная тусо́вка. The hippies are holding a huge do today. 2. group, lot. 3. place or joint to hang around, party. После́дняя по вре́мени возникнове́ния тусо́вка называ́ется *Вавило́н*—кафе́ на у́лице Ге́рцена в Москве́. The latest place to appear is called the *Babylon*, a café on Herzen Street in Moscow. 4. problem. План выруба́ть—тусо́вка, дава́й ва́йна заце́пим. Getting dope's a problem—let's go for some wine.

• Believed to have derived from old Russian *тасо́вка*, lit. *shuffling (of cards, for example)*, meaning *to move from place to place for a party*. Also used in criminal and other argots.

тусо́вочный *adj.* referring to someone who likes to go to parties or hanging out. тусо́вочная герла́ party chick. тусо́вочный прики́д party gear. тусо́вочное состоя́ние party mood. тусо́вочное ме́сто joint, place where people get together or hang out.

тусо́вщик *m.* person who likes to hang out, party-goer, member of а тусо́вка.

• See also *тусо́вщица.*

тусо́вщица *f.* 1. female member of a group. 2. party-chick.

• See also *тусо́вщик.*

туфта́ *f.* crap, rubbish, garbage.

туфто́вый *adj.* rubbish, rubbishy, garbage, crappy.

ты́ква *f.* head, nut, bonce.

• Lit. *pumpkin.* See also *башка́, бестолко́вка, ре́па, ча́йник.*

тэн *m.* tenner, ten-rouble note. Наколо́л одного́ ло́ха на тэн. I conned some cretin out of a tenner.

тэ́нок *m.* variant of **тэн.**

У

убива́ться *v.i.* [*pf.* **уби́ться**] to smoke a lot of hash.

уби́ться *pf.* of **убива́ться**.

ублю́док *m.* bastard, swine.

убо́й *m.* great, fab, brill, excellent. Портвяшо́к—по́лный убо́й. Port is pure great.

• Lit. *slaughter.* Mit′ki term: usually used with the adjective *по́лный.* See also *крутня́к 2, обса́д, улёт.*

уга́р *m.* 1. high, a great time. Я люблю́, там, по вся́ким клу́бам пройти́сь, когда́ есть настро́ение, есть уга́р. I like it, well, going round all sorts of clubs; when I'm on a high it's excellent. 2. *interj.* Sorted! Wicked! Excellent!

• Lit. *carbon monoxide fumes.* Example taken from *ПТЮЧ.*

углова́тый офице́р *m.* homeless military officer. С вы́водом войск из Восто́чной Евро́пы в семе́йство углова́тых офице́ров влили́сь но́вые лю́ди. When troops were withdrawn from Eastern Europe new people joined the community of homeless officers.

• The phrase is coined from the title of an official publication: *Семья́ военнослу́жащего снима́ет кварти́ру и́ли у́гол, Family of a serving officer seeks flat or corner to rent.* Here *у́гол* means a room without bath.

уголо́к *m.* 25-rouble note.

• Lit. *corner.*

угора́ть *v.i.* [*pf.* **угоре́ть**] to be well pleased, delighted, die for, adore.

• Lit. *to have carbon monoxide poisoning.*

угро́хать *v.t. pf.* to kill. Что э́то за за́понки, и ско́лько они́ могли́ сто́ить, е́сли из-за них угро́хали твоего́ бо́сса? What sort of cufflinks were they, and how much could they be worth, if someone did in your boss for them?

• See also *гро́хнуть.*

удо́лбанный *adj.* high, out of it on drugs. Там все ходи́ли как удо́лбанные к утру́. They all went about as if out of it all night.

удолба́ться *v.i.pf.* to get high, out of it (on drugs).

• See also *обдолба́ться.*

удри́нчаться *v.i.pf.* to booze, get sloshed, sozzled.

• See also *дри́нкать, удры́нкаться.*

удри́нченный *adj.* sozzled, smashed, sloshed, pissed, drunk.

удры́нкаться *v.i.pf.* to booze, get sloshed, sozzled.

• See also *дры́нкать, удри́нчаться.*

ужа́сник *m.* horror movie, film.

ужа́стик *m.* variant of **ужа́сник**.

уку́ренный *adj.* doped up, high. Вон идёт чува́к уку́ренный. Here comes a doped-up guy.

улёт *m., interj.* excellent, fab, brill, great.
• See also *крутня́к 2, обса́д, убо́й*.

улета́ть *v.i.* [*pf.* улете́ть] 1. to get high. 2. to fly, be made up.
• Lit. *to fly away*.

улете́ть *pf.* of **улета́ть**.

улётный *adj.* excellent, fab, brilliant, class, sound.

ума́т *m., interj.* great, sound, far out. в ума́т big time, pure, dead. Мы вчера́ удри́нчались в ума́т. Yesterday we got blind drunk.

уматно́й *adj.* stunning, brilliant, wicked, great. уматно́й приќид wicked gear.

ума́тный *adj.* variant of **уматно́й**.

универ *m.* uni, university.

упако́ванный *adj.* 1. well dressed, done up. Иностра́нец был седо́й, краси́вый, я́вно упако́ванный по са́мое не́куда. The foreigner was grey-haired, good-looking and obviously dressed up to the nines. 2. well furnished. А тепе́рь упако́ванные ха́ты так запира́ют, что ни плечо́м, ни ло́мом и уж тем бо́лее ключо́м не возьмёшь. But these days people lock up their luxury flats so securely that you can't get in by barging the door, breaking in, let alone with a key.
• Lit. *packed up*. See *упакова́ть 1*.

упакова́ть *v.t.pf.* to do up, dress up to the nines. 2. to arrest and (hand)cuff someone. В тече́ние не́скольких мину́т спецна́зовцы гра́мотно упакова́ли всех граби́телей. In a few minutes the special squad had expertly arrested all the robbers and put the cuffs on.
• Lit. *to pack up*.

упакова́ться *pf.* of **упако́вываться**.

упако́вка *f.* patrol car, cop-car, paddy wagon. Менты́ подогна́ли упако́вку пря́мо к Сайго́ну. The fuzz drove the patrol car straight up to the Saigon.
• Lit. *packing*.

упако́вываться *v.i.* [*pf.* упакова́ться] to get done up, dressed.

упо́р: до упо́ра *m.* as much as possible, like nobody's business. Они́ рабо́тали до упо́ра. They worked like dogs.

упы́хаться *v.i.pf.* to smoke a lot of drugs.

у́рел *m.* [*pl.* урела́, у́релы] yob, lout, neanderthal.
• See also *урла́, урлага́н, урла́к*.

урла́ *coll.f.* yobs, louts, neanderthals.
• See also *у́рел, урлага́н, урла́к*. For an example, see *бэк*.

урлага́н *m.* yob, lout, neanderthal.
• A combination of *урла́* and *хулига́н* (*hooligan*). See also *у́рел, урла́к*.

урла́к *m.* [*pl.* **урлаки́**] yob, lout, neanderthal.
• See also *у́рел, урла́, урлага́н.*

урлово́й *adj.* variant of **урло́вый.**

урло́вый *adj.* loutish, yobbish, neanderthal.

усе́чь *v.i.pf.* to get (it), see, click. Усёк? Clicked? Get the message? Я это усёк. I got that. Ты нам пла́тишь и мы тебя́ оставля́ем в поко́е. Усёк? You pay us and we'll leave you alone—get my drift?
• Lit. *to cut off.*

уторча́ться *v.i.pf.* to get high.

уто́рченный *adj.* high (on drugs).

утю́г *m.* 1. currency dealer, often dodgy. 2. bully-boy.
• Lit. *(smoothing) iron.* See also *кида́ла.*

утю́жить *v.t.impf.* to con, swindle, steal. утю́жить фирму́ to con foreigners.
• See also *бомби́ть фирму́.*

учёбка *f.* recruit-training battalion.

учи́лка *f.* teacher, lecturer.

у́ши *n.pl.* [*gen.pl.* **уше́й**] 1. earphones. 2. name for the junction of Sretenka and Sadovoe kol'tso in Moscow, with monument to Nadezhda Krupskaya. висе́ть на уша́х *impf.* to bore to death. С утра́ на уша́х виси́т, всех доста́л. He's been talking all day; bored the hell out of everybody. поста́вить на́ уши *pf.* to rob, steal (someone or something), do over. Что лу́чше, че́стно рабо́тать, ска́жем, фрезеро́вщиком, за 200-300 рэ вка́лывать, как вол, и́ли поста́вить чью-нибудь кварти́ру на́ уши? What's better—earning an honest wage working like an ox as, say, a milling machine operator, for 200-300 roubles, or doing over someone's flat?
• Lit. *ears.* Sense 1 is an abbreviation of *нау́шники.*

Ф

фа́за *f.* see **сдвиг по фа́зе.**

фаза́н *m.* army recruit, member of the barrack-room pecking order.
• Lit. *pheasant.* See also *дед, де́мбель, дух, слон, черпа́к.*

фазе́нда *f.* small suburban house, villa, cottage, dacha. Я всё ле́то на фазе́нде паха́л. I spent all summer working at the dacha.
• This is one of a range of Spanish vocabulary items from a popular Mexican soap-opera series. This item is said to have been used in *Рабы́ня Иза́ура (Isaura the Slave Girl)* and to indicate that Soviets were slaves on their own land.

фа́зер *m.* dad, old man, father. Мно́го лет я пыта́лся ста́вить фа́зеру пра́вильную му́зыку, а он говори́л: э́то не му́зыка, э́то вой соба́чий. А пото́м я въе́хал: е́сли бы он при-коло́лся к мое́й му́зыке—э́то бы́ло бы ужа́сно. Он и не до́лжен к ней прика́лываться. For years I tried to get Dad to listen to the right sort of music, but he used to say: that's not music, it sounds like a dog howling. Then I twigged: if he got into my sort of music, then it would be terrible. He's not meant to be into it.

файф *m.* fiver, five-rouble note. Е́сли на та́чке е́хать, то ну́жен файф. If we're going to take a taxi, then we'll need a fiver.

файфе́шник *m.* 1. a mark of five at school or college (i.e. an excellent grade). 2. fiver, five roubles.
• See also *файф, файфу́шник.* Contrast with *хвост* 1.

файфо́вый *adj. used as noun* five.
• See also *файф.*

файфо́к *m.* variant of **файф.**

файфу́шник *m.* variant of **файф.**

фак *m.* fuck, shag, screw, lay.
• Vulgarism.

фа́канный *adj.* bloody, damned.

фа́кать *v.t.* 1. [*pf.* **фа́кнуть**] to fuck, screw, shag, lay. 2. [*pf.* **зафа́кать**] to get to, annoy, bore to tears. Зафа́кала ме́стная урла́. The local yobs have really got on my wick.
• Vulgarism. See also *фа́чить, фа́каться.*

фа́каться *v.i.* [*pf.* **фа́кнуться**] 1. to fuck, screw, shag, lay, sleep with. 2. to bugger around, arse around (busy oneself) with.
• Vulgarism. See also *фа́кать, фа́читься.*

фа́кер *m.* skirt-chaser, womaniser.
• See also *фа́кмен.*

фа́кмен *m.* skirt-chaser, womaniser.
• See also *фа́кер.*

фа́кнуть *pf.* of **фа́кать.**

фа́кнуться *pf.* of **фа́каться.**

фа́к-сейшн *m.* orgy, group sex. А го́луби, подо́нки, нае́вшись пшена́,/устро́или фа́к-сэйшн у моего́ окна́. And the pigeons, the little gits, gorged on millet,/started an orgy outside my window.
• Vulgarism. Example taken from song lyric.

фа́к-сэйшн *m.* variant of **фа́к-сейшн.**

факту́ра *f.* appearance, look(s). Жаль, е́сли така́я факту́ра пострада́ет. It'd be a pity if looks like those went to waste.
• Lit. *style, manner.*

фан *m.* fan.
• See also *фэн.*

фан- *in compounds.* фан-клуб fan club.

фана́т *m.* 1. hard-core football or ice-hockey fan. 2. swine, bastard, derogatory term of address. Ну ты, фана́т! Here, you bastard!

фана́теть *v.i.impf.* to be wild, nuts, crazy (about someone). Я вообще́-то за Валéру недáвно фанáтею. I've been wild about Valera just recently.

фанéра *f.* 1. dosh, readies, dough. 2. Concert, where artists mime instead of playing live. И никакúх обмáнов фанéрой. And no miming.
* Lit. *plywood, veneer.*

фараóн *m.* cop, pig, policeman.
* Lit *pharaoh.* Dated criminal argot.

фáрить *v.t.* [*pf.* зафáрить, пофáрить] to look, take a look, stare. Пойдём, пофáрим, есть там сигарéты úли нет? Let's go see if there's any cigarettes or not.
* Borrowed from the dated underworld use of *фáры* (eyes), (lit. *headlights*).

фарц *m.* [*pl.* фарцы́, фарцá] black marketeer, reselling goods and currency acquired from foreigners (especially during Soviet rule).
* See also *фáрцман.*

фарцá *coll.f.* see **фарц**.

фáрцман *m.* variant of **фарц**. Возвращáлись турúсты из музéев, мотáлись поднóсчики багажá, бéгали интурúстовские шестёрки, крутúлись фáрцманы. Tourists were returning from the museums surrounded by porters, lackeys from Intourist were running around and black marketeers hovering.

фáчить *v.t.* [*pf.* зафáчить] variant of **фáкать**.

фáчиться *v.i.* variant of **фáкаться**. Пóлдня фáчился с э́тим магнитофóном. I've spent half the day buggering about with this tape-recorder.

фáшики *m.pl.* fascists, Russian neo-nazis.

фен *m.* phenamine, a psychoactive drug.

фéнечка *f.* (and **фéнька**) 1. a hippy's decoration, usually a wrist-band, bracelet, plaid, beads, etc. Какáя у тебя́ фéнечка на рукé клёвая! That's a cool wrist-band you've got on! 2. prank, trick. Ты знáешь, у негó послéдняя фéнька какáя? Have you heard his latest (escapade)? 3. and **фéня**, joke, funny story. Я тебé сейчáс такýю клёвую фéнечку расскажý! I'll tell you a really funny thing!
* See also *фéня* and *фéнька.*

фéнька *f.* friendship beads, bracelet.
* See also *фéнечка.*

фéня *f.* 1. prank, joke. У Сайгóновцев есть излю́бленная фéня: при появлéнии патруля́ надевáть большóй я́ркий значóк с нáдписью: 'Меня́ ужé сегóдня свúнчивали'. The Saigon lot have a favourite prank: when the fuzz come, they put on a big bright badge saying 'I've been picked up once already today'. **до**

фе́ни [+ *dat.*] it's all one, it's all the same, couldn't care less, couldn't give (a damn). Иногда́ ка́жется: молодо́му поколе́нию всё до фе́ни, кро́ме ба́бок, тусо́вок и ка́йфа. Sometimes it seems that the young couldn't care a damn about anything except women, parties and gear. 2. criminal lingo, slang.
  • See also *фе́нечка 3, дофени́зм, дофени́ст*.

фиг *m.* euphemism for хуй. Он ни фига́ не зна́ет. He knows damn all.

фигня́ *f.* crap, garbage, rubbish, bull(shit).

физру́к *m.* P.E. teacher.

фирма́ *f.* 1. *coll.* something or someone from the West, foreigner, westerner. **по фирме́** good quality stuff, gear, as if made by a foreign company. 2. *interj.* great, brill, sorted, (well) sound. Ви́дел у него́ та́чку? Фирма́! Have you seen his car? It's wicked!
  • Lit. *firm.* See *бомби́ть фирму́* for an example of *фирма́ 1*.

фирма́ч *m.* [*pl.* **фирмачи́**] 1. foreigner, particularly from the West. 2, businessman.

фи́рменный *adj.* made in the West, good, sound, high quality.

фирмо́вый *adj.* high quality, bearing well-known brand name.

флаво́вый *adj.* flower, relating to 'flower children' (*цвето́чное движе́ние*).
  • Dated.

флэт *m.* [*pl.* **флеты́**] pad, joint, place, apartment. У меня́ открыва́ется флэт. I've just got a place. Засиде́вшись на флэту́, в метро́ опозда́л. I missed the metro as I stayed too long at the pad.
  • See also *флэтя́ра*.

флэ́товый *adj.* 1. home, referring to a pad. **флэ́товый сэйшн** a party in a flat. 2. *used as noun* hippy who prefers to be alone, do his own thing, or stay at home.

флэтя́ра *f.* flat, pad.
  • See also *флэт*.

фонта́н: не фонта́н *m.* not so good, not so hot, not that great, not much to get carried away about. Сапоги́, коне́чно, не фонта́н, но на одну́ зи́му их хва́тит. The boots weren't up to much, but they'll do for one winter.
  • Lit. *not a fountain.*

францу́женка *f.* French teacher, lecturer (female).
  • Lit. *Frenchwoman.*

фрей: би́тый фрей *m.* a cagey old bird, old hand.

френч *m.* variant of **фрэнч**.

фри лав *m.* free love, sex with no strings. А тепе́рь я за неё не то́лько все фри ла́вы отда́м, а что уго́дно. But now I won't just give her all the sex she wants, but whatever else.
  • See also *фрила́в*, *фрила́вность*.

фрила́в *m.* variant of **фри лав**.

фрила́вник *m.* believer in free love.
  • See also *фрила́вщик*.

фрила́вность *f.* carefree sex life, free love. В тот день пришёл коне́ц мое́й фрила́вности. That day was the end of my free love.
  • See also *фри лав*, *фрила́в*.

фрила́вщик *m.* variant of **фрила́вник**.

фрэнд *m.* [*pl.* **фрэнды́**] pal, mate, buddy, friend.

фрэндо́вый *adj.* of, belonging to a friend. Это фрэндо́вые трузера́—ви́дишь, жмут меня́ в по́ясе. These are my mate's trousers—you see, they're too tight for me round the waist.

фрэнч *m.* Frenchman, frog. Как же! Запла́тит френч неусто́йку! What! The frog will pay the lost amount!
  • See also *френч*.

фрэнчо́вый *adj.* French, froggy.

фуз *m.* gadget for guitar to produce a fuzzy sound, distortion box. Хочу́ я всех моча́лок застеба́ть, нажа́в ного́й свое́й на мо́щный фуз. I want to wind up all the hags giving it severe fuzz with my foot on the pedal.
  • Lyric by Бори́с Гребенщико́в.

фунфу́рик *m.* medicine glass (usually 30 ml.) with glue or perfume.
  • See also *панфу́рик*.

фунфури́ст *m.* someone who gets drunk on cheap substitutes (such as cheap medicine) for alcohol.

фунфы́рь *m.* glass containing slightly over a tenth of a litre.
  • Possibly a blend of *фунфу́рик* and *пузы́рь* (*bubble*).

фуфа́йст *m.* member of a right-wing youth movement, which appeared around 1986. The men wore tarpaulin boots and sweater-coats to protest against Western culture.

фуфло́ *n.* 1. rubbish, crap, shit. 2. useless person, git.

фуфло́вый *adj.* rubbish, useless, no good.
  • See *абза́ц* for example.

фэйс *m.* [*pl.* **фэйса́**] face. А где-то в кабака́х сидя́т мои́ фрэнды́,/фэйса́ у них небри́ты, попи́саны хэнды́. Somewhere in the pubs my friends are sitting,/unshaven faces and scarred hands.
  • See also *фэйсу́шник*.

фэйсану́ть *pf.* of **фэйсова́ть**.

фэйсова́ть *v.t.* [*pf.* **фэйсану́ть, отфейсова́ть**] to hit, smack, give one in the face.

фейсу́шник *m.* variant of **фэйс**.

фэн *m.* fan. Фэ́ны гру́ппы бу́дут ра́ды вы́ходу но́вого альбо́ма, как фа́кту, а головоло́мщикам придётся не раз прослу́шать за́пись, что́бы поня́ть, что к чему́. Fans of the group will be glad at the release of the new album as a fact, but those not in the know will have to listen to the recording several times to figure out what's what.
  • See also *фан*. Example from *Ниоткуда*.

фэнс *m.* a great or sound bloke, someone having popular approval in urban working youth culture.

X

хаба́рик *m.* fag end.

хаба́рить *v.t.* [*pf.* **захаба́рить**] to pinch out a cigarette (to smoke later). Солда́ты дру́жно захаба́рили оку́рки. The soldiers pinched out the fag-ends all at once.

ха́вать *v.i.* [*pf.* **заха́вать, наха́вать, сха́вать**] to eat, swallow, take. Он вчера́ лист цикло́ды заха́вал. He took a sheet of cyclodole yesterday. На́до поха́вать пригото́вить. We need to make something to eat. Наха́вался колёс и шизу́ет. He's taken a load of tabs and is freaking out.

ха́вка *f.* food, grub, scran.

хайлайфи́ст *m.* rich young person in the smart set, high-flyer.
  • Folk. See also *хайлафи́ст*.

хайлафи́ст *m.* variant of **хайлайфи́ст**.

хайр *m.* [pl. **хайры́**] hair, hair-do. Попу́тного ве́тра тебе́ в хайр. The wind's blowing your hair. У него́ хайр лонго́вый. He has long hair.

хайрану́ться *v.i.pf.* to get a hair cut.

хайра́стый *adj.* 1. long-haired. хайра́стый чува́к a long-haired bloke. 2. *used as noun* hippy.
  • See also *хайра́тый*.

хайра́тник *m.* headband. У́зкое, с изя́щными черта́ми лицо́ окружено́ ни́мбом дли́нных воло́с, перехва́ченных на лбу́ тесьмо́й—хайра́тником. A narrow face with elegant features, surrounded with a halo of long hair caught up on the forehead with a braid headband.

хайра́тый *adj.* variant of **хайра́стый**.

халя́ва *f.* 1. freebie, free lunch, something given out free. **на халя́ву** for nowt, free. Пойдём на сва́дьбу—пожрём на

халя́ву. Let's go to the wedding: we'll get sozzled for nothing. 2. chick, bird.
• For first definition, see also *на ша́ру.*

халя́вщик *m.* scrounger, cadger, moocher.

ха́нька *f.* 1. a liquid drug obtained from poppy. 2. drugs, junk, gear.

хард *m.* 1. hard drive. На́до бы́ло на хард записа́ть. We should have put it on the hard drive. 2. hard-core music.
• See also *винт 5.*

хардко́р *m.* hard-core music. Но сейча́с хардко́р вдру́г оказа́лся са́мым весёлым и оптимисти́ческим сти́лем те́хно. But now hard core suddenly turned out to be the happiest and most optimistic techno style.
• Example from *Окорок.*

хардко́ровый *adj.* hard core.

хардо́вый *adj.* hard.

хард-ро́к *m.* hard rock. И ещё была́ гру́ппа Колумба́рий (го́род Северодви́нск). Хард-ро́к. О́чень 'хард'. And then there was the group, Columbarium (from the town of Severodvinsk). Hard rock. Very 'hard'.
• Example from *Rock Fuzz.*

харко́та *f.* nobody, nonentity, insignificant person.
• Punk term. See also *харко́тинка.*

харко́тинка *f.* variant of **харко́та**.

ха́та *f.* place, joint, pad, apartment.
• Lit. *peasant house.* See *стано́к* for an example.

ха́халь *m.* lover, fancy man, lover-boy. Чтó-то к ней ха́хали зачасти́ли. For some reason fancy men have started going to see her often.
• Dated.

хвост *m.* the lowest mark given for work in school or college. У меня́ в э́том семе́стре хвост по а́лгебре. This semester I got a really bad mark in algebra.
• Lit. *tail.* Contrast with *файфе́шник.*

хвостану́ть *v.i.pf.* to die, kick the bucket.
• Punk term.

хер *m.* dick, knob, prick. Пошёл на́ хер! Fuck off! Piss off! Up yours!
• Vulgarism. See also *прик, хрен, ху́й.*

хи́дать *v.i.* [*pf.* **захи́дать, прохи́дать**] to hear.
• Combination of the English *hear* and *-(д)ать.*

хи́лый *adj.* 1. insufficient. 2. weak.

хиля́ть *v.i.impf.* to come, go. Смотри́, кака́я шма́ра хиля́ет. Look at what's coming—what a slapper. Хиля́й отсю́да! Get lost! Beat it!
- See also *каня́ть*.

хи́мик *m.* 1. prisoner transferred from a prison camp to construction work. 2. chemistry teacher, lecturer (male).
- Lit. *chemist*. Sense 1 was coined during the Khrushchev era, when the chemical industry was developed by prison labour. See also *хими́чка*.

хими́чка *f.* chemistry teacher, lecturer.
- See also *хи́мик 2*.

хипа́н *m.* hippy.
- See also *хиппа́н, хиппа́рь, хи́ппи*.

хи́пеж *m.* angry scene, scuffle, set-to, bust-up, brawl, quarrel. В тюрьме́ кормёжка трёхра́зовая, по́стная, но дистрофи́ей никто́ не страда́ет, в свобо́дное вре́мя—кому́ ка́рты и домино́, кому́ ша́шки и ша́хматы; развлече́ния э́ти ограни́чиваются, но е́сли без ссор, без хи́пежа, то смо́трят сквозь па́льцы. In prison you get fed three times a day, it's pretty basic, but doesn't poison anyone. In your spare time some play cards or dominoes, some draughts or chess; these activities are limited, but if it goes on without any arguments or brawls, they turn a blind eye to it. **подня́ть хи́пеж** *pf.* to raise hell, scream blue murder. По́днял хи́пеж из-за како́й-то ерунды́! He cried blue murder all over some rubbish or other.
- See also *хи́пиш*.

хи́пиш *m.* variant of **хи́пеж**.

хипп *m.* hippy.
- See also *хипа́н, хиппа́н, хиппа́рь, хи́ппи*.

хиппа́н *m.* variant of **хипа́н**.

хиппа́рь *m.* hippy.
- See also *хипа́н, хипп, хиппа́н, хи́ппи*.

хи́ппи *m.* hippy.
- See also *хипа́н, хипп, хиппа́н, хиппа́рь*.

хиппи́зм *m.* the hippy way, philosophy.

хиппо́вский *adj.* hippy, relating to hippies or the hippy culture.
- See also *хиппо́вый*.

хиппо́вый *adj.* hippy, relating to hippies or the hippy culture.
- See also *хиппо́вский*.

хиппота́ *coll.f.* hippies.

хип-хо́п *m.* hip hop.

хич *m.* hitch, lift. Он отпра́вился в хич. He set off hitch-hiking.

хичха́йкер *m.* hitch-hiker.

хлам: в хлам dead drunk, out of one's face, sloshed, legless, pie-eyed.
- See also *в хлами́ну*.

хлами́на: в хлами́ну variant of **в хлам.**

хо́дка *f.* previous conviction, record. Собо́р означа́ет ве́рность воровско́й профе́ссии, а коли́чество куполо́в—число́ хо́док в зо́ну, пе́рстень на па́льце с заштрихо́ванным квадра́том говори́т о том, что его́ облада́тель отсиде́л от звонка́ до звонка́, крест в пе́рстне—карма́нный вор, че́реп—отличи́тельный знак разбо́йника. A (tattooed) cathedral means loyalty to the criminal world, the number of cupolas it has—the number of convictions, a ring on the finger with a shaded square means that its owner has served a full stretch, a cross on the ring means a pickpocket, and a skull—the specific mark of the bandit.

хокке́й: всё хокке́й everything's fine, okay.
- Possibly from English *Okay.*

хом *m.* home.

хому́т *m.* [*pl.* **хомуты́**] 1. policeman; volunteer patrolman. 2. army sergeant.
- Lit. *horse-collar.*

хомута́ть *v.t.* [*pf.* **захомута́ть**] 1. to detain, arrest. 2. to take on, recruit, talk into. Я покоси́лась, а у коло́нны стои́т хорошо́ подда́вший шта́тник и его́ шика́рно хомута́ют две интерде́вочки. I looked sideways and saw a really drunk American at the column, with two foreign-currency tarts chatting him up.

хому́тская *adj used as f.noun* police-station.

хомутьё *coll.n.* police, pigs, cops.
- See **хому́т.**

хоро́ший *adj.* real, pure, utter. Она́ то́же сво́лочь хоро́шая. And she's an utter swine too.
- Lit. *good.* See also *поря́дочный.*

хрен *m.* dick, prick, knob. ста́рый хрен old git.
- Vulgarism. Lit. *horseradish.* See also *прик, хер, хуй.*

хрено́вый *adj.* crap, crappy, lousy, rotten.

хромачи́ *m.pl.* high military boots (without laces).

хрущёба *f.* Apartment built in early 1960s, the time of Khrushchev. Век хрущёб ко́нчился, но в них прихо́дится жить мно́гим. The age of Khrushchev slums is over, but lots of people still have to live in them.
- A combination of the Soviet leader *Хрущёв* [First Secretary 1953-1964] and *трущо́ба* (*slum*). See also *хрушёвка* and *хрущо́ба.*

хрущёвка *f.* variant of **хрущёба.**

хрущо́ба *f.* variant of **хрущёба.**

хуёвый *adj.* crap, crappy, rubbish, rubbishy, lousy.
- Vulgarism.

хуй *m.* dick, prick, knob, cock. Пошёл, иди на́ хуй! Fuck off! Fuck you! Go fuck yourself! посыла́ть [*pf.* посла́ть] кого́-нибудь на́ хуй to tell someone to get lost, do one. Ни хуя́ себе́! Not bad at all! Bloody brilliant! Он ни хуя́ не зна́ет. He knows fuck all, bugger all. Хуй с ним! To hell with him! Sod him!
   • Vulgarism. See also *прик, хер, хрен.*

хуйня́ *f.* crap, bull, bullshit, bollocks.
   • Vulgarism.

ху́нта *f.* gang of street criminals. На́ша ху́нта в э́том райо́не всех гоня́ет. Our local junta in this manor makes life hard for everyone.
   • Lit. *junta.*

хэ́ви-мета́л *m.* heavy-metal.
   • See also *металли́ст.*

хэнды́ *m.pl.* hands.

Ц

цветно́й *adj. used as noun* screw, pig, jailer.
   • Lit. *coloured.*

цвето́чный *adj.* flower, hippy. цвето́чное движе́ние the flower generation.

центр *m.* town.
   • Lit. *centre.*

центра́ *coll.f.* see **центрови́к.**

центри́ть *v.i.impf.* to go into town, into the centre of the city.
   • See also *центрова́ться.*

центрова́ться *v.i.impf.* variety of **центри́ть.**

центрови́к *m.* places in central Moscow. Хи́ппи в основно́м наро́д с центровико́в (Пу́шка, Го́голя, Я́шка). Hippies are basically people who hang around certain places in the centre (Pushkin Square, the Gogol monument, Sverdlov Square).

центрово́й *adj. used as noun* person whose activities are conducted in the centre, in town.
   • Lit. *central.*

центря́к *m.* 1. main vein in the arm. 2. variant of **пластили́н.**

цепану́ть *pf.* of **цепля́ть.**

цепля́ть *impers.v.t.* [*pf.* зацепи́ть, цепану́ть] to take effect (of a drug). Не то, чтобы кры́ша е́дет, но уж бо́льно бы́стро цепля́ет. It's not that I'm losing it, but it's working pretty fast already. Меня́ цепану́ло. It hit me.

цивил *m.* 1. civilian clothes, civvy gear. Он постри́гся и циви́л на себя́ наде́л. He had his hair cut and put on civvy clothes. 2. ordinary person, square. Занайта́ли у клёвых циви́лов. We stayed the night with some great folk.

циви́льный *adj.* 1. civil, ordinary, square. циви́льная флэтя́ра a flat in civvy street. циви́льный клифт normal (i.e. non-military) coat. 2. great, brilliant.
• Lit. *civilian.*

цивильня́к *coll.m.* square people. На стриту́ то́лько цивильня́к—ни одного́ волоса́того. There were only squares in the street—not one hippy.

цикл *m.* [*pl.* **циклы́**] cyclodole (tablets).

цикла́ *f.* variant of **цикл**.

циклу́ха *f.* variant of **цикл**.

циркули́ *pl.m.* pins, pegs, legs.
• Lit. *pair of compasses.*

Ч

чайлд *m.* [*pl.* **чайлды́**] kid, nipper, child.
• See also *чилд, чи́лдрен, чи́льдрэн.*

ча́йник *m.* 1. head, nut. noggin. Получи́л по ча́йнику. I got one on the nut. А ча́йник у него́ хорошо́ ва́рит. He's well clued up, he's got a head on his shoulders. 2. dolt, dunce, thickhead, idiot, thickie. У Ма́ни обы́чно пожра́ть не́чего. Зато́ штакета́ (для ча́йников объясня́ю—ги́льзы папиро́сные), как на фа́брике таба́чной. At Manya's there's never anything to eat. But it's like a cigarette factory, the amount of cigarette papers (I'll explain that for dunces: paper for rolling cigarettes) you find.
• Lit. *tea-pot.* See also *башка́, бестолко́вка, ре́па, ты́ква.*

чебура́шка *f.* half-litre bottle. Объявле́ние на пу́нкте приёма посу́ды гласи́ло: 'Чебура́шки не принима́ем'. There was a notice at the bottle depot: 'Half-litre bottles not accepted'.
• Named after the popular children's cartoon character.

чейндж *m.* swap, exchange.
• See also *ченч.*

чейнджану́ться *v.i.pf.* [+ *inst.*] to swap, switch, exchange.

чекана́шка *m.,f.* 1. nutter, nut-job, head-case, screwball, 2. half-drunk nutter, who participates in every demonstration.

чекану́тый *adj.* mad, daft, crazy.

чеку́ха *f.* 1. (doctor's) line, prescription (for a drug). Я бы пошёл в дра́гу, да чеку́хи нет. I'd go to the chemist's, but I haven't got a prescription. 2. stamp.

челно́к *m.* 1. trader who buys goods abroad and takes them back to Russia to sell. 2. courier employed to smuggle inferior (usually cheap) goods into the black market. Из ци́кла 'Ничего́ себе́ профе́ссия': манеке́нщица, панк, челно́к. Among the not-bad-at-all jobs, there is model, punk, courier.
- Lit. *shuttle.*

ченч *m.* variant of **чейндж.**

чепо́к *m.* variant of **чипо́к.**

черножо́пый *adj. used as noun* person from Asian or Caucasian republics, black-arse. С черножо́пыми в Черёмушках дра́лись, вот плечо́ и вы́били э́ти су́ки па́лкой. We had a fight with the Asians in Cheryomushki, the bastards put my shoulder out with a stick.
- Vulgar: lit. *black-arsed.* See also *чёрный.*

черну́ха *f.* 1. black magic, black art. Занима́ется вся́кой черну́хой. He goes in for all sorts of weird stuff. 2. opiates-based drug, often causing very swift addiction. Подсе́л на черну́ху. He got hooked on opiates. 3. and **тупо́й кайф** black rush. Така́я черну́ха идёт. I've got such a rush. 4. lie.

черну́шник *m.* 1. con-man, crook, liar. 2. perv, pervert, dirty-minded person. 3. opiates addict.
- See also *черну́шница.*

черну́шница *f.* 1. crook, swindler, liar. 2. perv, pervert, dirty-minded person. 3. opiates addict.
- See also *черну́шник.*

чёрный *adj. often used as noun* black, person from Asian or Caucasian republics. На ры́нке одни́ чёрные торгу́ют. There were only Asians trading at the market. 2. and **чёрная** and **чёрное** opiates. 3. **чёрный тюльпа́н** *m.* military helicopter.
- Sense 3 (lit. *black tulip*) appeared in reports of the war in Afghanistan.

черпа́к *m.* army recruit, member of the barrack-room pecking order.
- Lit. *ladle.* See also *дед, дух, слон, фаза́н.*

чёрт *m.* 1. weirdo, freak, eccentric, odd person. 2. clown or dunce in a labour camp, often occupying a low rank in the camp structure.
- Lit. *devil.* Also a rude term of address. For an example of sense 1, see **масть.**

чёс *m.* concert tour to many small towns.

четверти́нка *f.* quarter-litre bottle of vodka. Ра́ньше бы́ло как: купи́л четверти́нку, взболта́л её, роди́мую...и в употреб-ле́нии про́сто и на душе́ хорошо́! What was it like before:

you've bought a quarter-bottle, shaken it, downed the whole lovely lot just like that and you felt great!

чешуя *f.* garbage, rubbish.
- Lit. *scales.*

чик-фа́ер *m.* lighter. У тебя́ чик-фа́ер и́ли спи́чки? Have you got a lighter or matches?

чилд *m.* [*pl.* чилды́] variant of **ча́йлд**.
- See also *чи́лдрен, чи́лдрэн.*

чи́лдрэн *m.* [*pl.* чи́лдрэна́, чи́лдрэны] kid, nipper. Твой чи́лдрэн? Is this your kid?
- See also *ча́йлд, чилд.*

чипо́к *m.* 1. café for servicemen. Пошли́ в чипо́к. Let's go to the NAAFI. 2. discount store.
- Also *чепо́к.*

чи́ра *f.* woman teacher.

чи́рик *m.* tenner, ten-rouble note. Довези́ до́ дому—чи́рик даю́. Drive me home and I'll give you a tenner.

чисти́льщик *m.* member of a fascist group of the 1980s, 'purifiers'. Чисти́льщики мочи́ли голубы́х. The purifiers gave the benders a real doing.
- Lit. *cleaner.*

чи́сто по жи́зни *adv.* well.

чи́стыми *adv.* clear, in cash. Я получа́ю чи́стыми о́коло десяти́ ты́сяч. I get about ten thousand clear.

чистя́к *m.* person with no police contact.
- Criminal argot.

чифи́р *m.* very strong tea used as narcotic.

чифирба́к *m.* vessel or brew (used for making **чифи́р**).

чифири́ст *m.* person who drinks **чифи́р**.

чмо *n. indec.* plonker, idiot.
- See also *чмо́шник.*

чмо́шник *m.* plonker, idiot.
- See also *чмо.*

чмы́рить *v.t.impf.* to make a jerk, mug of. И Черёмухин на́чал въезжа́ть, потому́ что он сам был воя́ка и знал, на что быва́ют спосо́бны отде́льные чмы́ри, поэ́тому, когда́ в его́ ро́те кого́-то чмы́рили, стара́лся э́то по возмо́жности пресека́ть. And it began to dawn on Cheryomukhin, as he himself was a serviceman and he knew what some jerks were capable of; so, when they made a mug of someone in his company he tried to nip it in the bud as best he could.

чмырь *m.* jerk. Тогда́ он попроси́л Кузьмина́ покопа́ться в па́мяти, но тот с усме́шечкой сказа́л, что из о́бщих враго́в был у них то́лько оди́н чмырь, кото́рому не то что с

Караевым, а с четвертью Караева не справиться. Then he asked Kuzmin to rack his brains, but he said, with a slight grin, that of their common enemies there was only one useless jerk, who wouldn't be able to handle a quarter of Karaev, never mind Karaev himself.

• Yiddish.

чокнутый *adj.* crazy, mad, nuts.

чувак *m.* guy, bloke, geezer, dude.

• Especially popular among *stilyagi*. See also *чувиха*.

чувиха *f.* young woman, chick, bird.

• Especially popular among *stilyagi*. See also *чувак*.

чудак *m.* dude, mister (as mode of address), geezer. Говоря друг о друге, молодые люди называют себя чудаками. (Мы тут с одним чудаком вчера...) When speaking of each other, young men use the word 'dude'. (Yesterday, this dude and I...)

• Lit. *eccentric, crank.* Play on the word *мудак, arse.*

чуйка *f.* Asian cannabis from the Chuiskaya Valley.

чума *f., often interj.* excellent, great, sound, cool, wicked, sorted.

• Lit. *plague.* See also *чумовой.*

чумовой *adj.* 1. excellent, great. Тусовка может оказаться парашливой, то есть неудачной, или удачной—чумовой. A gig can turn out to be either crap, that is, poor, or successful—in other words, fab. 2. no good. Это совершенно чумовой вариант! That version is utter rubbish!

• See also *чума.*

чурка *m.,f.* native of Caucasian or Asian republic.

• Lit. *block, lump.* See also *нацмен.*

чухан *m.* young person who is not a member of a gang or has no street cred; ponce. Уже второклассники в школах делят окружающих—за вычетом малых детей, стариков и женщин —на пацанов и чуханов. Second-year kids already divide the people around them (except for little kids, old men and women) into the real boys and the no-marks.

• See also *чушпан.*

чушпан *m.* variant of **чухан**.

Ш

шабить *v.i.impf.* to smoke, have a smoke (cannabis).

• See also *подкуриваться, пыхать.*

шайба *f.* type of powdered drug compressed into a rough tablet, tab. Шайбу-то сам скатал? Did you sort the tab?

• Lit. *puck, washer.*

шайка *f.* gang, mob.

шáла *f.* cannabis.

шалмáн *m.* dive, wino hang-out, low-class joint, often a bar or café.

шáра: на шáру *f.* for nothing, as a freebie.
* Variant of *на халя́ву.*

шарáга *f.* workshop.

шары́ *m.pl.* [*gen.pl.* **шарóв**] eyes. Шары́ вы́катили со стрáху. His eyes popped out with fear.

шварценéйгер *m.* big stiff; person with brawn and little brain.
* From Arnold Schwarzenegger, said to portray such characters in films. See also *арнóльд, качóк.*

шелухá *coll.f.* 1. young gang members who are coerced into committing criminal acts by older gang members. 2. young louts. 3. *sing.f.* rubbish, nonsense.
* Lit. *peel, skin, scale.*

шерсть *coll.f.* 1. prisoners thought to have compromised themselves and who are despised or distrusted by others. 2. prisoners who infringe the prison régime or do not cooperate.
* Lit. *wool.* See also *отрицáловка.*

шестери́ть *imp. v.t.* to treat like or be a skivvy, slave, gofer.

шестёрка *f.* 1. a creep, a convict subservient to influential prisoners. 2. a gofer, skivvy. 3. a VAZ-2106 car.
* For example of sense 1, see *масть.*

шизá *f.* 1. crazy turn. 2. nonsense, garbage, rubbish. Пойдём отсю́да—не стóит бóльше э́ту шизу́ слу́шать. Let's go, there's no point in listening to this rubbish any longer. 3. *m.,f.* and **шизану́тый** *adj. used as noun* schizo, lunatic, loony, looney-tunes, psycho. Э́тот мэн—настоя́щая шизá. That guy's a real loony. 4. schizophrenia. Мне постáвили шизу́. They diagnosed me as a schizo.
* Abbreviation of *шизофрени́я* (*schizophrenia*).

шизану́тый *adj.* loony, psycho, schizo, schizoid, lunatic, round the bend.
* See also *шизá.*

шизану́ться *v.i.pf.* to freak out, lose it, go ga-ga, mental, round the bend.

шизовáть *v.i.impf.* to freak out, lose it, go ga-ga, mental, round the bend.

шизóвка *f.* hippy stuff. Написáл для журнáла замечáтельную шизóвку. I wrote some great hippy stuff for the magazine.

шизóвый *adj.* 1. mental, weird, far-out. 2. hippy.
* See also *зашизóванный.*

шип *m.* dick, prick, knob.

ши́рево *coll.n.* 1. junk, gear. 2. *n.* fix, hit; junk, injected drugs.
* See also *ширя́лово.*

ширну́ться *pf.* of **ширя́ться**

ширя́лово *n.* fix, hit.

• See also *ши́рево.*

ширя́ние *n.* hit, fix, injection of a drug.

ширя́ться *v.i.* [*pf.* **ширну́ться**] to shoot up, hit up, inject a drug.

• From *ширя́ть, to dig, peck, push.* See also *втира́ться, гнать по ве́не, дви́гаться, коло́ться, тре́скаться, шмы́гаться.*

шить *v.i.impf.* to accuse falsely, to pin something on someone, to frame, stitch up. Ма́ло ограбле́ния—так тепе́рь ещё и уби́йство мне шьёте! It's not enough that you're pinning the thefts on me—you're trying to frame me for murder as well.

• Lit. *to sew.*

шко́ла *f.* college, university, uni. Не пойду́ сего́дня в шко́лу. I'm not going in to lectures today.

• Lit. *school.*

шко́льная во́дка *f.* Moscow vodka.

• Lit. *school vodka.* The phrase derives from the fact that the vodka first appeared for sale on the first day of the academic year, 1 September 1985. See also *андро́повка.*

шко́нка *f.* plank bed.

• Criminal argot.

шку́ра *f.* bit of skirt, a rude reference to young women. Догада́лась, шку́ра? Так могу́ и ли́чико разукра́сить! Do you get it, bitch? You know I can spoil that pretty face of yours.

• Lit. *skin, hide.*

шлема́к *m.* crash helmet.

шмак *m.* one rouble, buck, quid.

шма́ра *f.* slut, tart, slag, slapper.

• Common.

шматьё *n.* variant of **шмотьё**.

шмон *m.* 1. stench, smell. Тако́й шмон в ко́мнате скве́рный. There's a really foul stench in the room. 2. search in prison cell or labour camp.

шмона́ть *v.t.* [*pf.* **обшмона́ть**] 1. to attack and rob teenagers. Поджида́ли малышей у шко́лы и шмона́ли. They waited for the kids coming out of school and robbed them. 2. to search. Шмона́ют ка́меру. They're searching the cell. Цветны́е шмона́ли зэ́ков на ва́хте. The screws searched the convicts in the guardroom.

шмони́ть *v.i.impf.* to smell, reek, stench. На́до на балко́не кури́ть, чтобы не шмони́ло. We'd better smoke on the balcony so it won't smell.

шмо́тка *f.* item of clothing. Я тут одну́ хоро́шую шмо́тку купи́ла, но по разме́ру не подхо́дит. I bought one decent garment here, but it doesn't fit.

шмотьё *coll.n.* clothing. Да, я была счáстлива, потому́ что перестáла ду́мать о копéйках, потому́ что появля́лась с настоя́щим мужчи́ной, пéред котóрым открывáлись двéри всех рестора́нов, потому́ что моё шмотьё вызывáло зáвисть всех прики́нутых. Yes, I was happy, because I stopped counting the kopecks, because I was going round with a real man, who could get into all the restaurants, and because my clothes were the envy of all fashionable people.

шмы́гание *n.* injecting, shooting up. Шмы́гание гря́зной маши́ной опáсно для вáшего здорóвья. Shooting up with a dirty needle is dangerous for your health.

шмы́гаться *v.i.impf.* to use, inject, shoot up. Давáй шмы́гаться. Let's shoot up.
- See *втирáться, гнать по вéне, дви́гаться, колóться, трéскаться, ширя́ться*.

шнóбель *m.* conk, hooter, nose.
- See also *пятáк, руби́льник*.

шнурóк *m.* 1. dope, mug. Этот шнурóк весь день на ры́нке кру́тится, да всё впусту́ю. That mug faffs about all day at the market, all to no purpose. 2. **шнурки́** folks, parents.
- Lit. *shoelaces*.

шнырь *m.* 1. man on duty. 2. scum, scumbag, low-ranking person in labour camp. Шнырь, ставь чифирбáк. Put the kettle on, scum. 3. a rude form of address.

шня́га *f.* heroin, scag; gear, junk, narcotics in general. **шня́гу замути́ть, запогáнить** to prepare, fix up a drug.
- See also *сульты́га*.

шоп *m.* shop. У нас валю́тный шоп откры́лся. A foreign-currency shop has opened at our bit.

шпанá *f.coll.* yobs, yobbos, louts.

штакéт *m.* [*pl.* **штакетá**] rolling paper.
- See *чáйник* for an example. See also *штакéтник*.

штакéтник *m.* cigarette paper.
- See also *штакéт*.

штáтник *m.* 1. Yank, American citizen. Чéстно говоря́, засомневáлась: а ну́жно ли, как америкáнцы? Ведь те же штáтники, францу́зы, нéмцы, да и ту́рки, наконéц, строя́т свою́ жизнь по свои́м, а не заи́мствованным мéркам. To tell you the truth, I started to doubt: do we need to be like the Americans? After all, at the end the same Yanks, French, Germans, and even Turks build their lives according to their own standards, and not those of others. 2. (professional) policeman.

У меня сосе́д—шта́тник из мили́ции. My neighbour's a copper.

- 1. from *Соединённые Шта́ты* (*United States*). See also *аме́рикос*. 2. abbreviation for *шта́тный сотру́дник, permanent member of staff*.

шту́ка *f.* grand, thousand roubles. Ру́ки о́чень натура́льно дрожа́ли, когда́ нали́чность отдава́л, штук под де́сять оказа́лось при себе́. His hands were shaking, very naturally, when he handed over his ready money; he turned out to have something approaching ten thousand on him.

- Lit. *item*. See also *кусо́к*.

штукату́рка *f.* war paint, thick layer of make-up.

- Lit. *plaster, stucco*.

шуз *m.* [also *pl.* **шузы́**, *gen.pl.* **шузо́в**] shoes, boots.

- See also *шузня́, шузня́к*.

шузня́ *coll.f.* shoes, footwear.

- See also *шуз, шузня́к*.

шузня́к *coll.f.* variant of **шузня́**.

Щ

щёня *f.* young, new rockers getting to grips with motorbikes.

Ю

юг *m.* [*pl.* **юга́, юги**] Yugoslav, Yugoslavian.

- Lit. *south*.

юга́ *coll.f.* Crimea or the Caucasus.

юго́вый *adj.* Yugoslav, Yugoslavian.

юкс *m.* quid, one-rouble note. Дай юкс на ко́фе. Give us a quid for coffee.

- Finnish *uksi* (*one*). See also *юксо́вый*.

юксо́вый *adj. used as noun* quid, one-rouble note.

- See also *юкс*.

Я

я́ма *f.* 1. stash, hiding place, place to hide stolen goods. У нас была́ я́ма—ме́сто, куда́ мы сбыва́ли кра́деные а́вто. We had a stash, a hiding-place where we stashed away stolen cars. 2. the centre of a market hall.
• Lit. *hole.* See *парке́т.*

янго́вый *adj.* young.

ящеробо́гий *adj. used as noun* scruff.

я́щик *m.* box, tv, television set. Моя́ тёща всю *Мариа́нну* по я́щику смо́трит. My mother-in-law watches all of *Marianna* on the box.

Sources and References

by UFO

'А для души - "райска"', *Аргументы и факты*, 41, 1992

'Азиза', *Собеседник*, 38, 1991.

Айвазян А., *Рок, 1955/1991*, СПб: «Триал», 1992.

Баймухаметов, С., 'Что с нами?...', *Смена*, 12, 1991, 68.

Баранов, А.Н., Караулов, Ю.Н, 'Русская политическая метафора (материалы к словарю)', М., 1991.

Берджес Э., 'Заводной апельсин', *Юность*, 3, 1991, 15-27; 4, 1991, 60-83.

Бестужев-Лада, И., 'Омрачение завистью', *Неделя*, 23, 1990.

Богачев, И., 'Скитаясь тихо по России...', *Наука и религия*, 4, 1988.

Быков, Д., 'Следи за собой', *Собеседник*, 43, 1991.

'Голоса', *Рейтинг*, 16, 1992.

Гриценко, И., 'Устами "завязавшего"', *Юность*, 4-5, 1992.

Журавлева, Н., 'Чума', *Аргументы и факты*, 14, 1992.

Исарова, Л., 'Запонки императора', *Смена*, 4-6, 1992.

Карпова, О., 'Бизнес шепотом', *Смена*, 4-6, 1992, 102.

Кашелкин, А.Б., Овчинский, В.С., 'По неписаным законам улицы...', М: «Юрид. лит.», 1991, 304-33.

Кич, К., 'Спортивный парень, или "Не надо нас подплечивать!" (интервью с Александром "Рикошетом" Аксеновым)', 12, 4, 1988.

Кичигин, С., *Собеседник*, 2, 1992, 4.

Колбовский, А., 'Генералы пока не разрешают', *Экран и сцена*, 13.09.90.

Колесова, Е.А., '"Аврора" и Система, //По страницам самиздата', М: «Молодая гвардия», 1990, 68-78.

Крайний, А., 'Неуставняк', *Комсомольская правда*, 23.09.90.

Краткий справочник американских идиоматических выражений, Л., 1991.

Крюков, Д., 'Черный блюз светлой памяти', *Юность*, 1, 1992.

Кузьмина, Ю., 'На роду написано?', *Наука и религия*, 3, 1990, 8-9.

Кунин, В., 'Интердевочка', *Аврора*, 2, 3, 1988.

Леонтьев, В., *Аргументы и факты*, 34, 1992.

Литвинов, С., 'Остров "везения"?', *Смена*, 12, 1991, 16.

Литвинов, С., 'Биржевые страсти', *Смена*, 1, 1992, 110.

Мазурова, А.И., 'Сленг хип-системы' // По неписаным законам улицы, М: «Юрид. лит.», 1991, 118-38.

Мазурова, А., Радзиховский, Л., 'Стеб остранения', *Знание—сила*, 3, 1991, 65-70.

Мазурова, А.И., Розин, М.В., 'Развитие, структура и сущность хиппизма' //По неписаным законам улицы, М: «Юрид. лит.», 1991, 99-118.

Мартынов, И., 'Меньше света!', *Юность*, 3, 1992.

Митрофанов, Е.В., Никитина, Т.Г., *Словарь молодёжного сленга*, 12, 24, 1992.

Морозов, Д., *Панк-рок, //По страницам самиздата*, М: «Молодая гвардия», 1990, 282-92.

Немира, В., Кто-куда?, *Собеседник*, 43, 1992, 6.

Ненашев, С.В., Пилатов, С.Г., *Дети андеграунда*, Л: Лениздат, 1990.

Новое в русской лексике. Словарные материалы-77, «Русский язык», М., 1980.

Новое в русской лексике. Словарные материалы-78, «Русский язык», М., 1981.

Новое в русской лексике. Словарные материалы-81, «Русский язык», М., 1986.

Новое в русской лексике. Словарные материалы-82, «Русский язык», М., 1986.

Овчаренко, В., 'Нелегал-коммерсант', *Юность*, 2, 1992.

'Подборка документов с экскурсом в историю вопроса', *Кабаре*, 2, 02.10.91.

Поляков, Ю., *Сто дней до приказа*, М: «Литфонд РСФСР», 1991.

Поляков, Ю., 'Парижская любовь Кости Гуманикова', *Юность*, 6, 1991, 21-31; 7, 1991, 48-56; 8, 1991, 35-51.

Пшеничный, О., 'Как я был фанатом Леонтьева', *Комсомольская правда*, 23.09.90.

Рожанский, Ф.И., *Сленг хиппи (материалы к словарю)*, СПб.-Париж: «Изд-во Европейского Дома», 1992.

Русский рок, СП «Внешсигма», М., 1991.

Сальникова, Л., 'Баллада о прекрасной даме', *Юность*, 9, 1991, 84.

Серов, А., *Семья*, 18, 1992, 24.

Снегов, С., 'Философия блатного языка', *Даугава*, 11, 1990.

Снегов, С., 'Язык, который ненавидит', *Просвет*, М., 1991.

Сочнев, К., *"Двойной маленький" для андерграунда,//Отрицательный угол* М: Молодая гвардия, 1990, 127-44.

Соколов, М., *Собеседник*, 2, 1992, 2.

Ричард, А., *Спиерс Словарь американского сленга*, М: «Русский язык», 1991.

Федоров, С., *Собеседник*, 2, 1992, 2.

Чайка, О., *Проникающее ранение, // Отрицательный угол* М: «Молодая гвардия», 1990, 63-86.

Шевчук, Ю., 'Все мы немножко с прибабахом', *Аргументы и факты*, 33, 1992.

Шульженко, И., 'Давайте вырядимся!', *Спутник*, 3, 1988.

Щуплов, А., 'Речевое облако России', *Голос*, 35, 1992, 12.

Эйто Дж., 'Словарь новых слов английского языка', М: «Русский язык», 1990.

Юкелис, О., 'Живет такой парень', *Аргументы и факты*, 33, 1992.

Additional Bibliography

by James Davie

Reference Works

The following works were consulted during the editing and revision of the Second Edition. Details regarding the original version of the dictionary are also included.

Bushnell, J., *Moscow Graffiti*, Boston: Unwin Hyman, 1990.

Быков, В., *Русская феня*, Смоленск: Траст-Имаком, 1994.

Chapman, R.L., *Dictionary of American Slang*, London: Pan, 1987.

Drummond, D.A. & Perkins, G., *Dictionary of Russian Obscenities*, Oakland: Scythian Books, 1987.

Елистратов, В.С., *Словарь московского арго*, М: «Русские словари», 1994.

Дубягин, Ю.П. & Теплицкий, Е.А., *Краткий англо-русский и русско-английский словарь уголовного жаргона*, М: «Терра», 1993.

Флегон, А. *За пределами русских словарей*, (second edition), London: Flegon Press, 1992.

Marder, S., *A Supplementary Russian-English Dictionary*, Ohio: Slavica, 1994.

Nikol'skii, V.D., *Dictionary of Contemporary Russian Slang*, Moscow: Panorama, 1993.

Ожегов, С. И., Шведова, Н. Ю., *Толковый словарь русского языка*, Москва: Азъ, 1995.

Oxford Russian Dictionary, Oxford: Oxford University Press, 1993.

Рожанский, Ф.И., *Сленг хиппи (материалы к словарю)*, СПб.-Париж, «Изд. Европейского Дома», 1992.

Shliakhov, V. & Adler, E., *Dictionary of Russian Slang*, New York: Barrons, 1995.

Сидоров, А., *Словарь современного блатного и лагерного жаргона*, Ростов-на-дону: «Гермес», 1992.

Thorne, T., *Dictionary of Contemporary Slang*, London: Bloomsbury, 1990.

The following **Russian youth fanzines and supplements** provided additional examples for the Second Edition:

Blitzkreeg, 1 (16), 1994.
Наш драйв, 1, ноябрь, 1995.
Ниоткуда, 2 (25), январь, 1996.
Окорок, 2, июль, 1991.
ПТЮЧ, 5, зима, 1995-96.
Rock Fuzz, 28, декабрь, 1995.
Штирлиц, 3, 1991.
Энск, 2 (27), 1993.
Я молодой, 6 (82), февраль, 1996.